THE TRUTHS OF
JUSTICE

By THE HON. RICHARD RITTENBAND

Advance praise for
The Truths of Justice:

"Any law student or layman with a serious interest in how our trial courts actually work can do no better than to read Judge Richard Rittenband's interesting and informative book, The Truths of Justice. In it, Judge Rittenband uses criminal and civil cases that have come before him to make instructive points and observations on a variety of subjects that bear on the conduct of trials and the administration of justice. In the process, he provides the reader with fascinating insights into the kinds of judgment calls that a tough but fair-minded judge must make in order to ensure that justice is done and the public interest protected. In writing this book, Judge Rittenband has made an important and highly readable contribution to a better understanding of why ours is a system of law we can be proud of."

James L. Buckley
Senior Judge, U.S. Court of Appeals for the District of Columbia Circuit
Former U.S. Senator from New York

"An unusually illuminating view of our system of justice—including actual cases by the judge who decided them. Rarely has there been so clear and lively a report and analysis from the inside."

Nat Hentoff
Syndicated columnist
Expert on the First Amendment and the Bill of Rights

ACKNOWLEDGMENTS

A heartfelt thank you to my friend, Larry Blakely, formerly of South Windsor and currently of New Salem, Mass., who urged me to write this book; and my friend, Judge Jim Buckley, of Washington, D.C. and Sharon, Conn., who encouraged me to continue. I would also like to express my thanks to Vincent Michael Valvo, editor and publisher of *The Connecticut Law Tribune*. His sound advice, ideas and suggested changes have produced a better and more readable book.

DEDICATION

To Rhoda, my wife and best friend, who has lived through it all and without whom this book would never have been written.

The Truths of Justice:
An Inside Look At How A Courtroom *Really* Works

The Hon. Richard Rittenband

ISBN 0-910051-33-48-8

First Edition, printed December 2002

TABLE OF CONTENTS

The Truths of Justice

INTRODUCTION

Senator Barry Smith is on trial for the murder of his lover, Amy Jones. The state has charged him with stabbing Amy to death in a motel room because he was afraid that she was going to go public with their affair and ruin his political career. unless he acknowledged he had made her pregnant and married her. The witness is Amy's husband, Roger Jones. Smith's defense attorney is Alex Collins.

Collins: "Now, Mr. Jones you've heard witnesses testify that your wife was deeply in love with Senator Smith. Senator Smith testified that he was in love with your wife and wanted to marry her. You've heard witnesses testify that your marriage to Amy was falling apart because she couldn't put up with your temper tantrums anymore. Isn't that true?"

Jones: "That's what they said, but it's not true. Amy was in love with me. We had a happy marriage."

Collins: "Do you really expect this jury to believe that you're the only one telling the truth in this courtroom and that everyone else is lying? Is that what you want us to believe?"

Perspiration began to appear on Jones' forehead. His face was flushed, and he looked uncomfortable. Before he could answer, Collins continued in a louder voice, moving closer to Jones.

"What is true, Mr. Jones, is that your wife was unhappy in your marriage; that she turned to Senator Smith and fell in love with him. You became insanely jealous, you followed her to the Holiday Inn where she met with Senator Smith, and you looked through the opening between the drapes and saw them making love. You waited for Senator Smith to leave, and then you burst into the room and confronted your wife. She admitted to the affair, you became enraged, and in a fit of rage you picked up this knife, state's exhibit 6, and plunged it into Amy's chest; and then plunged it in again and again and again, didn't you?"

Jones started to cry. He put his face in his hands, then looked up

11

with tears streaming down his face and shouted: "Yes! Yes! I did it! God help me; I did. I didn't mean to. I loved my wife."

Only on television, only with Perry Mason or Ben Matlock does this happen.

Most people in America learn about our court system from television dramas or movies. Although there is a certain amount of realism in *Law and Order, The Practice* and *Judging Amy*, it is still entertainment. A real judge, as occurred in one episode of *The Practice*, wouldn't tell members of a civil jury that they're a bunch of jackasses because of the high verdict they rendered. Real judges don't yell at and belittle the plaintiffs and defendants as Judge Judy does.

There are several differences between television dramas and the reality of an American courtroom. In **the real world**, participants are not all handsome and beautiful—and only on television do people confess under withering cross examination. As hard as we try, we have never been able to start and finish a trial in one hour minus commercials. No one confesses on the witness stand, judges don't have affairs with defense attorneys, and defense attorneys don't have affairs with prosecutors. Newspapers report serious criminal trials, but usually only the result and not the conduct of the trial itself. The televising of the O. J. Simpson trial was for many their first glimpse of an actual trial, but the circus atmosphere, the lack of control of the courtroom by the trial judge and the ineptitude of some of the attorneys, primarily the prosecutors, are hardly reflective of what really takes place in a courtroom.

Despite the fact that court decisions permeate every aspect of our society, I believe it is safe to say that the majority of our citizens never actually see the inside of an American courtroom. Those who have, have had limited experience, perhaps when going through a divorce, facing a traffic offense or being involved in an accident case. Many civil and criminal cases are settled on the eve of trial, so, unless you've been a juror, you've probably never seen an actual trial take place. It's unfortunate that more citizens are not selected as jurors because hundreds of jurors have told me after the conclusion of the trial that their service, although sometimes demanding, was a fascinating and educational experience which they will remember for the rest of their lives. However, even their experience was limited to one case and, thereby, only one type of case.

This book will analyze some of the so called "myths" of our justice system. It is commonly believed, among other things, that:

1. People tell the truth when under oath.
2. You can lie and get away with it.
3. America is a safer place now that the crime rate is going down.
4. People often win huge verdicts for minor injuries.
5. Criminals can be cured with sufficient treatment and counseling.
6. Only the powerful and wealthy get a fair trial
7. Too many people get off on technicalities.
8. "I don't want the public defender. I want a real lawyer."
9. The criminal justice system is not tough enough on criminals.
10. When a police officer makes an arrest, the criminal is back on the street before the officer finishes his/her shift.
11. Issues of divorce, custody, alimony, child support and property division are always decided in favor of the wife.
12. Juries are stupid.
13. We're not tough enough on drunk drivers.

This book, therefore, is to give you a taste of reality, to inform jurors and non-jurors what life is really like in our justice system. This book describes the conflicts in our society, the violence, the drugs and the other dangers facing our citizens; "telling it like it is" from the perspective of a trial judge who has been on the firing line daily, who has seen first hand the problems threatening our way of life and the actual workings of the justice system which is trying very hard to solve these problems. There are no actors or actresses here, no scripts to be followed and no glossing over the truth. Rather, it is a view of what is actually going on in the streets and homes across America, how we are reacting to it and what more we should be doing. It's about real people with real problems facing a real jury and a real judge in a real courtroom, which is the last resort for resolving the conflicts and problems in our troubled society.

So, let me take you on a journey through our court system including a word picture of actual cases. Some of what you see may surprise you.

The Truths of Justice

Chapter One

MURDER IN THE CONNECTICUT WOODS

"Murder itself is past all expiation the greatest crime, which nature doth abhor." **Goffe**

It was spring time in Connecticut, warm in the day but colder at night. On a cold April night, the early morning hours of April 26, 1986, at approximately 2:00 a.m., David Copas, age twenty-five, had driven Laura Bieu, a sixteen year old high school student, to Hop River Road, a dirt road deep into a wooded area in Coventry, a rural town in eastern Connecticut. The scene can best be set by part of the sentencing statement of State's Attorney Patricia Swords[1] in the murder trial of *State of Connecticut v. David Copas.*

". . . . The defendant brought her to this very isolated spot approximately seven tenths of a mile from any home in the area and along the dirt portion of Hop River Road.

We will never truly know what occurred out there between the defendant and the victim, but suffice it to say that nothing the victim did or could have done out there justified the vicious, brutal and cold blooded attack on this sixteen year old girl. By the defendant's own account, all of the stab wounds he inflicted occurred during the first part of the attack, and by that I mean when they were both standing out on the dirt portion of Hop River Road.

It is obvious from the number and the location of the defense wounds on the victim that she vigorously attempted to fight for her life, and although the defendant has refused to admit it, the fact that

[1] Attorney Swords, a consummate professional, did an excellent job in this case. She is now a Superior Court judge.

Note: The names used in this chapter are the actual names of the people involved.

the victim had at least three stab wounds in the middle of her back indicates I think very clearly that she was attempting to run away from the defendant, but he was able to run her down and stab her.

We're going to hear a lot this morning from the defense, I can expect, about the defendant and his unhappy past and how the Court should be merciful because of his deprived childhood and young adulthood. I would ask the Court before we get into all of that, however, to place yourselves in the position of the victim out there on Hop River Road at two o'clock in the morning in this dark, desolate area seven tenths of a mile from any home. Imagine that you're five feet two like she is and a hundred and ten pounds and you've been brought there by someone who is nine years older than you, who is seven inches taller and fifty pounds heavier.

Purportedly, you're out there to smoke marijuana. Imagine how frightening these circumstances are to a young woman and add in what we know about the defendant's well documented history of aggression and history of violence and the fact that he is now armed with a knife. Imagine the terror, the fear, the suffering that Laura Bieu must have felt in the final thirty minutes of her life; for thirty minutes is the amount of time that Doctor Katsnelson, the assistant medical examiner, estimated she lived after the first stab wound.

Imagine the pain of the repeated blows, twenty-two in all, to Laura's head, her face, her arms, her back, her hands, as she was struck repeatedly by the defendant's knife and then when Laura lay crumbled on the side of the road, imagine the further intense pain when the defendant takes that large rock and drops it on the right side of her head, and then as she's calling out for her mother, so he knows she's still alive, he drags her by the feet, off the road into the woods over the dirt and the rocks and the fallen trees, bumping her head as she's going along and finally leaves her twenty-three feet off the road.

Imagine the additional pain when *he then commences to drop more large rocks on top of her, some of which have been estimated by the State Police to have been fifty pounds,* and that includes another rock to her head as well as rocks to her shoulders, stomach and legs, but even that wasn't enough for the defendant . . . . He began to kick her because he was so angry at her, and he finally stopped when he started to hear his car dying on the side of Hop River Road, and that's what caused him to stop his attack. Not through any remorse but because of his own self-serving interest in being able to get out of there without anybody finding him.

This was not a swift and painless death. Rather, it was a hurtful, vengeful, painful, cold blooded death, and the defendant's response to these cold blooded and vicious actions has been characteristically cold blooded, uncaring, calculating and self serving.

Much of this information was gained from the defendant's confession as well as physical evidence found at the scene. Of course, there were only two people there at the time of the murder, Laura and David, and obviously Laura couldn't speak from the grave. A few days after the murder a fisherman found Laura's semi-nude, stabbed and bludgeoned body partly covered with heavy rocks in the woods off Hop River Road. Suspicion quickly focused upon David Copas since he was the last person to see Laura alive. Earlier in the evening Laura and a few of her girlfriends had been dropped off at a bowling alley in a nearby town. Much later in the evening Copas had agreed to give Laura and two of her girlfriends a ride home. He dropped the girl friends at the home of one of them. The other was to stay overnight. It appeared that Laura wanted to get out of the car and stay with them, but the girl who lived there had not obtained permission for her to do so. Reluctantly, Laura drove off with Copas. This scene was vividly described at the trial by the two girlfriends who now bitterly regret that she was not allowed to stay with them.

Further investigation also pointed to Copas, and he was eventually taken in for questioning by the Eastern Division of the State Police Major Crime Squad. The questioning took place at the local town hall which was commandeered for that purpose. Sometime around 1:00 a.m., Copas confessed to the murder although it would later turn out that the circumstances surrounding the taking of the confession would become controversial. Copas was then arrested.

The Truths of Justice

He sought legal representation from Attorney John Doe, a local lawyer who was primarily a tax attorney with little if any experience in criminal law. Doe, faced with the confession, did not move to suppress it and had his client plead guilty to a charge of murder in the first degree. This was not a death penalty offense, so the state's attorney at that time argued for the maximum prison sentence, life, which is considered sixty years. Attorney Doe argued for forty years, and the court, Judge Eugene Kelly, now deceased, sentenced Copas to fifty years in part because by pleading guilty Copas had spared Laura's family from the ordeal of a trial.

However, some time after the sentencing, Copas filed a writ of habeas corpus served on the Commissioner of Corrections seeking immediate relief from confinement in this case on the basis of the denial of his right to counsel under the provisions of the Sixth Amendment to the United States Constitution. Right to counsel has been interpreted to mean right to adequate or effective counsel. The court that presided over the habeas trial (habeas is heard before a judge without a jury) agreed with Copas that Attorney Doe's representation of him was ineffective assistance of counsel, and ordered a new trial.

One of the major points cited by the habeas judge was that Attorney Doe should have presented a defense of *Extreme Emotional Disturbance*, and if the jury had agreed with this defense, the defendant would have to be convicted of manslaughter: which crime carried a maximum sentence of twenty years in prison. The State appealed this decision to the State Supreme Court which affirmed the decision of the habeas court.

The new trial was scheduled to begin on May 1, 1997. I was assigned to preside over the trial. Since it was a charge of murder, the defendant was entitled to a twelve person jury. Because the trial was expected to take a month, I ordered selection of six alternate jurors who would sit with the jurors and replace any that became sick or for some other urgent reason were unable to serve for the remainder of the trial. On trials of lesser offenses, we usually had a jury of six with two alternates. The trial itself did take a full month, the jury coming in with a verdict on May 30, 1997. I'm happy to say that all of the jurors stayed right with the trial to the end, and it turned out that we did not in fact need the alternates.

Under Connecticut law, jury selection takes longer than in federal court or other states as described in the chapter on *"Jury Selection"*. In this case we started selection in the middle of March and completed it just short of the May first trial commencement date. The defendant who had remained incarcerated since 1986 was represented by the Chief Public Defender for the Tolland Judicial District, Phillip Armentano, and an attorney and professor of law at the University of Connecticut School of Law, Timothy Everett, who was also director of the UConn Criminal Law Clinic.

Both attorneys were highly competent and experienced in criminal law. I was confident that they would conduct themselves admirably, and I was not disappointed. I could not imagine another habeas petition claiming their performance was ineffective. I did, however, insist that the defendant appear in non-prison clothing. The jury was not supposed to know of his prior conviction for this murder or the fact that he was in custody which itself can prejudice the jury into thinking he is a dangerous and violent man. I had recently granted a habeas petition because the defendant was allowed to appear in prison garb. Mr. Copas was wearing a dark blue pin striped suit.

During jury selection, Attorney Armentano asked a prospective juror whether she "could give my client over there the presumption of innocence." She replied: "Which one is he? They all look like lawyers."

MOTION TO SUPPRESS THE CONFESSION

There was one major motion that had to be heard before we began jury selection, and that was a motion made by defense counsel to suppress the defendant's confession.[2] Hearings were held on January 28, 29, 30 and 31, 1997 in which considerable testimony was taken. Each side filed briefs (memoranda of law) on March 7, 1997 (they had to wait until the transcripts of the hearing were ready). I issued

---

2 The defendant did not testify at the suppression hearing or at the trial.

a sixteen page decision on March 14, 1997. The defense filed five motions. The basis for the first motion was that the statements made by the defendant were not preceded by adequate warnings of his right to remain silent and his right to have an attorney present, and that the defendant never knowingly, voluntarily and intelligently waived those rights. I gave great credence to the testimony of State Police Detective Michael Malchik whom I found to be honest and consistent in his testimony, very professional with good attention to detail and a good memory. He was also very experienced.

I found that the defendant, on his way from the hospital where he had been picked up by the police for transfer to the town hall indicated either that he might need an attorney or that he wanted an attorney. He was told he could call one at the town hall. He was provided with a telephone when he arrived, made several phone calls and then advised Malchik and his partner, Detective Roland Pelkey, that he didn't want to speak to an attorney, but did want to speak with his wife.

At about midnight, his wife was taken into the room where hair samples were being taken from Copas pursuant to a search warrant. She and the defendant talked privately for twenty minutes. No interrogation had taken place at that time. She returned twenty five minutes later for another private session with her husband. The defendant then told Malchik that he would tell him about the murder of Laura Bieu as long as his wife could be present. He said he did not want an attorney, and that he trusted his wife's judgment.

At 1:00 a.m. Malchik read the defendant his constitutional rights, commonly called the Miranda warnings.[3] The defendant signed a waiver of all of his Miranda rights with his wife signing as a witness. He then gave an oral confession in the presence of his wife. This was followed by a tape recorded confession. At the beginning of the recording, he read his Miranda rights and waived them. Thereafter, he gave a written confession on a form that included a recitation of his Miranda

[3] So named from the United States Supreme Court decision in **Miranda v. Arizona** which requires the police to warn the defendant of his right to remain silent, his right to an attorney, etc.

rights and a waiver of them above the written statement which was signed by the defendant.

I concluded that the defendant had voluntarily, knowingly and intelligently waived his constitutional rights, federal and state, including his Miranda rights. The state police had "scrupulously honored" the defendant's rights against self incrimination. The other motions were based upon more technical grounds. After considering all the evidence, I denied all of the motions to suppress except one. I ruled that statements made by the defendant at his habeas trial in January, 1992 were not admissible. His testimony there was in effect involuntary because he had to testify in order to exercise his right to effective assistance of counsel. He should not have to give up his Fifth Amendment rights in order to show a violation of his rights under the Sixth Amendment. I, thus, adopted the dissenting opinion of Justice Thurgood Marshall in a 1974 United States Supreme Court case.

The granting of this last motion turned out to be irrelevant. The confession had been admitted into evidence, and this was sufficient with physical evidence and testimony to prove that the defendant had murdered Laura Bieu.

THE TRIAL

Once the state had established that the defendant was the last person to see Laura alive, that forensic examinations of blood and other items had implicated the defendant and that other statements made by the defendant showed his guilt, and once the confession had been admitted into evidence, it was clear that the state had established the defendant guilty of murder beyond a reasonable doubt. Then, came the main thrust of the defense case, the affirmative defense that at the time of the murder the defendant was suffering from extreme emotional disturbance, and if proven, the defendant would be found guilty of the lesser offense of manslaughter carrying a twenty year maximum sentence.

The burden was on the defendant to prove this defense, but he

21

had to do it only by the lesser burden of proof known as ***preponderance of the evidence.*** This is the standard of proof in a civil case, a burden far below that carried by the state in its case, namely ***beyond a reasonable doubt.*** Preponderance of the evidence means to prove that it was ***more likely than not*** that the defendant suffered from ***extreme emotional disturbance.*** That means that the evidence had to tip only slightly more than fifty percent in the defendant's favor.

In my charge, or instructions to the jury, I explained the elements of the defense of extreme emotional disturbance that the defendant had to prove:

"**1.** The defendant was exposed to an extremely unusual and overwhelming state that is more than mere annoyance or unhappiness; and

2. the defendant had an extreme emotional reaction to that state, as a result of which there was a loss of self-control, and his reason was overborne by intense feelings, such as passion, anger, distress, grief, excessive agitation, or other similar emotions. You should consider whether the intensity of these feelings was such that the defendant's usual intellectual controls and that his normal rational thinking no longer prevailed at the time of the act.

. . . . the word 'extreme' means the greatest degree of intensity away form the normal state of the defendant . . . . You must also find that ***there was a reasonable explanation or excuse for this disturbance.***"

Each side presented expert witnesses. The defense presented testimony from one psychiatrist and one psychologist. The state presented one psychiatrist and two psychologists.

Such testimony is often facetiously dubbed "psycho-babble" in the judicial system. What the witnesses should do is describe the principles and premises of psychiatry and psychology in laymen's terms as much as possible. Although some judges have heard these technical terms used in other cases, we are really as much laymen as are the jurors, and in any case it is the jurors who have to understand it all.

The witnesses in this case had outstanding credentials and reputations. Several of them had been on the staff of or were now independently associated with the world renowned psychiatric hospital known as **The Institute For Living** in Hartford. The claims boiled down to this: the defense claimed that the defendant suffered from the mental disease of borderline personality disorder, and his lead psychiatrist said that what the defendant committed was a "*reactive homicide*", that he became enraged after being slashed in the hand with a penknife by the victim which caused him to take the knife away from her and stab her.

In his confession, the defendant stated that after they had had "consensual sex" earlier, when they later reached the woods, the victim got out of the car and claimed that the defendant had soiled and diseased her, and, then, she came at him with the knife. The state, on the other hand, claimed it was not a reactive homicide, and that the defendant, although a sociopath, did not suffer from a "borderline personality disorder". A person with that disorder would show remorse which the defendant had never done.

The defense also presented evidence to show the defendant's difficult childhood as well as problems he had in his teen years and early twenties to support the contention of borderline personality disorder. School records, prior medical records and testimony from his siblings were also introduced as well as statements the defendant made to the psychologists and psychiatrist who had examined him for this trial. The state claimed that these statements by the defendant were all self serving and, therefore, unreliable. There was, of course, other evidence over the thirty day trial, but the above is a summary of each side's position on the issue of **Extreme Emotional Disturbance.**

KEY FACTORS LEADING TO VERDICT

"Reactive Homicide": In its rebuttal the state called Assistant Chief Medical Examiner, Dr. Katsnelson, as a witness. The State Police, in the execution of the search warrant at the Town Hall, had taken several color photographs of various parts of the defendant's body.

One was the palm of the defendant's right hand showing the cuts where Laura allegedly had stabbed him and which produced "his uncontrollable rage". Dr. Katsnelson, testified, however, that these wounds were ***not defensive wounds but instead were offensive wounds.*** He testified that the wounds had been incurred by the defendant while he was stabbing Laura twenty-two times, that the wound in the center of his palm was a blister or boil created by the head or handle of the knife when his strokes hit bone before sliding off into flesh and that the wounds across his fingers were sustained when the knife hit Laura's body on the downward swings.

This testimony completely undermined the defense psychiatrist's claim that it was a "reactive homicide". The psychiatrist should not be blamed since his information came from the defendant's confession and subsequent interviews with the defendant in which the defendant lied when he said that Laura had first come at him with a knife. It was also hard to believe that a sixteen year old girl much smaller and lighter than the defendant would take a pen knife and initiate an attack on him. This testimony by Dr. Katsnelson had further effect than the issue of who used the knife first. It showed the defendant to be a liar as a result of which the jury gave little credence to his defense.

Remorse: The defendant's now ex-wife reluctantly testified that she had visited her husband while he was in prison about the time of his first conviction in the case. It was apparently a conjugal visit because while she was taking a bath, she tried to pin him down as to the real reason he had killed Laura Bieu. His reaction was to move his hands from her shoulders to around her neck to which he started to apply pressure. Frightened, she got out of the tub, at which point he told her: "Don't worry about Laura Bieu. She got exactly what she deserved." I looked at the jury and saw both shock and disgust in their expressions.

On the night of the crime, the defendant later returned home and wanted to have sex with his wife shortly after he had committed the murder. One of the state's psychologists cited this, as well as the statement to his wife during the conjugal visit, as evidence of a lack of remorse on the part of the defendant. You will recall that more than one psychologist/psychiatrist had stated that if the defendant were suffering from the mental disease of "borderline personality disorder", he would have shown remorse.

The jury received the case after final arguments and my charge to the jury on the law early Wednesday afternoon. About noon on Friday, May 30th, they returned a verdict of **guilty of murder**, having rejected the defense of Extreme Emotional Disturbance. I continued the case for sentencing for six weeks and ordered the Office of Adult Probation to conduct a thorough pre-sentence investigation (PSI) and present a report to the court and the attorneys at least two days prior to the sentencing date.

SENTENCING

The hearing was held on July 18, 1997. The state's attorney, Patricia Swords, urged the court to impose the maximum sentence of sixty years which in Connecticut is considered life in prison. This, of course, would be an increase over Judge Kelly's sentence of fifty years. Therefore, under the U.S. Supreme Court ruling in North Carolina v. Pearce, I had to describe on the record those factors not available to Judge Kelly which would justify an increased sentence.

This is based upon the concern that, otherwise, a defendant would be penalized for exercising his or her constitutional rights by going to trial. There were many reasons for the increase as pointed out by Attorney Swords. I had been present at a trial over a period of thirty days and heard evidence that Judge Kelly had not, including graphic details of the crime which were not explored in full at a sentencing in which the defendant had pleaded guilty. I knew that the defendant had lied in his confession which nobody knew except for the defendant until Dr. Katsnelson testified.

The defendant's comment to his wife that Laura Bieu had "gotten what she deserved" was not available to Judge Kelly, nor were the many instances of disruptive behavior while he was in prison awaiting trial. There were other factors too numerous to mention, but I was convinced there was sufficient justification for a longer sentence to be imposed if I chose to do so. I also heard emotional pleas by Laura's grandparents.

Defense attorney Phillip Armentano concentrated on the fact that the defendant had suffered from child abuse and that he had become very close only to his grandfather who had died when the defendant was fifteen years old. It was this loss, according to the psychiatrist who testified on his behalf that devastated him and led to an escalation of his use of marijuana, alcohol and other drugs. He stressed that the defendant should have received more counseling and psychological treatment when he was younger and that when it was given, it was unsuccessful.

It appeared to me that he had undergone several periods of treatment and counseling over the years. Attorney Armentano also claimed that this was not a cold blooded murder and that although the jury apparently did not agree that he was suffering from extreme emotional disturbance, he still had a diminished capacity to control his behavior. The defendant's sister had written a letter to the court which I had read along with other letters from both sides, and the defendant's brother addressed the court.

The brother portrayed the defendant as a victim of a society which did not recognize his need for mental health care. I thanked him but thought, *"Here we go again. The murderer has become the victim."* What about Laura Bieu and her family, the real victims in this case?

Attorney Everett, the legal scholar in this case, pointed out that the issue in <u>North Carolina v. Pearce</u> was still up in the air in Connecticut, and he too urged me to impose a sentence of less than fifty years. Attorney Swords then responded in rebuttal (much of her initial remarks are quoted at the beginning of this chapter) that the defense claim that the defendant has a diminished capacity to control his own behavior even today, eleven years after the crime, illustrates his dangerousness and his need for the maximum period of incarceration.

Decision Time: Everyone had been heard, either in person or by statement, and it was now time to do what judges are supposed to do, make a decision. Rather than describe it, I will quote selected remarks from the transcript.

What I know which Judge Kelly did not know, number one, is the absolute viciousness of the crime itself . . . . Now, I'm using photographs from the trial, and sheriff, I would like you to take these to Mr. Copas.

First is a picture of Laura Bieu when she was smiling, happy, and certainly unmarked, and Mr. Copas, as a result of your actions, this is what you turned her into on the night of April 26 . . . . And here's a picture just of her face where she's lying on her back with a face horribly bloodied and cut and disfigured. Here's another photograph of her at the murder scene with the rocks piled on top of her, one sneaker missing and the same facial characteristics as well as certain parts of her body that were exposed.

And here is another picture after she's been cleaned up, of her face at the autopsy, and all you have to do is look at these photographs to determine the viciousness, the horrendous nature, the heinous nature of this crime; and Mr. Copas, I notice you're not looking at these photographs. I'm ordering you to do so. Attorney Everett, show them to him in the order I've described. I don't care if this makes you uncomfortable, Mr. Copas. Look at them and see what you did. I hope you never forget them . . . .[4] (He looked at them quickly and then turned away.)

According to Dr. Katsnelson it took Laura Bieu thirty minutes to die, and I only have to read from your confession to see what was going on. 'I hit her in the face with the back of my hand. She fell down. I started stabbing her in the body, face and leg.' There were wounds to the back . . . as a matter of fact, the one that Dr. Katsnelson said was probably a fatal wound was the wound to the back that went into the chest and punctured her lung. You go on to say 'she was down on the ground and all bloodied. I picked up a large rock and threw it at her, hitting her in the head.'

Now what I don't understand is behavior from a human being like

---

[4] During the trial when the crime scene and autopsy photographs were shown to the jury, one juror became ill and/or emotionally upset. He asked for a short recess which I quickly granted.

this: you see her lying there with the stab wounds . . . . Let's assume there was a burst of anger here. You knew her condition at that time, but you did not know that these wounds were fatal. She was still crying out. She was still alive. I realize this would have implicated you, and maybe what I'm going to say is unrealistic, but someone who cares about human life at that point would have done something to summon help for Laura Bieu, and if it had been done, conceivably, she could be alive today.

Instead you finished the job, bashing in her skull with a rock, and this is why I'm talking about the heinous nature of the crime. After you hit her in the head, quote, 'she wouldn't stop moving, and it looked like one of her eyes was missing, so I dragged her by the feet into the woods and piled rocks on her. She was still alive, thrashing around and calling for her mommy. I started kicking her, and she just wouldn't stop moving. My car stalled. I ran out to the road. I rolled the car about an eighth of a mile toward route 6. I can still hear human moaning.' "

I pointed out to Copas that in Laura's moaning, she said something to you like 'Why are you doing this?' "The tragedy of it is that you cut short a life that had great promise . . . and thanks to you, Mr. Copas, nobody will ever see Laura again. Nobody will ever see her smile. Nobody will ever see her graduate from high school and college. Nobody will ever see her get married, and nobody will ever see what her children might have looked like, and I would add, too, that no one will see whether or not she could ever realize her wish to be a veterinarian . . . . She won't laugh, she'll never celebrate another birthday. She won't look at the sunset. She won't look at the ocean, all the things that we enjoy as parts of our lives are over for her. She's dead! And it's because of your actions.

Now, this is not Cambodia. This is not Bosnia. In the United States, human life is still precious, and you took away the life of a human being, and . . . it seems to me that could have been avoided.

. . . I will grant you, Mr. Copas, I think you've done a lot to improve yourself while you've been in prison . . . but you also have nineteen disciplinary violations including threats at an officer . . . Dr. Grenier's report indicates that you are presently suffering from "borderline personality disorder, narcissistic and antisocial traits", and that's after almost twelve years in prison . . . . Although you have done some things to improve your skills, acquiring computer skills, paralegal training, etc., when it comes to improving yourself to get over some of these psychological problems, apparently what you have done in twelve years hasn't really worked, which gives me much less confidence that it will work in the future . . . . *The sentence of the Court is that the defendant be committed to the custody of the Commissioner of Corrections for the remainder of his natural life, which has been defined in our Connecticut statutes as a period of sixty years."*

I pointed out to him that although I did not have the authority to sentence him to life without parole, Connecticut statutes do not permit parole for someone convicted of murder. I said that statutes can change, and if parole does become available, my recommendation is that the defendant not receive parole. I added that the parole board looks carefully at the recommendation of the sentencing judge and ordered that a transcript of the proceedings be prepared, I will sign it, and it shall become part of the defendant's file.

"Society has to be protected. I consider Mr. Copas to be a dangerous man, a menace to society . . . . The doctors found that he has an *antisocial attitude,* that he could lose control and that he's dangerous. His prison record shows a willingness to fight and be assaultive . . . . I'll accept that he had a very difficult childhood, but apparently his sister and brother who were subjected to the same childhood don't have a lasting problem as a result of all this abuse . . . . The problems of his childhood, with alcohol and drug abuse, the problem of making it in this world where there's so much unemployment and poverty *cannot be used as an excuse for killing another human being* . . . . This man apparently has an I.Q. of one hundred twenty-one. He should have been able to do something with that high an I.Q., but now it will be forever lost to society . . . so the real victim here, is not Mr. Copas. It's Laura Bieu whose young life was tragically cut short at the age of sixteen . . .

The Truths of Justice

In any event I acknowledge I'm far from perfect, and the Court cannot come up with all of the solutions to the ills of society, but I can do my utmost to protect society, and by giving him the full maximum and my recommendation of no parole, I hope that he will remain incarcerated to the point where he cannot do something like this again. Hopefully, when he is released he'll be at an age where he's incapable of doing anything violent. Shortly after this sentencing, the Department of Corrections also eliminated credit for good time in prison. Mr. Copas should be eight-five when he is released.

Finally, my heart goes out to Laura Bieu's family and to the young, innocent girl herself for losing what life has to offer. I became a little emotional (although I managed to keep it hidden) when I looked at the autopsy photos, when I heard the recording of the confession and when I heard from Laura's grandparents.

David Copas' conviction was upheld on appeal to the state Supreme Court, and he remains in prison for the rest of his life.

Note: In talking with the jurors after the trial, they indicated that their service had been a disturbing but fascinating experience. They said they were impressed by the conduct of the trial and opined that the courtroom is the last vestige of dignity and decorum.

Chapter Two

YOU BE THE JUDGE

In many states there is a program called Accelerated Rehabilitation (AR). It is a program for first time offenders which, if granted and there is compliance with the terms, results in the charge being dismissed. It keeps your record clean. You can use it only once. The defendant pleads neither guilty nor not guilty. Whether to grant it or not is generally left up to the discretion of the judge except that certain crimes such as murder, robbery, assault 1, Burglary 1 or 2, sexual assault l, or driving under the influence of liquor, are specifically barred from the program. There are four considerations the judge should take into account when deciding whether or not to grant the program:

1. Whether the offense is too serious to warrant granting the pro gram. Most misdemeanors (punishable by no more than a year in jail) are eligible. Most felonies (punishable by more than a year in jail) are not although Class D felonies such as Burglary 3 and Larceny 3 are eligible.

2. The background of the offender aside from any convictions (which, as stated above, would make the individual a second offender and, therefore, ineligible).

3. Opposition to the application, generally from the victim of the crime and or the state's attorney.

4. The likelihood of the defendant offending again.

As noted in a later chapter entitled "**Stalking and the Strange Case of Kathy Gerard**", I granted her application for AR. Here, I am going to give you ten cases in which I actually decided whether to grant or deny the application and, if granted, what conditions I put on successful completion of the program. The maximum period of the program or probation is two years. I ask you to sit in my chair and decide whether you, if you were the judge, would grant or deny the application, and if you grant it, what, if any, conditions you would require the defendant to do to successfully complete the program. Assume the defendant has no prior criminal record of conviction including no conviction under the Youthful Offender program the results of which are sealed as to the public but not as to the judge. There are no right or wrong answers. It is up to your discretion. The fact that you disagree with my decision does not mean you are wrong. The results of what I did in these cases will appear on a subsequent page. They are only opinions or decisions by one Superior Court judge who has had experience on the firing line. If you disagree with my decision, you might well be agreeing with another judge who has made a different decision in a similar case.

1. A young woman, who happened to be a well known TV reporter, was jogging in 1994 along a well traveled road in a rural area at approximately 7:30 a.m, the morning after a heavy snow storm. The road had been plowed, and she was where she should have been, jogging on the side facing the traffic. She was hit and killed by the defendant, a young married man on his way to work who was not under the influence of alcohol but who was recovering from a bad cold and had taken over the counter anti-cold medication. He was charged with Negligent Homicide, a misdemeanor which carries a maximum sentence of 6 months. The defense attorney argued eloquently that although the result was serious, the offense itself was not being only a misdemeanor and although the victim was wearing bright clothing, the defendant just didn't see her in time to avoid hitting her. The state's attorney took no position on the application but yielded to the victim's husband, a Hartford police detective, who spoke fervently and articulately in opposition.

2. A Department of Corrections guard who, while treasurer of the Correction Guards' Union, had embezzled $25,000. A representative of the union was in court opposing the application although well aware that the defendant, if convicted, the application being denied, would probably lose his job. The state's attorney also opposed the application.

3. The defendant had been charged with possession of less than 4 ounces of marijuana. He was a student at the University of Connecticut.

4. The defendant had been given a ticket for a minor motor vehicle violation. While talking to the black state trooper who had stopped him, he called him a black son of a bitch/bastard, etc. He was facing a charge of interfering with a police officer/resisting arrest, which was a misdemeanor. Neither the trooper, the state police division nor the state's attorney took a position on the application.

5. A local doctor, a general practitioner, had been charged with 7 counts of fraud/ misuse of drugs. He had become addicted to pain killers. He would prescribe a liquid type of pain killer, have the patient return with the filled prescription, and then inject the patient with a shot of water while telling the patient it was a pain killer. He later injected himself with the actual pain killer. There were letters from former patients objecting to the application as well as in court objection by the state's attorney. His license to practice medicine in Connecticut had already been suspended.

6. Youthful Offender status, for sixteen and seventeen year olds, is similar to AR. It is up to the discretion of the judge as to whether or not to grant it. If granted, there is a guilty plea, rarely any incarceration, and if the youth complies with the conditions of probation and does not violate any laws, the record is automatically erased when he or she reaches age twenty one. Similar to AR, the judge has to consider the seriousness of the offense. In this case, two young men, one sixteen and one seventeen, shortly after obtaining their driver's licenses, had each driven a car racing with each other on a rural road. One driver lost control, hit an embankment and a tree resulting in the death of one of his teenage passengers. The victim's parents had expressed their opposition through the state's attorney, and the state's attorney, herself, opposed the application. The youths had prominent attorneys who argued eloquently in favor of youthful offender status.

7. A young woman had gone to the state police claiming she had been raped by her boyfriend. She filled out a sworn statement describing what happened. The state police investigated and became suspicious of her statement. Subsequently, she came in and withdrew the statement. She was questioned extensively as to whether her withdrawal was voluntary. She insisted it was. She was then arrested for filing a false statement, a misdemeanor. There was no objection to her application for AR.

8. Misconduct with a motor vehicle: when an operator of a motor vehicle, with criminal negligence, causes the death of another person, a class D felony which carries a maximum sentence of 5 years. The driver of a pick up truck was at his home with some friends drinking beer, when they decided to go somewhere together in the truck. One of his friends weighed approximately 350 pounds. Because of his size, he decided to ride in the back of the pick up. The driver specifically instructed him to put up the tailgate of the truck before they left. The friend failed to do so. The truck proceeded down the driveway over a storm drain as it entered the highway at a point where there was a sharp incline in the highway. The sudden move upward and the 350 pound weight of the victim caused him to slide down the back of the truck, the tailgate being down, and fall onto the highway on his back striking the back of his head on the highway killing him. Alcohol was not a factor in the accident at least as to the driver. He passed a Breathalyzer test. The state took no position on the application, and the victim's widow supported the application.

9. Ridicule on account of race, creed or color: "Any person who, by his advertisement, ridicules or holds up to contempt any person . . . on account of the creed, religion, color, denomination, nationality or race of such person . . . shall be fined not more than fifty dollars or imprisoned not more than 30 days or both." I believe the defendant was also charged with breach of peace. Both charges were misdemeanors.

A somewhat heavy set black woman in her late thirties or early forties, had entered an Italian restaurant and ordered a grinder (sub) to go. While she was waiting for it, she took a seat in an empty booth, which was apparently the last available non-smoking booth. Enter the defendant, a white middle aged businessman with a companion for dinner. He went over to the booth and asked (she claimed "demanded") the woman to leave the booth. She said no and explained that it would only be a few minutes because she was just waiting for her grinder. There were no counter seats. Her refusal infuriated the defendant who called her either a nigger or a black bastard, told her she had no right to the booth and again demanded that she leave with such words as "Who the hell do you think you are, you lousy nigger?" By this time, the woman's grinder was ready, she got up, paid for it and left with the comment to the defendant: "Sir, this has been a very interesting experience. Have a nice day."

All of the words spoken by both parties were loud enough to be heard by other patrons of the restaurant as well as a waitress who testified to all of this at the hearing on the AR application. You would think the defendant would drop the whole matter at this point. Not so. He strode after the woman and accosted her in the parking lot. She testified that he poked his finger in her face and yelled at her "Why don't you go back to Africa where you came from? You people are really screwing up this country." At that point the woman had had enough. She went inside and called the police. With the account given by the waitress as well as the woman, the defendant was arrested. He was represented by a highly respected and competent attorney who had a good reputation for integrity. He argued that this outburst by the defendant was out of character for him, that he was under business pressure at the time, and that by virtue of the light penalty if convicted, it did not rise to a serious offense. The state took no position because the victim was there in opposition to speak for herself. She described the humiliation she felt and was especially angry at his pointing his finger in her face. Then, she stated "And, I'm a Christian, your honor. I'm a Christian." I wasn't sure what to make of that statement, and rather than get into a discussion of religion with the possibility that the defendant would announce his religion, I made no comment.

10. The **SPUDZOOKA INCIDENT:** Two young men, in their twenties, one a senior at the University of Connecticut and the other a recent graduate, had gotten very drunk on a Saturday night on the campus, "hammered," I believe is the appropriate word. One of them had taken a piece of relatively small sewer pipe, and somehow had transformed it into a replica of an Army or Marine bazooka used

in combat primarily to destroy enemy tanks. I don't recall whether they were engineering students, but under the circumstances that could be a logical conclusion.

Not having military ordinance to put into the bazooka, they decided to use potatoes instead which as you will see, can still be deadly. Thus, was born the name "SPUDZOOKA." The maker of the spudzooka sat in the passenger side of the automobile. The other individual was, of course, the driver. They then drove past the Police/Fire Complex and fired the spudzooka at the police part first. The "spud" hit the brick wall of the building and fell harmlessly on the ground causing no damage. Still drunk and still obviously unsatisfied, they drove back to where they had started and took another run past the complex. This time they hit their target. The "spud" crashed through a window of the fire complex smashing it and sending shattered glass flying around.

No one was near the window at the time so no one was injured, and the damage was negligible. Following their arrest, they were subsequently presented in court before me pursuant to an AR application. A representative of the police department and a representative of the fire department showed up to oppose the application. The defendants' attorneys said in support of the application that the charges of breach of peace and reckless endangerment were only misdemeanors, it was just a college prank, no one was hurt, and the defendants were just drunk and meant no harm. Aside from this incident, they were good citizens of the University campus.

The decisions I made appear on the following page. You may wish to check your decisions against mine.

RESPONSES TO AR APPLICATIONS

1. Negligent Homicide. The jogger who was struck and killed. Defense counsel tried to convince me that it was just a misdemeanor, that although the result was serious, the crime was a low grade misdemeanor. Unbeknownst to the defense attorney, I had researched U.S. Supreme Court decisions and was able to quote

Justice William O. Douglas to the effect that a misdemeanor was not always a minor crime. I also stated that except in very unusual circumstances, a death was too serious a matter to warrant wiping the slate clean. By eliminating any record of the crime, it would be devaluing the life and memory of the victim. **APPLICATION DENIED.** The defendant then pleaded guilty and was given a suspended sentence. He was found guilty of a misdemeanor, but could not apply for AR again in view of the fact that he now had a record.[1]

2. **Embezzlement of $25,000 by the treasurer of the Corrections Guards Union. APPLICATION DENIED.** The defendant was in a position of trust which he violated. That violation of trust plus the amount embezzled made the crime too serious.

3. **Possession of less than four ounces of marijuana. APPLICATION GRANTED.** This is a common practice among young people. I routinely granted AR, usually to University of Connecticut students, on this charge so they could keep a clean record. I recognize that this is a gateway drug that can lead to use of other, more dangerous drugs, and the young person receives a lecture from me to that effect. Further, they are warned that if they do it again or commit any other crime, they will not be eligible for AR.

4. **The driver who called the state trooper a black son of a bitch/bastard. APPLICATION GRANTED.** There was no opposition from the state, the state police, the particular state trooper or anyone else. However, I put the defendant on probation for the maximum 2 years and added a condition that within 60 days, he make a $1,000 contribution to the NAACP.

5. **The doctor who had stolen drugs from his patients. APPLICATION DENIED.** The offenses, which were multiple, were just too serious. I did not think he should go to jail, however. He himself was an addict, and he had lost his license to practice medicine in Connecticut. I gave him a suspended sentence with two special conditions of probation: a substantial number of hours of community service to be performed, and I directed his attorney to send by

---

[1] In 1998, the Connecticut legislature amended the Accelerated Rehabilitation statute to **preclude the granting of the program in any case where a death resulted** from the defendant's actions.

certified mail notice of his convictions and his loss of his Connecticut license to the medical licensing authorities in the 49 other states and the District of Columbia so they would be aware of this if he applied for a license. I also ordered him to undergo drug addiction treatment.

6. The two youthful offenders seeking youthful offender status. APPLICATIONS DENIED. The death of the teen age passenger was too serious to warrant a clean record.

7. Making a false statement to the police about being raped. APPLICATION DENIED. Even though it was a misdemeanor, the consequences of her action, if the state police had not become suspicious, would have been disastrous for the young man she accused. He would have had to hire an attorney to represent him, his reputation would be harmed, and he would no doubt be offered a deal to plead guilty to a misdemeanor such as sexual assault 4 with perhaps, some jail time. The alternative would be to go to trial and, if the jury believed her, even though he knew she was lying, he would be facing substantial prison time. If he accepted the deal, he might still serve some time and would have a record.

Today, he would have to register as a sex offender under Meagan's law and his employment prospects would be seriously diminished; all for something he didn't do. I fully recognized that he could have pressured her to recant her statement. However, the state police had questioned her extensively on that, and I did as well, making sure the young man was not in the courtroom while I was questioning her. I had to conclude that there was no evidence that she had been pressured, and that she recanted because the state police had questioned the veracity of her original complaint.

8. Misconduct with a motor vehicle, the death of the man who fell out of the pick up truck. APPLICATION GRANTED. Although I still believe, as a general rule, that a death is too serious to warrant AR, there are exceptions, and decisions should be made on a case by case basis. The widow supported the application, the state did not oppose it, and I was convinced that the victim's own negligence was the proximate cause of the accident. If the case had gone to trial, the negligence of the victim would have been a valid defense to the charge of misconduct with a motor vehicle.

9. Ridicule on account of color or race. APPLICATION DENIED. This case and the case of the black state trooper shows that racism is still alive and flourishing. We have a long way to go to eliminate it. The difference between this and the case of the black state trooper is that here the actions of the defendant went beyond a simple outburst. He made his remarks in a public place, and he continued them, even to the point of following the victim outside into the parking lot. The victim vigorously opposed the application, and the independent waitress in effect supported her. Overall, it was just too serious to warrant AR. He pleaded guilty. I gave him a suspended sentence and probation with conditions of community service and a $1,500 contribution to the NAACP.[2]

10. The Spudzooka incident. APPLICATION DENIED. This was more than just a college prank. If a firefighter had been near the window when it was broken and been hit by flying shards of glass, he or she could have been seriously, and even fatally wounded. I accepted guilty pleas, and gave them each a suspended sentence and probation. Two special conditions of probation were that they each address the incoming freshman class or the convocation audience if University officials agreed, to describe what they did, what their penalty was, apologize for what they did, and thereby warn the students of the consequences of drinking too much. In addition, they were each to spend 100 hours washing fire engines or police cars as the University police and fire departments directed.

---

2 During World War II, General Dwight D. Eisenhower was Supreme Commander of the Allied Expeditionary Force (SHAEF). Part of his job was to develop good relations with the Americans, British, French and other allied nations in order to have a command and armies free from inter-nation rivalry, prejudice and tension. He has been given great credit, and rightly so, for his diplomatic skills in welding together disparate nations and personalities into an effective and victorious fighting force. Historian Stephen Ambrose in his prize winning biography of "Eisenhower, Soldier, General of the Army, President-elect, 1890-1952" recalls an incident in England in 1942. ". . . Eisenhower heard of a fracas between an American and a British officer on the AFHQ staff. He investigated, decided that the American was at fault, ordered him reduced in rank, and sent back to the States. The British officer involved called on Eisenhower to protest. "He only called me a son of a bitch, sir, and all of us have now learnt (sic) that this is a colloquial expression which is sometimes used almost as a term of endearment." To which Eisenhower replied, "I am informed that he called you a British son of a bitch. That is quite different. My ruling stands."

Chapter Three

LYING UNDER OATH

"Oh, what a tangled web we weave when first we practice to deceive." — **Sir Walter Scott**

Lying under oath has recently become a hot topic in our society. It happens more often than most people think. It strikes at the very heart of our judicial system. It interferes with the right of every person to have a fair trial. When a witness lies as to the identity of a person who committed a crime, and that witness is believed, the falsely accused person can go to jail for the rest of his or her life and under certain circumstances can be executed for a crime he or she did not commit. Life and liberty are at stake when perjury is committed in a criminal trial. Not too long ago it was discovered that several Philadelphia police officers had trumped up evidence against defendants and lied about this evidence on the witness stand. As a result, several innocent people were wrongfully convicted and imprisoned. When these incidents came to light, the investigation widened, and more such incidents were discovered. Prisoners were released, their cases were either dropped or they were given new trials; but who could make up for the shame and agony they suffered and the freedom they lost for many months or years? A similar situation was exposed in New York state among members of the state police years earlier. Of course, this is not to say that all police officers do this. Most of them are honest, hard working individuals who do a very difficult, dangerous and frustrating job, but when it does happen, even though it may be rarely, the defendant is deprived of his or her right to a fair trial with sometimes devastating results.

And what of the man who is falsely accused and convicted of sexual assault based upon the perjured testimony of the "victim?"; or those who were falsely accused but eventually acquitted? The long time head of the White House travel office comes to mind. He underwent severe emotional distress and embarrassment to say nothing of the huge legal fees he had to pay to protect his rights. I can recall Ray Donovan, Secretary of Labor in the Reagan administration who had to resign when he was investigated for labor racketeering and subsequently went to trial. He was acquitted, and as he met the media on the steps of the New York courthouse, he said: "Now, tell me. Who's going to give me back my reputation?" As a judge in criminal court I have seen many situations in which a defendant proclaims his innocence. He or she is charged with a serious crime based upon what the defendant considers false testimony by a witness or an accuser. The defendant knows he or she is innocent, but also knows if he or she is found guilty, it will mean a long prison sentence. Does he or she want to risk that?

The defendant's attorney works out a plea bargain with the prosecutor, a reduced charge with no jail time or maybe a year in jail. This would give the defendant a criminal record, and he or she would either be on probation or would spend a year in jail and then be on probation. The defendant would be away from his or her family, and if the breadwinner, unable to support the family. He or she would probably lose his or her job. Knowing you are innocent, it doesn't sound very appealing, does it? But what if the jury chooses to believe the lies of the accuser? Then, the defendant would be facing ten to twenty years in prison, plus having to spend substantial sums for legal representation during the trial. What would you do?

Judges take lying under oath very seriously, but it is up to the prosecutor to bring the charge, and that will happen only when there is a clear case of perjury, and, of course, only when the perjury is discovered. Even then, dockets are crowded with people charged with crimes of violence, and those cases have to take precedence. People are charged with and convicted of perjury, but it is rare. Hopefully, more prosecutions will take place for this crime, and hopefully, increased prosecutions will serve as a deterrent to those who are thinking of lying under oath. Then, again hopefully, we can reduce the incidents of miscarriage of justice.

Why do people lie under oath? There are several reasons. They are basically dishonest and have no respect for the quality of integrity, the rule of law or fundamental fairness. It is in their best interest to lie. They want to avoid the consequences of their actions that would occur if the truth were known. They may be bitter against the other person and want revenge, and, of course, old fashioned greed has its place. By lying in a civil case or a family case (i.e., divorce, custody, visitation), they can obtain money in a civil case, pay more or less alimony or support in a divorce case or convince the judge that their spouse is a horrible person who is not entitled to the custody of the couple's children or visitation with them. Sometimes a spouse will make unfounded charges in order to pressure the other spouse into a more advantageous settlement, one that favors the spouse making the false charges. Is this right? Of course it isn't, but we know it happens all the time.

Finally, the other compelling reason people lie under oath is that they think they can get away with it. Those who lie on the witness stand think that judges and juries are not very bright. Well, I have a surprise for them. Juries in Connecticut whose members have had to go through a very probing, individual questioning by the attorneys turn out to be intelligent, sophisticated, experienced and honest. They can usually tell when witnesses are lying. Judges are former attorneys who have spent many years in the "trenches" where they have constantly had to evaluate the truthfulness of their own clients, have had to evaluate and sometime attack the credibility of opposing witnesses, and, of course, have had to evaluate the credibility of their own witnesses in order to decide whether or not to put them on the witness stand subject to cross examination by the opposing attorney. Most attorneys have heard all the lies and excuses before. Judges bring this experience with them to the bench. Further, trying cases is a constant learning process. The more experienced the judge is, the better he or she is at knowing a lie when he or she hears one. Several parties and witnesses have learned this the hard way. A few examples from cases I have tried will demonstrate this.

State of Connecticut vs. David Copas. (See **Murder In the Connecticut Woods** for the details about this case.) In his confession Copas stated that he and Laura had arrived at the wooded area and that when they got out of the car, she claimed that he had diseased her and then she pulled out a pocket knife and stabbed him repeatedly in his right hand. This so enraged him that he grabbed the knife away from her and stabbed her. The psychiatrist who testified for him, who was a prominent and eminently qualified psychiatrist, said that his killing of the girl was a "reactive homicide" which demonstrated his extreme emotional disturbance. Of course, the only testimony by an eye witness was in the form of Copas' confession. There seemed to be no one to challenge his version of what happened. Well, not quite. In rebuttal, the state produced as a witness the assistant state medical examiner who displayed on a screen a slide, in color, showing Copas' right hand palm up, based upon a photograph taken by the state police at the time of the crime in 1986. It showed the wounds on Copas' hand that he claimed were caused by the victim attacking him with the pen knife. The medical examiner, however, testified that these were offensive wounds, not defensive wounds, and that they had been sustained by Copas when he stabbed Laura twenty-two times. This showed that Copas had lied in his confession and that Laura had not attacked him. This, of course, undermined his psychiatrist's testimony that it was a reactive homicide. The jury found that he was not under extreme emotional disturbance and found him guilty of murder. I sentenced him to life imprisonment, and under Connecticut law he will not be eligible for parole. In my sentencing remarks, I emphasized that he had compounded his horrible crime by lying about it.

Lying under oath is, of course, not limited to criminal matters. In 1996 I tried the family relations case of *Dr. John Doe vs. Jane Doe*. It was a contested divorce case which was tried for fifteen days, a lengthy trial as divorce cases go. Jury trials are not allowed in family matters, so it was tried before me sitting as the court. In such a situation, there are, of course, no instructions to the jury on the applicable law given by the judge, and it is the judge rather than a jury who decides what facts are. Beyond that, all of the normal rules of trial are applicable. In Connecticut, as in most states, we have what is known as no fault divorce. Neither party has to prove that the other party was at fault. It is only necessary to prove that the marriage had broken down irretrievably with no hope of reconciliation. Fault is not an issue in the court granting a dissolution of the marriage. Both parties generally want the divorce, and the only testimony needed on this issue is of one party stating that the marriage had broken down irretrievably. Although custody is sometimes at issue, it was not in this case. As in most cases, the principal fight was over money, how much child support should be awarded for two minor children, how much alimony should be awarded, if any, and how the property or assets should be distributed. Visitation with the children was not a contested issue. Although the husband and wife were clearly "disillusioned" with each other, it was also clear that they each loved their children very much and that the children loved them.

The couple was in their mid-thirties. They had met at college and had been married for ten years. The wife was employed as a nurse, and the husband was an M.D. in private practice. The husband was considered brilliant in his chosen field. He was an expert in his field and had published popular books on the subject. Unfortunately, along with his brilliance came a certain amount of arrogance which he amply demonstrated while testifying.

In order to determine the amount of child support and alimony to be awarded, the judge must determine the earning capacity of the husband as well as the wife. The wife received a salary, which made earning capacity easier to determine. The husband had worked for a hospital, but was now in his first year of private practice. Therefore, his previous salary was irrelevant. A determination of his earning capacity is based upon the income and expenses he has had, and most importantly what he is expected to earn in the next year. To a great degree that is based upon the credibility of the witness. As stated in my written decision, I concluded that Dr. John Doe had committed several what Winston Churchill once called "terminological inexactitudes". In other words he was caught lying under oath.

The wife's attorney was questioning him about an alleged sexual affair that he had with one, Deborah Smith, a doctor who had attended a physician's convention in Chicago Memorial Day weekend of l993 which was also attended by Dr. Doe. He had met her on a previous occasion, but the affair of which he was accused occurred in Chicago on that weekend. In a deposition held prior to the trial, he had admitted having sexual relations with Mrs. Smith in July, 1993 after, as he claimed, that his marriage had broken down irretrievably, but had denied under oath that he had had sexual relations with her Memorial Day weekend, 1993. A deposition is the questioning of a party or witness prior to trial usually held at an attorney's office with most of the questioning being done by the attorney for the other party. The person testifying, often called the deponent, takes the same oath to tell the truth that he does in court.

Dr. John Doe was a prolific letter writer, particularly good at writing love letters complete with romantic expressions and protestations of love. Some might even call them steamy. He wrote many of these to Mrs. Smith following his return from Chicago. What he knew but chose to overlook was the fact that Mrs. Smith and **her husband** were also having marital problems. Mr. Smith found the letters and sent copies of them to Mrs. Doe. At the trial these letters had, by agreement of the attorneys, been pre-marked as exhibits and admitted into evidence. Dr. John Doe had been informed of this by his attorney, but either through arrogance or overconfidence, or both, he must have forgotten about them. After his denial of a sexual affair in Chicago with Mrs. Smith in response to Mrs. Doe's attorney's questions, I chose to intervene with my own questions. As the ultimate finder of fact, the judge has the right to ask questions during a court trial. The colloquy went like this.

"Doctor, you're sure that you did not have sexual relations with Mrs. Smith in Chicago Memorial Day weekend of 1993?"

"That's correct."

"Just so I understand your answer, Doctor, that means that there was no kissing, no touching, no feeling, no foreplay, no hugging?"

"That's right."

"It was merely a platonic relationship. Is that correct?"

"Yes."

"Doctor, did you see Mrs. Smith during the first three weeks you were home after Memorial Day weekend?"

"No."

"What type of contact did you have with her during those three weeks, if any?"

"By telephone a few times, and I may have sent her a letter."

I must have been prescient in pinning him down on what was sexual relations, not realizing, of course, that the definition of sexual relations would in 1998 become a national issue. I picked up one of the letters written by Dr. Doe.

"Doctor, let me read to you a letter to Mrs. Smith from you dated June 21, 1993, three weeks after you returned from Chicago. It starts out with "My sweet angel", and then you continue to pour your heart out to her telling her in various ways how much you love her. Doctor, do you really want this court to believe that after a weekend that was purely platonic in which you didn't even kiss or otherwise touch Mrs. Smith, in which there was no physical contact, and after three weeks at home in which you had no physical contact with her, that on June 21st you suddenly fell head over heels in love with her?"

He looked at me. "Well, your honor I was desperate. I was desperate."

I looked at him. "You mean desperate for the emotional sustenance you were not getting from your wife?"

"That's it. That's it, exactly."

"That's what I thought." I replied.

Then, I shifted to another aspect. "Doctor, I notice that at the end of your letter to Mrs. Smith, you close by saying 'I miss you more than you will ever know. Love, John.' I also have here a valentine card that you sent to your wife approximately four months earlier in which you end with 'I love you more than you will ever know. Love, John.' Tell me, Doctor did you love them both equally or is this just a phrase you tossed around?" There was no response. Is it any wonder that I did not find him to be credible?

Dr. John Doe had claimed that his earning capacity was $90,000 per year gross, less $40,000 in office and related expenses for an annual net of $50,000. After reviewing the documents and all of the testimony, I concluded that his gross earning capacity was $201,000. Giving him the same $40,000 for expenses, I concluded that his net earning capacity was $161,000. Also, in Connecticut, although there is no fault divorce, the judge is allowed to take fault into consideration when awarding alimony, attorneys' fees and in distributing assets. The key word here is "irretrievable" as in "the marriage has broken down irretrievably". The wife had testified that she and her husband were trying to keep their marriage together through counseling, taking a vacation together, etc., but that starting right after Memorial Day weekend of 1993, things started going down hill again between her and her husband. He became even more distant, difficult to talk to, and by July, the marriage had completely broken down. It is entirely possible that without Mrs. Smith, the marriage would eventually have failed anyway, but I concluded that as of Memorial Day weekend, 1993, the marriage was still salvageable, and if it were not for the adultery the husband had committed that weekend, the marriage would not have broken down irretrievably in early June as it did.

Based upon the husband's net earning capacity, and in accordance with the state's child support guidelines, I awarded $550 per week child support. I also awarded $500 per week alimony with no limitation, $20,000 lump sum alimony and $25,000 in attorneys' fees to reimburse some of the money advanced to the wife by her parents, both sums to be paid over a relatively short period of time. The wife received the marital home. The husband had already purchased another house for himself. About a year later, the husband sought modification of my orders before another judge claiming that he was grossing less than $201,000. He **claimed** that his gross earnings were $176,000 which is still a far cry from $90,000. The modification was denied. The case was appealed to the Appellate Court, but before it could be heard the parties settled with only minimal changes to my original orders.

One final word on Dr. John Doe. At one point shortly after my decision, the parties returned to me for approval of a minor modification, which I granted. I asked Dr. John Doe what had happened to his relationship with the former Mrs. Smith. "Oh," he said, "we broke up. She wanted to get married." I read to him another one of his letters to her in which he ended with "Love, from your future husband, John." When I pointed that out to him, he had no comment. [The full text of my decision in this case is included at the end of this book as Appendix A.]

Marcus Sanchez had received a sentence of seven years, execution *suspended*, for possession of cocaine. He was put on probation for a period of three years during which he was required to submit to such substance abuse evaluation, counseling and treatment, either out-patient or inpatient as may be directed by the Office of Adult Probation. This is one of the standard conditions of probation in a drug case. The goal is, of course, to rehabilitate him by curing his addiction to illegal drugs. Mr. Sanchez had violated his probation by continuing to use cocaine and by not complying with the drug treatment orders of the probation department. He had admitted to his violations, a pre-sentence investigation and report had been done, and I had read the report. He appeared in front of me in Willimantic, Connecticut for sentencing. I had the options of terminating his probation, sentencing him to the full seven years that had been suspended, continuing him on probation or sentencing him to a portion of the seven years with the remainder being suspended and a new period of probation being imposed to commence upon his release from custody. He was represented by the public defender. Sanchez was a man in his early forties, approximately five feet ten inches tall with a stocky build.

"What am I supposed to do with you, Mr. Sanchez? I can't put you out on the streets again where you can get cocaine and where you might steal to get the money to get cocaine. You'd be dangerous to other people. As for more drug treatment, you've already had three opportunities for inpatient treatment and failed them all. I understand the problems with outpatient treatment. When you get home after counseling, drugs are available on the streets, and you use them again. I generally give a break to someone who has not had inpatient treatment; but you've had three chances. What happened at New Perceptions?"

"One of the nurses gave me a hard time, so I left." he replied.

"All right. What about New Horizons?"

He responded with another excuse.

"What about Stonington House?" Another excuse.

"Mr. Sanchez. You've had three chances for inpatient treatment and you've blown them all. These beds are at a premium. There's a long waiting list. I can't put you back in and deprive some other drug addict who's never had an opportunity for inpatient treatment. It wouldn't be fair to him. I can't put you back on the streets. The only alternative is to put you in jail. It would be warehousing you, but I don't see where there is any other choice."

By this time his attorney had moved away from him. All eyes were focused on Mr. Sanchez who said:

"Your honor, may I say something?"

"Certainly. Please do."

"I was abused as a child."

"Well, that's too bad." I replied. "That's news to me. I didn't see that anywhere in the pre-sentence report. Did you tell that to Mr. Woods?"

"Yes, I did, but he probably forgot to put it in."

"Well, I doubt that. I know Mr. Woods. He's an attorney in addition to being a probation officer. He's very thorough."

"Also, your honor; I have found the Lord. All I want to do is his work. All I want to do is help people. I want to spend the rest of my life helping people."

"That's wonderful, Mr. Sanchez, and I'm going to give you an opportunity to do just that. I can't think of any group of people who need more help than your fellow prisoners. I'm going to give you five years to do that. Mr. Sanchez, you are hereby committed to the custody of the Commissioner of Corrections for a period of seven years. Execution of that sentence is suspended after five years. I'm putting you on probation for a period of three years." I then described the conditions of his probation including drug treatment as may be directed by the Office of Adult Probation.

His mouth was still open as he was led away.

"Oh, one more thing, Mr. Sanchez." He turned toward me.

"May God be with you."

I was later informed that the next day people on probation suddenly started to show up on time for meetings with their probation officers.

Civil cases are not immune from people lying under oath. The classic anecdote is of the plaintiff being on the witness stand, and in response to a question from the defendant's attorney, he, the injured plaintiff, demonstrated how high he could lift his right arm because of the accident. He struggled, obviously in great pain, to lift his right arm level with his right shoulder. The defense attorney then asked how far he could lift his arm before the accident. "Oh, before the accident", he replied, "I could lift it all the way up to here." as he effortlessly raised his right arm way above his head reaching toward the ceiling.

Back to reality. In a Hartford courtroom before me and a jury of six, the plaintiff was suing Shoprite supermarkets for injuries she sustained as the result of her fall on a liquid substance in one of the aisles. Mrs. Calendar was a short, blond woman, rather attractive who appeared to be in her mid-thirties. She got up from her seat at the counsel table with much difficulty, and leaning heavily on her cane she took short steps as she struggled to the witness chair. She described in answer to her attorney's questions the restrictions placed upon her as a result of the accident.

"I could no longer hold my granddaughter in my arms because I might drop her. I've had to have someone next to me when I hold her in case I start to drop her." She began to sniffle, and her voice broke. Her attorney paused as she took out her handkerchief to blow her nose.

"What else?" asked her attorney.

"I've been unable to go back to work as a waitress, I haven't been able to do household chores, I can't go shopping. I can't even go for a walk."

"What about recreational activities?" her attorney prompted her.

"I can't go skiing, I can't go horseback riding any more, and you know, I used to go flying. Not as a pilot, but as a passenger in a small plane owned by a friend of mine. There's a little step that you have to use in order to boost yourself up into the cockpit. With my bad right knee, I've been unable to do that."

On cross-examination, defense counsel quickly got her to admit that she and her husband had never actually skied or gone horseback riding. They had merely gone to the ski area to inquire about lessons and had visited the stables to "look the place over and find out the cost". Then the other shoe dropped. Over strenuous objections by the plaintiff's attorney, I admitted into evidence a videotape taken by a private investigator for the supermarket the previous October. The trial was the following February. The videotape, in color, was played for the jury on a television set brought into the courtroom. The first series showed the plaintiff leaning against her kitchen counter just inside the white storm or screen door holding her granddaughter in one arm and a cell phone in the other hand talking continuously. The door then opened, and Mrs. Calendar, with granddaughter in one arm and continuing to talk on the cell phone, proceeded with no apparent discomfort to walk across a large wooden deck in the rear of her house, and then down a steep flight of wooden stairs not using the handrails and, of course, bending her right knee as her right foot stepped onto and off of every other step. About halfway down, she sat down, again bending her right knee. And, you guessed it! She placed her granddaughter on the same damaged right knee, still talking on her cell phone. There were other scenes of the plaintiff taking out the garbage cans - again with no problem.

She even returned to Shoprite, (apparently there were no hard feelings left over as a result of her "accident" there), driven there by someone else in a large van. The next scene showed her pushing a grocery cart, and admittedly leaning on it while she pushed it, from the store to the side of the van. On the side of the van there was a small step by itself on which a passenger would have to step to boost herself up into the van, similar to the step a passenger would have to take to boost herself up into the cabin of the airplane. The plaintiff stepped onto this step, right foot first, up into the van with ease. The jury returned a verdict for the defendant.

Okay, you may say. She was caught in a lie, and justice was done; and, besides, this was a civil case. Only money was at stake. It wasn't a criminal case where someone's life or liberty was at stake. True; but does that mean it's all right to lie in a civil case but not in a criminal case? You've just read what could have happened to a mother and two children if the husband's lies were not discovered. In an accident case in which the plaintiff is seriously injured perhaps suffering the loss of use of his or her arm or leg, the plaintiff is restricted from working and carrying on life's usual activities. Although with permanent injury, the plaintiff never gets back the use of his or her arm or leg, he or she should at least be compensated for the lost earnings, both past and future, for the pain and suffering and the restricted activities the plaintiff will suffer for the rest of his or her life. People's entire lives have been turned around for the worse because of the negligence or fault of another. Shouldn't these people be compensated in so far as money can do it? What if Mrs. Calendar's lies had never been exposed? Well, you might say, "that's okay; it's only the insurance company's money." But if we slough off fraudulent claims against insurance companies, guess whose insurance premiums will rise? Yours and mine, that's who. Why should we be forced to pay for someone else's fraud?

Here's an example of how a plaintiff could have been cheated. It was a trial before me and a jury in the fall of 1998. Plaintiff had been hit in the rear of his automobile on a superhighway causing his car to collide with the guard rail. The offending driver had no insurance, so the suit was against the plaintiff's own insurance company based on the uninsured motorist provisions in his policy. There was no question that the other driver was at fault. The issue was one of damages. The plaintiff had been employed at the main post office operating a zip code machine. This required him to bend his neck forward from a standing position to type in the zip codes. It was his neck that had been injured. The orthopedic surgeon who had testified for him said that he had a 10% permanent partial disability of his neck. The plaintiff testified that he was unable to perform his job without severe pain in his neck. As a result he was forced to take a lower paying job as a counter person at a post office branch where presumably he would not have to bend his neck.

The offer from the insurance company had been $35,000 which his attorney recommended he accept. He was in his late forties or early fifties with a life expectancy of at least twenty-five years. The insurance company had referred him to another orthopedic surgeon for an "independent medical examination." That doctor testified that his evaluation was that the plaintiff had suffered no permanency. But if that were so, why would the plaintiff have voluntarily taken a drop in grade and a lower paying job? If there were no permanent injury to his neck, he would have remained in the job he held at the time of the accident. Did the insurance company's doctor lie under oath?

Probably not. These examinations are somewhat subjective in nature, and the doctor could have honestly believed there was no permanency. However, this case shows how critical the credibility of witnesses is in a trial. A professor of economics from a local college had testified that the plaintiff's lost earnings and his future lost earnings amounted to $99,000. The jury did not believe the testimony of the doctor who testified for the insurance company and awarded the plaintiff $143,000; the $99,000 plus $6,000 in medical bills plus $38,000 for past and future pain and suffering. To his credit the plaintiff had declined the offer of $35,000.

There are, however, times when plaintiffs tend to exaggerate, and this is not lost on the jury. A plaintiff in an intersection accident testified that his main complaint resulting from his knee injury (he was retired) was that he could no longer go water skiing. I looked at the members of the jury and did not see any signs of sympathy in their eyes. To top it off the door to the courtroom was open. It became noisy in the corridor, so the plaintiff who had been limping because of the injury to his knee leaped up and closed the door without any sign of limping or discomfort. This, too, did not go unnoticed by the jury.

The Truths of Justice

Civil cases are, of course, not all accident cases. There are civil cases of sexual assault, stalking and harassment, discrimination in employment and a host of others. They also usually turn upon the credibility of the witnesses. If they lie under oath and are, nevertheless, believed, justice is not done. Many of these cases are highly emotional, and if the party who has been wronged or falsely accused loses because of perjured testimony, the effect of such loss can be devastating, not only financially, but also emotionally, and the losing party can have his or her reputation severely damaged.

I have given you examples of lying under oath when the lies have been discovered; but what about all the other cases in which the verdict has been based upon perjured testimony and it is not discovered. What can be done about it? Well, hopefully, we can all work together to restore a sense of moral values to society, and honesty will once again be an important part of those values. The other alternative is to prosecute those individuals who have been caught lying under oath and require them to serve time in jail. To some this may seem harsh, but until the penalty for lying under oath is sufficiently severe and prosecutions for this offense are actually brought, then there will not be a sufficient deterrent to this crime that undermines our entire justice system.

Chapter Four

JURY SELECTION

Article First, Section 19 of the
Connecticut Constitution states:
"The right to question each juror individually
by counsel shall be inviolate."

C onnecticut is unique in this regard. It is the only state in the nation to have this provision in its constitution. It is the only state that guarantees this right. In federal court and in many states it is the judge who asks the questions of prospective jurors. The attorneys may submit questions for the judge to ask, but it is within the judge's discretion as to whether or not he or she will ask these questions; and the attorney cannot suggest what questions should be asked to follow up on the answer. Often the questions are asked of an entire jury panel of 25 to 50 prospective jurors sitting together in the courtroom.[1]

This has become a controversial issue in Connecticut. Many judges, attorneys, legislative and governmental officials strongly advocate a constitutional amendment to abolish the right of attorneys to question prospective jurors individually. These advocates are people of high intellect, experience and a sincere desire to see that justice is done. What is their purpose in this? *To save time!* In federal court a full jury is often selected in a day or less. In Connecticut, jury selection can take two days to two months. A non-capital criminal offense or a civil trial requires only six jurors plus usually two alternates; but in a murder case where twelve jurors plus at least two alternates are selected, it can take even longer.

No doubt those advocating abolishment of the present system have in mind the often cited words of William Gladstone who said:

---

[1] Connecticut also has statutes dealing with jury selection the provisions of which are not common to federal trials nor to most states:
"In any criminal/civil action tried before a jury, either party shall have the right to examine, personally or by his counsel each juror **outside the presence of other prospective jurors** as to his qualifications to sit as a juror . . . ." Sec. 51-240 and 54-82f.

The Truths of Justice

"Justice delayed is justice denied." Civil jury cases generally take at least three to four years to come to trial. Imagine how the process can move ahead more quickly with jury selection time drastically reduced; and what about the criminal defendant who is in pre-trial detention awaiting trial? He or she and the alleged victim would want the trial to take place as soon as possible.

However, despite these arguments, I respectfully disagree with my colleagues on the bench and others who advocate this change. The right to question prospective jurors individually is fundamental to the right to a fair and impartial jury.

The late Edward Bennett Williams, a prominent Washington D.C. attorney, originally from Hartford, was nationally recognized as an outstanding criminal defense attorney. He successfully represented several high profile defendants including labor leader Jimmy Hoffa and Army Captain Medina of My-Lai massacre fame. Williams was often quoted as saying: "If you went to the sidewalk in front of the Baltimore courthouse and picked the first twelve people walking by, you could get as good a jury as you could from going through the voir dire process." If he said that, or something similar, I again disagree.

Voir dire is another phrase that identifies jury selection. In French it means "to speak the truth." If that is our goal, and it should be, we are more likely to learn the truth about potential jurors when jurors are questioned individually by the attorneys for both sides.

The ideal juror is one who is intelligent, has had broad experience in life, is willing to judge other people, who is not inflexible, who is willing to serve and pay attention to the trial instead of thinking of his or her job, business or other areas of his or her personal life, and *above all is impartial.* Bias for or against any party or witness is anathema to the concept of an impartial jury. Bias or prejudice on the part of even one juror severely undermines the individual's right to a fair trial. How best to determine whether this bias exists? Here are a few examples of individual questioning of jurors:

Example One: The defendant is a Hispanic male charged with burglary. The prospective juror is a middle aged white woman who lives in a suburb of Hartford.

"Q: How long have you lived in South Windsor, Mrs. Jones?

A: Three years.

Q: Where did you live before that?

A: In Hartford.

Q: Where in Hartford?

A: In an apartment building I owned at the corner of Broad and Park streets."

The attorney is well aware that Broad and Park streets is an area inhabited overwhelmingly by Hispanic immigrants from Puerto Rico.

"Q: Why did you decide to leave there and move to South Windsor?

A: I didn't like the element . . . the people I had to take as tenants."

This juror was excused by the defendant's attorney.

Example Two: The defendants are two black men in their early twenties who are on trial for murder. The jury is deadlocked, 11 to 1 for conviction. The lone holdout is a middle aged black woman. The other jurors, in trying to persuade her to vote for conviction tell her: "The evidence is overwhelming as to their guilt. There's no question, no doubt that these two men committed the murder."

"I know, I know," she responded, her words a mixture of anger and frustration.

"Then why won't you vote guilty," the foreperson asked looking equally as frustrated.

By now, tears were streaming down the holdout juror's face. "I just can't. I just can't bring myself to put two more brothers in jail."

Another juror spoke up. "Why didn't you tell the judge that during jury selection? Don't you remember when he asked if any of us had a bias against or **for** the defendants because they are black?"

"Yes," she replied. "I should have, but I didn't. Maybe I didn't think it would ever come to this, or maybe I was just afraid."

Of course, she was afraid, or at the very least uncomfortable. The woman who didn't like Hispanics probably felt the same way. How would you feel if you were in a large, open courtroom seated with 30 or 40 other prospective jurors and were asked that question? Would you raise your hand and publicly admit that you were a racist? On the other hand, if you were questioned individually, no other jurors present, with only the judge and the two lawyers present (except for the anonymous clerk and court reporter), and the lawyers were permitted to ask a series of probing questions, the truth as to the juror's bias is much more likely to be revealed. If this kind of bias is not discovered, then either the defendant, or in the latter case, the state ("the people") are denied their right to a fair and impartial trial.

There are, of course, other factors that impact upon a juror's ability to serve. In a recent murder case in which I presided (see **Murder in the Connecticut Woods**, elsewhere in this book), the defendant claimed that he had acted under extreme emotional distress. If he were to succeed in that defense, the charge would have to be reduced to manslaughter which carries a maximum sentence of twenty years. Therefore, his mental condition, later to be described by psychiatrists and psychologists on both sides, was a critical issue in the case. In voir dire, defense counsel asked the man whether he believed there was such a thing as mental illness.[2] The juror said yes, which was followed by the question "do you know anyone who is suffering from a mental illness?" The juror broke down in tears and said in between sobs, that his daughter was confined to a mental hospital in Massachusetts. I immediately excused him with the comment that jury service was not supposed to be cruel and unusual punishment.

In the same jury selection, another man became very emotional and broke down because he had recently been divorced from a woman he still professed to love.

I submit that such information would not have been revealed without the individual questioning by the attorneys. In general remarks to a panel of prospective jurors, these jurors would have felt intimidated, frightened, embarrassed or at least too uncomfortable to reveal this information before thirty other jurors and without the probing questions that attorneys generally ask.

Does this type of voir dire set forth in the Connecticut

---

[2] I later chastised the attorney for a question that called for such an obvious answer. I told him that if any juror said no, he would be disqualified for not being competent to serve, and suggested he lead into this subject in a different way.

Constitution result in longer sessions of jury selection? Of course it does, but the concept of speedy justice has to take second place to the right of both parties to have a fair and impartial trial.

When judges give their instructions on the law to the jury that has heard the actual case, sometimes called the judge's charge to the jury, we tell them respectfully that they are the finders of the facts; that a major factor in determining what the facts are is the credibility they ascribe to each witness. They are told to observe the witnesses' demeanor on the witness stand, the manner in which they respond to questions, the consistency or inconsistency of what they say, their memory or lack of memory, their ability to observe, *any bias the witness may have for or against either party*, the witnesses' interest in the outcome of the case; in other words, to evaluate them as to their credibility, to size them up. We also instruct jurors again that sympathy for either party or bias for or against either party has no place in the juror's decision.

This is what we tell the jurors to do in assessing the credibility of witnesses. Isn't it then logical to expect the attorneys to be able to use the same factors in determining the credibility of a prospective juror who will decide their clients' fate; to ensure that the jurors selected are honest, competent and most importantly unbiased? Of course it is. To do this, we must give the parties, through their attorneys, the tools with which to make that determination. Those tools should include the right to question each prospective juror individually outside the presence of other prospective jurors.

Chapter Five

CONSUMER BEWARE!

It was August, and the weather was hot. The dog days of summer were upon us. The judge handling criminal cases in Part B was on a two week vacation, and the other judges took turns filling in for him. I drew Wednesday of the first week and Tuesday of the following week. When I arrived at court that Wednesday morning, I was presented in my chambers with a pre-sentence report done by the Office of Adult Probation concerning one, Justin Potter. Mr. Potter had previously pleaded guilty to nine (9) counts of operating a home improvement business without a license. That was only part of the story.

Mr. Potter, who was in his late twenties, had made it a habit of stopping at the homes of elderly people, usually in their eighties, and offering to repave their driveway at a reduced rate. He told these people that he had just finished another job, and had a half a load of gravel left in his truck. He would, therefore, offer to do their driveway with the left over gravel at a much lower cost than usual. The price would run between $500 and $3,000 depending upon the size of the driveway and the lack of sophistication of the homeowner. In short he would charge whatever he could get. He always demanded the money in advance, preferably in cash, or if it had to be by check, he would immediately drive to the bank to cash it. Then, he would work on the driveway until he ran out of gravel with the promise to return the next day to finish the job. He not only left the work incomplete, but what work he did do was usually defective. As I'm sure you're imagining, that was the last the homeowner saw of Justin Potter. He had fleeced nine people out of a total of $16,143.

I stated for the record the following:

"The special investigator for the Department of Consumer Protection found that the driveway pavement was uneven and the apron had not been paved. And this goes on and on and on, and there's an 89 year old woman here who got fleeced out of $2,000.

The Truths of Justice

The victim's daughter says that the offender owes her 89 year old mother the $2,000 that he "extorted from her". . . those are her words. He applied asphalt to the driveway without permission from the mother, then intimidated her into signing a contract and giving him a check for $2,000. The extra asphalt had no value to her mother, and the driveway itself is neither improved nor harmed by the work that was done, and so on and so on. I won't go into more detail, but the total monies, according to the Probation Officer, comes up to $16,143."

The state was represented by Assistant Attorney General Robert Marconi rather than the state's attorney's office because the charges emanated from the Department of Consumer Protection. The defendant was not represented by an attorney, so it would have been difficult to have a pre-trial conference without an attorney present for the conference. Further, I did not want to forewarn Mr. Potter as to what I was going to do. Attorney Marconi explained the plea bargain agreement that he had developed with the defendant. Each count of practicing home improvement without a license carries a $50 fine plus up to six months in jail. The plea bargain agreement was that in exchange for a guilty plea to all counts, Mr. Potter would receive a suspended sentence and a period of probation during which he would repay the victims at the rate of $700 per month total for all of them. The state would also nolle (not prosecute) all other charges including more serious offenses such as larceny, etc.

My response: "Okay. Well, I have read the pre-sentence investigation, and I am rejecting the plea bargain agreement. I'm sorry for all your hard work, Attorney Marconi, but in reading the pre-sentence investigation, I think what this defendant did was absolutely horrible . . . what disturbs me is the underlying offense which is . . . *nine separate situations* where the defendant, in the only word I can use, defrauded, fleeced people out of their money. One woman was 89 years old . . . And I understand, Attorney Marconi, that your arrangement was for the purpose of getting restitution for these victims . . . But I think crimes like this should not go unpunished. I think a message has to be sent that this type of fleecing of people, defrauding

61

innocent victims, will not be tolerated, and the person who does it has to go to jail.

Now the problem with that, obviously, if he goes to jail, he is not going to make the restitution. But I believe a suspended sentence and the requirement that the payments be made at the rate of $700 per month won't work. He won't make the payments or will skip the state because everything he has done has been *fraud* and fleecing victims . . . he has lied to the probation officer, and he has never delivered anything he promises. He's promised to get her copies of his income tax returns and later he says he never filed because he didn't report the income. He agreed to provide the probation officer with a copy of his valid Rhode Island permit, but he failed to do that . . . . It's rampant throughout here, lies, flat out lies. And maybe he thinks he can take advantage of an 89 year old woman with lies, but he's not going to take advantage of an experienced probation officer, an experienced assistant attorney general, and he's not going to take advantage of this court."

"You have three options, Mr. Potter. You can accept a two year sentence of incarceration plus probation and a payment over a period of time, to be worked out. You can withdraw your plea of guilty and go to trial on these charges. Your third option is no incarceration, but you have to come up with the sixteen thousand one hundred forty-three dollars in a lump sum by next Tuesday. Now, I really think you should go to jail; but in order to get the full $16,143 to make restitution to these victims you will be required to come up with a bank or certified check payable to the State of Connecticut in the amount of $16,143 by next Tuesday. I'm continuing this case until next Tuesday, August 12th. Further, I am now setting a bond of $150,000 for Mr. Potter. Sheriff, take him into custody right now until he posts that bond; because quite frankly, sir, if you walk out of here we'll never see you again or the $16,000."

"Now, Mr. Potter, those are your choices. Pay a bondsman ten percent of the bond, $15,000 so you can be released immediately and then come back for trial at a later date - that is assuming you can find a bail bondsman who will risk $150,000 for $15,000. Your other choice is to add $1,143 to the $15,000, make it payable to the State of Connecticut, and I will give you a suspended sentence, or you could withdraw your plea of guilty and go to trial. Would you like to be heard on that, Mr. Potter?"

To say that Mr. Potter was uncomfortable would be an understatement. He actually sputtered when he talked. "Sir, I don't have that — I could borrow the money off my grandfather . . . ."

"Where you get the money is up to you, Mr. Potter. I notice from your pre-sentence report that your fiancé has two sons one of whom is allegedly involved in a similar scam in Darien, Connecticut and the state of Maine and one in Massachusetts. Also, you've indicated that your fiancé doesn't have to work and that she owns a new BMW free and clear. Perhaps, you might want to talk with them. However, none of them nor your grandfather are obligated to come up with the money. The bottom line, sir is that I want to see $16,143 payable to the State of Connecticut or it will be a jail sentence; and I'm not taking a chance on your skipping."

Potter replied: "I could pay the people back with the bond money. I'm not going to run, I want to give the money back, I don't want to run, sir, your Honor."

"Well, sir, I don't believe you."

"I don't want — I'm not going to run. I just want to pay it off."

"Sir, you're not getting the message. *I don't believe you.*"

"Can I have until tomorrow?"

"No. If you want to contact anyone, you'll have to do it by telephone. There are plenty of phones in the jail, or they could come to visit you; but you're going to stay put until you come up with the money. Take him into custody, sheriff. This matter is continued until next Tuesday."

"But your Honor..."

"This is a tough bargain, Mr. Potter. I realize that, but when I read through this pre-sentence investigation report, you're getting a better deal than you gave these nine people."

The following Tuesday he presented a certified check payable to the State of Connecticut for the proper amount. The money was distributed to the victims through the Attorney General's office and the Department of Consumer Protection. The victims were made whole again, at least financially. As for Mr. Potter, I sentenced him to nine consecutive sentences of six months each, and suspended the sentences. I put him on probation for two years, a special condition of which was that he not operate a home improvement business in Connecticut without a license. I warned him that if he were caught, he would be sentenced to six months for that offense plus he would have to serve the fifty four months which I had suspended, a total of five years. I doubted we would see him again in Connecticut.

Admittedly, he served only seven days in jail, but the important thing was to secure restitution for the victims, and I had to give him an incentive to obtain it. This result gave me substantial satisfaction. I had used the power of the court to obtain justice for the nine victims. This was more important to me than mere punishment of Mr. Potter. I had done what judges are supposed to do, protect the people from injustice.

Between the Wednesday and the following Tuesday of this case, another judge criticized me, telling me that I had trampled Mr. Potter's civil rights. I told him I had done it by the book and pointed out the provisions in the rules that gave me the authority to take the action I did. Further, this criticism was more than offset by letters from some of the victims thanking me for what I had done. It may seem like a small matter as crimes go, but it showed that the courts can provide justice for the victims of crime. I would do exactly the same thing if the same situation arose again, although next time I would try to have the offender serve more time while still obtaining restitution.

Chapter Six

"YOU RUINED MY LIFE!"

C hristopher Jones, in his early thirties, had been arrested for
Assault II with a motor vehicle, which means that in the
course of driving while intoxicated, he had injured someone, in
this case two individuals who were both seriously injured. In what
was probably a moment of weakness another judge had given him
a suspended sentence, two years suspended with two years probation during which he was to perform 400 hours of community
service. Just prior to the expiration of the two year probationary
period he had been arrested for violation of probation for failure
to perform the community service. He had in fact performed *no*
community service.

Subsequent to his latest arrest he had performed 40 hours of the
400 hours while his case had been continued. He was presented
before me on the charge of violation of probation. Since it was obvious he had not performed a condition of probation, he admitted the
violation, and I formally found him in violation. I had a few choices:
continue him on probation to permit him to perform the remaining
360 hours, sentence him to jail for up to the two years that were suspended or just terminate his probation.

I was incredulous. He had received a tremendous break from the
previous judge by avoiding any jail time, and he blew it by performing almost none of the community service. He now faced up to two
years in prison. I had learned that shortly after the original sentence
he had informed the probation officer that he had no intention of
performing the community service. His excuse was that he was too
busy to do the community service because he had to work, sometimes two jobs he said, to support his wife and child. He was not
apologetic to the probation officer, and in court, before me, he was

neither apologetic for failing to do the community service nor apologetic for injuring the two individuals. To say that he had a bad attitude is an understatement. I questioned him closely about finding time on the weekend to do the community service. His reply was that he worked seven days a week, and he couldn't do it.

"What about the 40 hours you did do since your arrest?" I asked. "You managed to do that." "I just don't have the time." he replied.

I made various suggestions to him, warned him of what could happen to him, but he remained adamant. Finally, I had had enough. I thought he had deserved jail time on the original arrest, and he surely deserved it now. I sentenced him to two years, execution suspended after eighteen months plus two years probation. There were no special conditions of the probation, but he was subject to the standard condition of not violating any laws of the State of Connecticut or the United States.

He looked shocked, and in a raised voice he said "**You've ruined my life.**" Suddenly, the man who had driven drunk and seriously injured two people was the victim. I looked at him intently. "Sir", I said "you are not the victim here. The two people you injured are the true victims. You don't seem to recognize that. You refuse to face up to your responsibilities. Hopefully, eighteen months in jail will make you think twice before you drive drunk again; and the public is safe from you while you're in jail."

He started to protest again, but I cut him off and ordered the sheriffs to take him into custody. A month later I received a written request from him for modification of his sentence. It was quickly denied.

Gordon Brown from west of Hartford was presented before me in G.A. (geographical area) 11 in Danielson near the eastern border of Connecticut on a charge of Assault ll with a motor vehicle. He had been driving while intoxicated and had struck a pedestrian. The injuries were in the medium range, between minimal and serious. The state's attorney and the defendant's attorney who was inexperienced in criminal law had come to an agreement for a guilty plea with no recommendation from the states' attorney, leaving the sentence totally up to the judge.

Brown was fifty years old, a well educated man, having graduated from a prestigious eastern university. His only prior conviction for stock fraud was from several years earlier and had nothing to do with Assault II except to demonstrate that he did not pay close observance to complying with the law.

I indicated that I was going to impose jail time because of the severity of the offense. The victim's attorney did not ask for jail time. The only thing in which he was interested was to learn the name of the defendant's liability insurance company. Mr. Brown had not given that information at the scene of the accident so I ordered him to do so.

He professed surprise at the possibility of incarceration, claiming that the probation officer in New London who conducted the pre-sentence investigation had indicated to him that he would probably receive a suspended sentence. I suggested that he might wish to withdraw his plea of guilty and go to trial, which he declined. I pointed out to him that he could easily have killed the victim, and the fact that he didn't was hardly a significant mitigating factor.

I was somewhat bothered by what the probation officer had said, and I found Mr. Brown to be at least ashamed of and remorseful for his behavior. I sentenced him to one year in jail suspended after 9 months plus three years probation during which he could not drive a vehicle while his right to operate was under suspension and during which he had to submit to such alcohol addiction evaluation and treatment, in-patient or out-patient as the Office of Adult Probation might deem appropriate.

Two months later his attorney and I were both guests at a wedding in Agawam, Massachusetts. We were seated at adjoining tables, and just before we took our seats she came up to me and said: **"You know, you ruined my client's life."** I calmed her down and told her why I had imposed the sentence and that I rarely, if ever, give a suspended sentence for this kind of serious offense. She replied that maybe it was her own inadequacy in representing him that resulted in the sentence.

I said no and pointed out that I felt I had to impose jail time in such a case, and then told her, which I did not truly believe, "Helen, it was because of you that I gave him nine months instead of a year." She seemed satisfied with that, and I was relieved that she had not burst into tears and put a damper on the wedding dinner. An attorney at my table had overheard the exchange and was irate that she had chosen to speak to me about it, particularly at a wedding. I agreed that the timing could have been better and said something about judges getting used to this type of behavior.

About a year later I happened to talk with Mr. Brown's probation officer who informed me that Mr. Brown had spent the first month or two of his sentence in the psychiatric ward of the jail, but had eventually straightened out, been taken to the alcohol rehabilitation program and was doing well. The officer informed me that the shock of going to jail had transformed him, and he doubted if he would ever drive drunk again. If that was true, then I had accomplished my goal with this "victim."

There have been other cases, of course, some even more serious, involving manslaughter with a motor vehicle. In one situation the drunk driver seriously injured one person and killed the other. I sentenced him to ten years execution suspended after five years with five years probation. Among other things I ordered him as a condition of probation to place flowers on the victim's grave once a month for each of the five years of probation on the same day of the month as when the death occurred. The purpose was to remind him every month for five years of what he had done.

His wife initiated divorce proceedings, and a few months later I noticed him in a courthouse corridor hobbling along to a hearing with his hand and legs in chains. I must admit that I had very little, if any, sympathy for him. Rarely will I impose less than three years for Assault II with a motor vehicle and rarely less than five years for manslaughter with a motor vehicle. On one occasion with assault with a motor vehicle, the defendant apparently became suicidal, and carried a 45 automatic with him on a trip to New York City. He returned intact, and in that case I gave him more than three years with a provision for a suicide watch and psychiatric counseling both in prison and when on probation. As you can tell from these incidents, I take these alcohol related offenses very seriously. This is also true of plain old "driving while intoxicated." I believe that these defendants had a choice. If they were alcoholics, they should get treatment and not wait for a judge to order it.

For those who are poor, there are plenty of governmental or charitable alcohol addiction programs which cost them nothing. *The choice comes in the decision to drive.* If an alcoholic knows he has a problem, he can take steps in advance to avoid driving himself to wherever he is going where he might imbibe alcohol. Connecticut allows work permits for convicted drunk drivers so they can support their families, but they face severe penalties if they are driving anywhere except to and from work or as part of their work.

There is talk of having some type of Breathalyzer as mandatory equipment in every motor vehicle so that if the reading of the driver tests over the legal limit, the vehicle will not start. Also contemplated is a shut off of the vehicle if the Breathalyzer shows that the driver has exceeded the limit while driving when the full impact of the alcohol has taken effect. Until this equipment is available and proves effective, and even after it does, we must strictly enforce the drunk driving laws.

Connecticut has recently strengthened its drunk driving laws.[1] The maximum legal limit has been lowered from .10 percent to .07 percent and to .02 percent for anyone under 21 years of age. Fines have been increased, and first time offenders must serve 48 hours in jail without the alternative of community service. The second offense calls for a mandatory 4 months in jail. It is now the third offense (rather than the fourth) that carries with it a mandatory one-year sentence and permanent suspension of one's driver's license.

This judge fully recognizes that lengthy jail sentences can take away needed financial support for the families who remain outside, and that is unfortunate. However, as difficult as that may be for them, these sentences are necessary to protect the innocent victims

---

[1] Connecticut should consider taking away ownership of the vehicle driven by the drunk driver, at least for the second offense.

of drunk driving. Ordinary drunk driving is neither assault nor manslaughter with a motor vehicle, but it is the first step toward it. It is usually only by chance that no one is injured or killed. If we don't stop drunk drivers at the drunk driving stage, they will soon reach the assault or manslaughter stage. We have a duty to protect innocent victims from this scourge of the road.

As I was writing this, I came across an item in the obituary section of today's morning paper. It was a memorial on the anniversary of the death of a fourteen year old girl. For those who need a reminder of the seriousness of drunk driving and a reminder of who the victims really are, check your local newspaper, and you will probably see something like this:

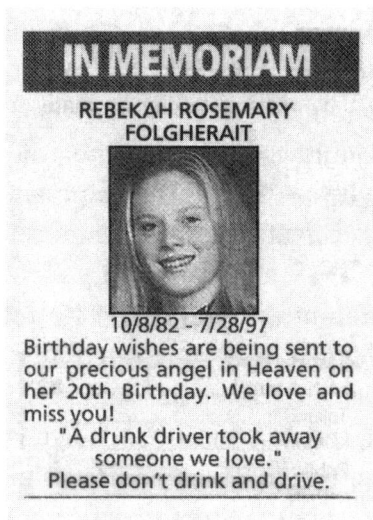

IN MEMORIAM

REBEKAH ROSEMARY FOLGHERAIT

10/8/82 - 7/28/97

Birthday wishes are being sent to our precious angel in Heaven on her 20th Birthday. We love and miss you!

"A drunk driver took away someone we love."

Please don't drink and drive.

Chapter Seven

DOMESTIC VIOLENCE

"I'm sorry. I won't do it again." "She wouldn't let me see my children." "I was drunk. I didn't mean to do it." "She was cheating on me." "She doesn't want to press charges". "She was leaving me." "I couldn't let her go. I still love her". "I would never hurt the kids".

These are some of the statements you hear from a man who has been accused of assaulting his wife, his ex-wife, his significant other (girlfriend) or his former significant other when he is presented in court. Sometimes, all you hear is a deafening silence or an "I don't know" as he sheepishly hangs his head. The man who had yelled at and threatened and then physically assaulted his wife, former wife, girlfriend or former girlfriend has become a quiet, allegedly remorseful and reserved individual when he appears before the judge.

The wives or girlfriends, present or former, will often say: "I'm afraid of him.

I'm afraid for the children, this isn't the first time he's done this, please keep him away from me or it's over between us, and he doesn't understand that". These cases are relatively easy to decide. However, the wives will sometimes say: "I want to keep the family together", or "he's that way only when he drinks", "all he needs is some counseling", or "this is unusual for him", or "I can get him to change", or "this isn't like him, he won't do it again", or "we can work this out between ourselves." These cases are a little more difficult to decide.

The most surprising issue that confronted me following my appointment to the bench was the amount of domestic violence that was taking place in our society. As a practicing attorney I rarely, if ever represented people accused of domestic violence. These defendants usually could not afford a private attorney and were generally represented by the public defender. Had this distasteful aspect of the community been lying below the surface for many years or was it an increase in the consumption of alcohol or the sharp rise in the use of illegal drugs that were to blame, or were people just becoming more frustrated more frequently in our increasingly complex and fast paced society, particularly in bad economic times? The answer is probably all of the above.

First, there was a dramatic increase in the reporting of domestic abuse following the much publicized Tracey Thurman case. Tracey Thurman was a young wife residing in Torrington, Connecticut who had frequently been beaten by her husband. She had complained to the police without much success. Then, her husband attacked her again, this time with the beating continuing outside in the driveway. Neighbors gathered. The police were called. Even after the first officer arrived the severe beating continued. Incredibly, the police officer watched without intervening.

Additional police arrived, the husband was arrested and taken into custody. He was subsequently sentenced to prison. Tracey Thurman was taken to the hospital lucky to still be alive. It was later determined that she had suffered permanent and disabling injuries. Parts of her body remain paralyzed. In a first of its kind legal action, Tracey brought suit against the police and the town of Torrington for failing to respond to her legitimate complaints of domestic violence and failing to protect her. The jury awarded her in excess of $2 million.

Shortly thereafter the Connecticut legislature adopted various domestic violence laws including a requirement that when police officers respond to a domestic violence complaint and there is some evidence of such violence or even threatened violence, they must make an arrest. As a practical matter, they usually arrest the man, but when both parties are injured, they often arrest both the man and the woman. The arrests are noted in the newspapers, and the individuals are presented in court charged with crimes ranging from disorderly conduct to threatening to assault.

Prior to seeing the judge, they are usually interviewed by the family relations division of the court. This office consists of trained and experienced professionals in domestic violence. They have heard all of the excuses before, and they interview the parties separately so there can be no direct pressure from the other party. They are usually successful in learning the truth as to what happened and in evaluating what course of action should be recommended. It is the rare person who can put one over on them. In many cases they recommend to the judge that the offender be entered into the family violence education program which consists of counseling, including anger management classes for up to one year.

If the individual successfully completes the program, the charges are then usually not prosecuted. In many of these cases, that is all that is needed, and the parties are never heard from again. If the incident is not the first one or the person has already completed a family violence program or has failed to complete the program, the matter is referred back to the state's attorney for prosecution.

In either event the family relations officer requests the judge to issue a protective order. The order is either ***partial*** in which the offender is ordered, in writing, not to harass, threaten or assault the victim, and if they are not living together, to not contact the victim in person, by telephone, by mail or through a third person. A ***full protective order*** goes one step further. It orders the offender not to enter the premises in which the victim resides. If the parties are living together, whether married or not, the offender is ordered to move out of the residence and to stay away from it. This may create a hardship for the offender and the family, but it is still necessary to keep the parties apart so as to defuse the situation while one or both are seeking treatment.

The protective order is designed to prevent a repetition of the violence while efforts are made to remove the cause of the original violence. The offender is also ordered not to possess a firearm during the pendency of the protective order by either transferring it to someone else or turn it over to the police for safekeeping. It is my practice to warn the offender, verbally, in court, that he must take these orders seriously, that possessing a firearm is punishable by up to five years in jail and that violating any portion of the protective order is punishable by up to one year in jail.

I state: "Do you understand , sir, that in this court, if you violate the protective order, you will go to jail. ***There will be no second chance***".

The offender and victim are each given a copy of the protective order, and a copy is sent to the police department of the town in which the victim resides.

This all takes place in **criminal court** after an arrest has been made. In **civil court**, an alleged victim doesn't have to wait for an incident and arrest to be made. If the individual is in fear for her or his safety, that individual can apply for a restraining order as long as the request is accompanied by a sworn affidavit setting forth the basis for the request. If the affidavit is sufficient to convince a judge that the applicant is justifiably in fear of her or his safety, that it sets forth facts sufficient to show that the applicant is in danger of imminent harm, the judge will usually sign the restraining order. The order is then served upon the alleged offender by a sheriff, and a copy is given to the local police department. However, there is one major difference between the restraining order and the protective order. There has been no third party intervention, such as the police, to determine whether the facts warrant the issuance of the order. We are basically taking the applicant's word for what happened, and as stated elsewhere in this book, people don't always tell the truth under oath. However, keeping with the old adage of being safe instead of sorry, the judge usually signs the restraining order. A hearing is scheduled for as soon as possible, usually within a week, to give the alleged offender the opportunity to refute the allegations contained in the affidavit. At that time, the restraining order is either revoked or continued for a period of ninety days.

The critical issue in all of this is the **enforcement of the protective or restraining order.** Let's discuss the protective order because that is the type of order most frequently issued. If the protective order is not enforced, then it is merely a piece of paper that means nothing. As I've stated in court many times, "If I don't act to enforce the protective order, I might as well be smoking something up here". I have told prosecutors that I will not accept a guilty plea to a different charge and then give a suspended sentence as part of a plea bargain. If the facts are there to prove a protective order violation, the offender will go to jail. The prosecutor can always nolle (not prosecute) the charge, but if there is a remaining charge of something else, such as assault, the offender will go to jail.

Changing the charge will not prevent jail time. The offender has the choice of pleading not guilty or withdrawing his plea of guilty if it was made upon the assurance of a suspended sentence. He will then claim the case for a trial, and it will go on the trial list with the hope on the part of the defendant that when it has reached the top of the list I will change my mind or the trial will be in front of another judge who will give him a suspended sentence. Generally, this delay doesn't work for the defendant, and for the most part prosecutors do co-operate with a judge who insists on jail time for someone who has violated a protective order.

My experience with prosecutors in this regard has been good. The prosecutors who have appeared before me have been tough on this offense. I sentence the defendant to jail for several reasons. First, the defendant **deserves** to go to jail. He has violated a very specific court order **after** he has had the opportunity for rehabilitation through the family violence program or has had some other form of treatment or counseling. Such a sentence also sends a message. It tells the defendant that this is a very serious matter, that we mean what we say. He gets a taste of jail which will hopefully deter him from doing it again. The news of the sentence gets out and sends a message to those who might otherwise consider committing an act of family violence.

Hopefully, the sentence will act as a **deterrent** to them as well. Finally, the sentence to jail will guarantee that the offender's family will be safe from his violence at least while he is in jail. Does this result in a financial hardship for the family when the "breadwinner" (if he had a job) is not bringing in a paycheck? Will he lose his job as a result of all of this? Probably, but it is my duty first and foremost to stop the family from being severely beaten or even being killed. The best way to do that is to guarantee that the offender does not have physical contact with the family.I have actually imposed jail sentences many times when there has been a violation of a protective order. A husband who was separated and was subject to a protective order went back to the house, dragged his wife out of her bed and beat her up. I sentenced him to the maximum of one year in jail on that charge. A man was under a protective order issued by Judge Cone in another court. He returned to her apartment, and she allowed him to enter. Everything was fine for a few days, then an argument ensued, and he hit her. That's when she called police. The prosecutor had obtained the transcript of Judge Cone's remarks at the time she issued the protective order.

Despite the defendant's claims to the contrary, Judge Cone had made it very clear as to what the protective order meant. The defendant knew very well that he would be violating the protective order if he went to her apartment even at her invitation. I sentenced him to eight months in jail.

There is an interesting sidelight to this case. The defendant was under a federal court order to be deported because of his conviction for selling narcotics. The order was being appealed although without much hope of succeeding. His attorney asked for a stay of execution of the eight month sentence so he could spend Thanksgiving with his family. I denied the request knowing full well that if he was released, he would disappear, either to his homeland or somewhere else in this country. One might ask: "What do you care? Good riddance to him".

There is something to that point of view, but I still wanted to send the messages I've mentioned. Further, if somehow he was able to win the appeal and stay in this country or managed to come back legally or even illegally I wanted him to get the message that violation of a protective order meant jail time, that he should stay away from this area no matter what happened and, further, that he can't play around with the system.

There are several other instances in which violence resulted from violation of a protective order. A man returned to the home despite the protective order, forced his wife into his car, drove to a secluded spot and was starting to rape her when he was interrupted by a police officer. The wife managed to get out of the car, but the husband then tried to run down the police officer.

He didn't succeed and was eventually apprehended. He not only received one year for violation of the protective order but substantially more time for the other offenses.

It is not always husband and wife or boyfriend and girlfriend. There was a young man who was an alcoholic. When he ran out of liquor and money to purchase it, he went to his mother's house and demanded liquor. Sometimes, she gave it to him. One night he escaped from an alcohol rehabilitation facility. The package stores were closed so he went to his mother's home and demanded liquor. When she refused, he dragged her down the stairs and threw her on the ground. Neighbors called the police. He was charged with assault and violation of a protective order. His mother pleaded with me not to send him to jail, to give him another chance at rehabilitation. I felt badly for the mother, but I was determined to protect her in spite of herself. I sentenced him to a year in jail. The mother left the courtroom in tears.

Here's an example of what happens when the protective order is *not* enforced. A former boyfriend, upset because his girlfriend had broken off their relationship, stalked and harassed her. She called the police, and eventually a full protective order was issued prohibiting him from going to her residence in West Hartford. He, nevertheless, violated the protective order by going to her residence again and threatening her. He was arrested and charged with violation of the protective order. A judge gave him a suspended sentence and put him on probation.

A few months later when she left her shift as a waitress at a Manchester restaurant, she stopped for gas at a nearby gas station. As she was leaving the gas station, she noticed him sitting in his car at the edge of the station. He followed her into Vernon. She blew her horn and made some gestures which alerted a police officer from Manchester who just happened to be in a cruiser behind the boyfriend. She pulled into the parking lot of a restaurant, and the boyfriend pulled up next to her. He had a pistol and started shooting at her.

Fortunately, the bullets hit the windows and windshield and did not injure the woman. By this time, the police officer had pulled up behind them. The officer got out of the cruiser, pointed his gun at the boyfriend and ordered him to drop his weapon. Incredibly, the boyfriend took a shot at the officer which missed. The officer returned fire wounding the boyfriend in the shoulder. The gun fell to the ground and the police officer quickly arrested him.

After being treated at a local hospital, the boyfriend was arraigned in front of me. I set bond at $2 million. The girl was lucky that the police officer was behind them and realized what was happening, and she was lucky that the shots fired by the boyfriend did not hit her. If the boyfriend had been in jail for violating the protective order, this incident would not have happened, at least not then, and perhaps spending a year in jail might have dissuaded him from doing it at all.

Of course, there are two sides to every story. Although those who violate a protective order should go to jail, there are situations in which *the victim is complicit in the violation* of the order. Two examples come to mind.

It was September of 1995. I was hearing motions on the criminal docket, Part A, reserved for the more serious crimes. A man in his early forties had been arrested in July for assaulting his wife and sexually assaulting her three different ways. After sexually assaulting her, he sat on her chest, put his knees on her arms and struck her repeatedly on both sides of her face with his closed fists. Another judge had previously imposed a protective order barring the man from having contact with his wife or entering the family home. He was before me requesting, through his attorney, that I lift the protective order so that he could return home to his wife and children.

I looked at the couple. The man was tall, dressed in a dark business suit, and appeared to be educated, somewhat sophisticated, with an income probably in the upper-middle class and not someone whom you would expect to see in court on these charges. The wife was tall, blonde and attractive and reminded me of Nicole Brown Simpson. The husband looked straight ahead, stood almost at attention, expressionless and didn't utter a word. His wife, the victim, however, was not so reticent. Incredibly, she pleaded with me to lift the protective order, to let him return to their home and take up married life again.

I said to her: "Mrs. X, I've looked at the state police photographs. I've seen the blood, the welts on your face and arms, and your back. It appears that he beat you within an inch of your life. Why do you want him back?"

"I want to keep the family together." she said. "I want to keep the family together."

"Are you afraid of him?"

She insisted she was no longer afraid.

"Why not?" I asked. "What has changed in the last month since the assault?"

"It was alcohol." she said, "and he's been getting counseling for it."

I looked at the photographs again. "This vicious and lengthy attack on you tells me that there's an underlying rage underneath all that alcohol, particularly when I look at the way he beat you on your face. There's a deep seated problem here that goes beyond the alcohol." I observed.

"But I want to keep the family together." she said.

"That's a very laudable objective," I said, "but your husband needs a lot of treatment or counseling before things will change for the better."

I turned to the attorney. "Counselor," I said. "How long has he been in counseling?"

"Since the beginning of August, your honor." he replied.

"It's only the beginning of September," I said, "a little more than a month. How many counseling sessions has he attended?"

"Four". he replied.

That did it. I must have had an incredulous look on my face when I said: "Four?" That's only half the number of classes that are required under the alcohol education program (for first time drunk driving offenders), and your client appears to have more problems than the average first time drunk driver."

"Mrs. X, I'm going to protect you and your children whether you **understand** it or not, whether you *like* it or not. Most people have been watching the O. J. Simpson trial on television. There was a situation of spousal abuse in which the wife kept taking him back after each beating. I'm not going to let that happen here. The protective order stands. It remains in full force and effect. Mr. X, your wife may want you back, but regardless, this protective order still requires you not to have any contact with her or go to the family home, and if you violate it in the slightest way, you will go to jail for one year, and I assure you that your wife's consent will not be considered a mitigating factor. ***This is a court order.*** It has nothing to do with your wife's wishes. If you violate a court order, you will go to jail. Further, I'm adding to the protective order. You are not only to continue with your alcohol rehabilitation. You are ordered to enter and complete an anger management program under the direction of the office of adult probation."

I again address the attorney. "Counsel, if you can satisfy this court, by affidavit or live testimony from a doctor, that your client has completely overcome his alcohol problem, and if you can satisfy this court in a similar manner that your client has his anger under control, I'll reconsider my decision. I will probably want an affidavit or live testimony from the doctor that your client no longer poses a threat to the safety of his wife." I was fully aware that such a statement would be almost impossible to get, but I wanted to stress the importance of the defendant making serious efforts to control his alcohol and anger problems.

Another example of the complicity of the female in the violation of a protective order is the case of Robert and Alice, who were boyfriend and girlfriend, a relationship that probably should never have developed in the first place. At times they blended together beautifully, and at other times they were like oil and water. It was these latter times that problems erupted. They would argue, become upset, and he would end up striking her in anger. She called the police, and an arrest was made.

A protective order was issued directing Robert to stay away from her. The problem was that she would not leave him alone. One day, at her request, they met and eventually ended up in a commercial parking lot in his car. This was during the day. They got into an argument concerning their respective families, and again in frustration, he lashed out at her slapping her with his hand so hard that it left a red mark on her cheek. Whether she was angry at him for his rejection of her or stung, both physically and emotionally, by his slapping of her, it was enough for her to call over a police officer who was walking nearby. Robert was arrested for assault and for violation of the protective order. At the time of the sentencing Alice claimed that he had instigated the whole incident, but, at the same time urged me not to send him to jail. He had already been through the family violence program, and was still not getting the message that under the court order he was to have no contact with her whatsoever.

I had specifically told him at the time the protective order was issued that he was not to have contact with her *even if she tried to initiate the contact*. I sentenced him to a year in jail for violation of the protective order and reaffirmed the continuation of the protective order. A few months later, his attorney moved for a modification of the sentence. At the hearing I learned that she was going to the jail to visit him on her initiative, not his. He wanted to know what to do.

I instructed him to take her off of his visitor's list, and refuse to see her if and when she showed up anyway. I could not issue a protective order against her because she had not broken the law. However, in view of the circumstances, I reduced his sentence to six months. At that time, I did not have the power to issue a continuing protective order (the law has been changed since then), but I did offer him some gratuitous advice, namely that he should reconsider his relationship with her.

Enforcement of protective orders is necessary to keep specific people apart and prevent future violence. Enforcement is also necessary as a deterrent to those who might violate them. A person who has had a protective order issued against him or her will hopefully think twice before violating one if he or she knows that it is more than just a piece of paper and that it is almost a certainty that he or she will end up in jail if the order is violated. However, enforcement of protective orders, as important as it is, it is not the long term answer to the problem of domestic violence. The answer is to *search out the root causes of domestic violence* and then remove them. This has been done with a good deal of success with the family violence program. However, this removal of the cause in specific cases is not always permanent, and it only takes place after there has been the first arrest. How do we eliminate these causes from our society? The first thing to do is recognize what they are. Now, I am the first to admit that I am not a trained psychologist or psychiatrist. Nonetheless, my experience as judge dealing with these problems on a daily basis has, I believe, given me an insight into the causes of domestic violence.

First is the "macho" problem. Webster's Ninth New Collegiate Dictionary defines macho as "a strong sense of masculine pride; an exaggerated masculinity: an exaggerated or exhilarating sense of power or strength". Many men are "macho" and react to any question of their masculinity or power with violence to demonstrate that they are "the boss". The military which is composed mostly of males have many men who consider themselves macho. In a 1999 report on "Sixty Minutes", statistics showed that the percentage of domestic violence is much higher in the military than in the general population, that there were more than 50,000 cases of domestic violence in one year. This macho attitude must be brought under control in order to eliminate a major cause of domestic violence.

Second is the problem of alcohol and drug addiction. People who are under the influence of either often take out their frustrations by striking out with violence. Being under the influence makes them lose control and do what they would otherwise not do. Of course that's not the entire problem. The example I cited of the wife who was assaulted and raped was blamed by the wife solely on her husband's drinking, but it was clear to me that there was an underlying anger, frustration or other condition that exploded into violence when the husband lost control because of his alcoholism. Marriage counseling, psychological counseling, anger management are all helpful in getting at the root of the problem, but this has to be accompanied by a program that will reduce and hopefully eliminate the addiction to alcohol or drugs.

Third is the growing frustration and problems in our increasingly complex society. Even in good times there are people who are overworked, who cannot handle the growing expectation that they must succeed, particularly financially. Sometime the competitive pressure is too much for them and causes them to strike out in anger and frustration when they fall short of their goal.

Advanced education, which is just not available to many people, is also becoming more and more important in the drive to succeed. If you don't have it, if you lag behind, your competitor, whether another employee or another business, will succeed where you don't. In bad economic times, this problem can be even worse. How many men who were downsized into unemployment begin to question their self worth or become angry at corporate America for putting them in their position? What about the frustration of a high powered insurance executive who is downsized, is in his fifties and who has to take what he considers a lesser job at a delicatessen counter in a supermarket to support his family? (This was an actual defendant who appeared before me.)

Take the man with a limited education who is laid off from his construction job because of a recession. He' s still young but cannot obtain another job. He and his wife and kids are forced to move to an inexpensive and run down apartment. He can't sit around the house where his young children are crying and his wife is beleaguered taking care of them in their non-air-conditioned apartment with the temperature in the nineties. He escapes to the local bar which is air-conditioned and after three or four beers his buddies convince him that his unemployment is not his fault (and it probably isn't). He then returns home, inebriated to say the least, and his wife, also understandably frustrated, criticizes him for drinking instead of looking for a job. "What kind of a man are you who can't support his wife and kids?" An argument breaks out, and he takes out his frustration by hitting his wife.

Finally, there is the woman in a bad and violent marriage or relationship who is afraid to leave her man. How can she support herself and the children? Where is she to go? What does she do when he has already beaten her and threatens to kill her if she ever leaves him, when she is in genuine fear of her life? It takes courage to leave him under these circumstances. Of course, she knows she must leave him, but where is she to go? There are shelters, but these are limited and generally temporary. If she has no family or friend on whom she can rely, what does she do?

She could go to the police and have him arrested and hope that he will stay in jail at least until his case comes up in court where hopefully a judge will either keep him locked up on a high bond because of his danger to society, in particular her and her children. In the alternative, the judge will issue a protective order barring him from the family apartment, and hopefully this judge has a sufficient reputation for enforcing protective orders with jail time so that the male will not violate the protective order. It is a risk for her, but it is one she must take to remove herself and her children from the violence that would otherwise occur.

I am also aware that there are times when the husband is wrongly accused of violence or threats of violence by the wife in order to obtain an advantage in a pending or about to be commenced divorce proceeding. Hopefully, a judge will see through this, but if he or she can't, it is usually better to keep the parties apart until the facts can be determined. The danger of leaving the wife unprotected is too high to do otherwise.

Do I have all the answers to the problems of domestic violence? Of course not. However, I do recommend the following to help alleviate the situation:

1. Judges must enforce protective orders with meaningful jail time.

2. More resources should be put into the establishment of shelters for victims of domestic violence and prospective victims of domestic violence. Charitable groups have done a good job as far as they could go. But, more is needed. Although I am generally an advocate of limited government, this is clearly an area in which the government *should* become more involved. One of the primary functions of government is to do for the people what they cannot do for themselves. That's why we have police, courts and prisons. Every citizen has a fundamental right to be protected from crime and violence, and victims of domestic violence are no exception. The state should establish facilities for women and children who are either threatened with or victims of domestic violence. These facilities should go beyond just being shelters. A trained staff should be available to find the woman a place to live, help her to obtain employment and give her the training necessary for her to qualify for employment, provide day care for her until she is able to manage on her own, provide her with an attorney to represent her in divorce and other legal proceedings, provide mediation and counseling for both husband and wife if it is likely to do some good, for even if they do become divorced, a non-violent relationship is essential for visitation etc,. Until the relationship becomes permanently non-violent, the resources of the state should be utilized to prevent further violence.

3. The parties should undergo counseling. In the case of the violent party, (generally the male but not always,) treatment for alcohol or drug addiction, psychological problems and anger should be mandatory, and it should be in-patient if deemed necessary.

4. As for the problems I have previously identified as leading to domestic violence, these need to be recognized early, and counseling/treatment should be given to prevent the violence from occurring. Recognition can come from the parties themselves, or from the family doctor. Religious institutions and employers should have people who are trained to recognize these problems, and should offer counseling and discussion sessions, either in group form or individually, to deal with root causes before violence erupts. Friends or relatives should feel free to intervene, although this needs to be done diplomatically and with great sensitivity. If payment for counseling is a problem, the religious and non-profit organizations could provide the needed assistance.

The difficulty, of course, that even when the problems are recognized, the person or persons who have the problem may be in denial and may continue to deny the existence of the problem. Further, even with recognition, the person cannot be forced to go to counseling. What can be done when a party refuses to recognize the problem or refuses to get help, I don't know. Wiser minds than mine will have to find a solution, for as you may recall, I said I do not have all the answers. These are only the thoughts of a judge who has been on the firing line concerning this serious and urgent malady in our society.

Chapter Eight

FAMILY

Divorce, Custody, Alimony, Support and Division of Property" I became disillusioned with my marriage so I made application for its dissolution."[1]

Divorce: Judges now say "A decree of dissolution of marriage may enter on the grounds of irretrievable breakdown." Dissolution may be a nicer word than divorce, but it still means a termination of the marriage. Whether the marriage is of short or long duration, a decree of dissolution can still have a devastating effect upon the parties, their children and the original family of each party. Some contested divorces can be very, very bitter, and even those that are uncontested in all respects have a certain sense of sadness to them. It is leaving someone you once loved, or at least thought you did, and it carries with it, in many cases, a sense of failure. Some are nervous, unsure of what the future may bring. Others are happy to get out of what has become an intolerable situation, and they look forward to the future with optimism as they get on with their lives. If there is a new spouse waiting in the wings, the future looks even brighter.

What are the causes of divorce? This calls for a complex answer. As a judge I have tried hundreds of divorce cases, and from my vantage point the more common ones follow:

Many young people are too young and immature to deal with the responsibilities of marriage. Some have been in love with the idea of being in love rather than really being in love with his/her spouse. Some are merely infatuated and believe it to be love when it really isn't. Of course, there are plenty of older people who get married, and are still immature at least when it comes to the male-female relationship. There are those who marry very, very young, and while one

---

[1] Webster's Ninth New Collegiate Dictionary defines disillusion as "the condition of being disenchanted" and dissolution as "termination". Noah Webster, one of Connecticut's more well-known historical figures was born in 1758 in the "Village of West Hartford."

spouse continues his/her education, the other one, usually the wife, stays home spending all of her time raising the children. The spouse with the education is making a success in the outside world, and pretty soon he has far outdistanced the spouse who stays at home in terms of knowledge and sophistication, so there is little left for them to talk about except for the kids.

Sometimes the wife spends so much time with the children, the husband feels rejected, creating stress in the marriage. A child may be born handicapped requiring so much attention by the mother that the father feels left out. If he is mature, he will be able to handle the situation. If he's not, and is not committed to his marriage vows, he may start to stray.

Take the man who deals with important business decisions all day, has a plush office and is viewed with respect by his company and his colleagues, who has secretaries or others who are there primarily to carry out his orders. Contrast that with his knowing that when he goes home, he will be met by a wife bedraggled from her daily activities of keeping the house clean, taking care of young children, or if older, taking them to and from activities, telling her spouse that he will have to get his own dinner while she takes care of the kids.

When they are finally put to bed, she is so tired that all she can do is tell him of the problems with the children or the house, with no time to hear about his latest triumphs. All she wants to do is go to bed to sleep. Facing that the next day, he looks at his secretary or a female colleague who is younger, very attractive and perfectly groomed who is also aware of his problems at work and his triumphs, and who can discuss them with him intelligently and with understanding, with perhaps the added spice of praise or comforting words.

His first mistake is to ask her and take her out for a drink. The other mistakes will soon follow. Take the wife who struggles at work to put her husband through medical or law school, and when he starts to make money he drops her for a nurse or someone else in the medical field with the lawyer turning to someone in the legal field.

Then, there is the spouse who is unusually possessive and jealous of someone else who is getting too close to him or her, leading to distrust in the marriage. A spouse may become abusive, a trait not recognized during the courtship. One spouse may want to control every aspect of their joint lives. The other spouse either gives in or asserts his/her independence thus leading to a clash of personalities.

Other factors can be alcoholism, drug addiction and stress from employment or stress from being unemployed. In some case the husband suffers a mid-life crisis. He realizes that his future is never going to live up to his dreams. His wife, instead of being sympathetic to his emotional distress, is instead critical telling him to act like a man.

Is this all right? Of course it isn't. The individuals should honor their marriage vows and provide understanding to their spouse. In a perfect world, that would happen, and there would not be a divorce rate of over 50 percent. But, of course, we do not live in a perfect world, and human weakness is an inherent flaw in our society.

No Fault Divorce: Several years ago, Connecticut adopted No-Fault divorce. Many other states have done the same. Some say that this makes it too easy for someone to obtain a divorce, that if it were tougher to obtain one, spouses would work harder to make the marriage succeed. In Connecticut one party can insist on sessions of marriage counseling. If the other party refuses, the divorce can be delayed six months.

Sometimes, counseling works. Other times, when a spouse has fallen in love with someone else or if the problem in the marriage has been long standing and been allowed to fester, the likelihood of successful counseling is slim. Before no fault, the party initiating a divorce action had to prove adultery, habitual intemperance, desertion or intolerable cruelty, and two witnesses were required to prove the case.

Since intolerable cruelty, the most common ground, usually took place in the marital home, there were no witnesses. Friends, neighbors or relatives of the party trying to prove the intolerable cruelty were not allowed to testify unless they actually saw the cruelty. If their only knowledge of it was from what the plaintiff had told them,

The Truths of Justice

the testimony was inadmissible as being hearsay. If there were no witnesses who could testify, the plaintiff could not succeed.

This left the defendant in a very good bargaining position. "I won't object to the hearsay testimony (in which case the judge would allow it into evidence) if you agree to my terms for settlement." This often led to unfair settlements. I can recall a case that I handled as an attorney many years ago before no fault divorces were permitted. I represented the husband. The wife was leaving him. A substantial age difference had left them incompatible. She was taking the two children back to Florida from where she had come. She also wanted alimony and half of the marital residence for which he had paid. I believed she was being unfair in her demands, and she had no witnesses that were qualified. I told her attorney that if she wanted the divorce, she would have to give up her interest in the house. "No house, no divorce." Accordingly, the husband received the house.

Because of the requirement to prove fault, which was often impossible, the existing system was widely considered unfair. Further, long[2], drawn out battles, often very bitter, trying to prove which party was more at fault, had adverse effects upon all the parties and a devastating impact upon the children.

The legislature then adopted no fault divorce. There is, therefore, no such thing as a truly contested divorce. All the plaintiff has to say is that the marriage has broken down irretrievably, and there is no hope of reconciliation. However, the nature of divorce as a contest did not go away. There were still issues of custody of the children, visitation of the children, support for the children, alimony, division of the assets and liabilities of the marriage and whether or not attorneys' fees should be awarded to the plaintiff or the defendant.

These issues are often hotly contested. If pre-trial sessions with special masters (attorneys who specialize in divorce) and later a judge, could not resolve the conflict, the trial would proceed as a "limited" contested matter.

---

[2] I used to tell clients, the race does not go to the swiftest, but rather to the one with the most stamina who is willing to return to court time after time to obtain what he/she wants.

An example that took fifteen days of testimony is the divorce case involving Dr. Doe which is described in the chapter *"Lying under Oath"*.

CUSTODY: The best interests of the child should always be the sole concern in deciding who should be given custody. Judges strive to fulfill this objective, but what the best interests of the child may be are not always clear. That's why we have hearings, take evidence and obtain evaluations from experts in the subject. Deciding custody of a child or children weighs heavily on a judge's mind. It is one of the more difficult decisions a judge has to make. We are well aware that our decision will have a major impact upon the child's future.

It is true that a substantial majority of custody awards gives custody to the mother. It is generally believed that the needs of a child, particularly a very young child, are better recognized and better met by the mother. After all, she is the one who gave birth, she is the one who is more likely to instinctively know and respond to the child's needs. By her very nature she is the one who can give warm, loving motherly care to a child. There is a certain bond that exists between mother and child that is unique. Further, the mother normally has more time to care for the child.

In days gone by, the father was the sole bread winner of the family, and it was traditional for the mother to stay home, take care of the children, and maintain the home. The mother was the one who could supervise the children during the day while dad was off at work, who would be home when the children returned from school.

With the advent of women in the work place starting with World War II and women becoming increasingly part of the world of commerce, much of that has changed. There are many households in which both parents work, sometimes the mother earning more money than the father. Women are finally becoming important in the world outside the home. They have attained positions of leadership in the professions, whether medical, legal, educational or other professions. They have entered the military, fly commercial airlines, and they have broken into the ranks of chief executive officers of major corporations.

The Truths of Justice

The status of women has changed dramatically since the forties, and the old traditions have largely disappeared. But not entirely. The special bond between mother and child hasn't changed, particularly in the child's younger years. When the children go to school, mothers often seek out a schedule that allows them to be at home when the children come home or shortly thereafter.

Suffice it to say that despite the absence of the mother during most of the day, mothers are still more likely to be given custody of the children. Except in unusual cases, they are often considered the better caregiver. In fact, in most uncontested and limited contested divorce cases, custody is uncontested. The father agrees that the mother should have custody. Even in joint custody the children may live with the mother, but the father has a right to be informed and consulted on such issues as medical treatment, schooling and activities.

Sometimes, there is shared custody in which the child stays with the mother three or four nights a week and with the father the remaining nights of the week. Of course, the parents would have to live near each other, and when the child reaches school age, some accommodation is usually made with the school system. In these cases, liberal visitation is granted to the other parent.

What happens when there is no agreement, and custody becomes a hotly contested issue? I can recall a case in which the wife remarried a man whose employer required him to be transferred to Michigan. I became involved in the early stages of the case and issued an injunction prohibiting the wife from taking the children until a full investigation and hearing could be held. The children were teenagers or close to it, and their feelings had to be taken into account. There were paternal grandparents here who could help with the supervision of the children. It was therefore not a decision to be made hastily.

The possibility that the wife might depart with the children without waiting for a final judgment was so serious that I ordered a lien on the marital home of the parents as to the ex-wife's interest to be enforced if she defied the court order. I was transferred to another court before there was a resolution of this issue so I don't know the result.

The Truths of Justice

However, in most cases in which the mother has been awarded custody, she is permitted, particularly when the children are too young for their desires to be seriously considered, to take the children with her to her new husband's new place of employment. Liberal visitation is allowed for the father, generally at his expense, and he is permitted extended visitation with the children in Connecticut at times when they are not in school assuming satisfactory travel arrangements can be made.

There are two examples of cases in which I decided custody after hearings which are exceptions to the rule of the mother being preferred for custody but which fulfilled the objective of considering the interests of the child as the sole deciding factor.

The Flower Case. Mr. and Mrs. Flower were granted a dissolution of marriage decree sometime prior to June 1, 1992. Custody of the minor child, Natalie, was granted to the mother with rights of reasonable visitation given to the father. Natalie was five years old at the time and was probably the only good result of the marriage. On June 1, 1992, Mrs. Flower made a complaint to the State Department of Children and Families (DCF) that Mr. Flower had sexually abused Natalie, and based upon the alleged sexual abuse she refused to allow visitation by Mr. Flower. DCF did conduct an investigation which included an evaluation by a child psychologist and found the charge to be groundless.

Dr. Coyle's report was dated November 1, 1992. I reviewed that report and heard testimony from DCF social workers as well as a State Family Relations Officer. Mrs. Flower continued to deny visitation despite the DCF evaluation and the report of Dr. Coyle. Another judge found her in contempt for refusal to permit the court ordered visitation, and two weeks later ordered that Mr. Flower have unsupervised visitation to take effect thirty days later. On February 24, 1993, Mrs. Flower continued to deny any visitation by Mr. Flower. She then failed to appear in court on April 14, 1993, even though she later admitted she had notice of the court hearing. As a result full custody was transferred to Mr. Flower.

To complicate things further, Mrs. Flower resided in Rhode Island, just across the state line, where she attempted to avoid service of notice by a sheriff. It wasn't until she was under threat of arrest that she finally came to court and transferred physical custody of Natalie to Mr. Flower. She subsequently moved to have custody of Natalie returned to her.

The hearing on her motion was assigned to me. The hearing lasted several days. I heard testimony from the parties, the two grandmothers of Natalie, DCF workers, psychologists and family relations officers as well as other witnesses including a teacher at Natalie's school. Mrs. Flower admitted that she had been wrong in her actions. I made the following findings:

"**1.** Mrs. Flower's conduct, however well intentioned it **may** have been, was not in the best interest of the child. Her refusal to allow visitation, particularly after her charges had been found to be unsubstantiated, demonstrated an unwillingness to permit a good relationship to develop between Natalie and her father.

2. Her failure to turn over to Mr. Flower, even after custody had been changed, the documents furnished by Natalie's speech therapist was not in the best interest of improving the child's speech.

3. Her failure to comply with the court orders as to counseling as well as failure to follow through with the recommendations of Newington Children's Hospital was not in the best interest of the child.

4. In addition, Mrs. Flower continued to make charges that DCF, after a thorough on-site inspection, found to be baseless, such as that Mr. Flower's home was lacking a proper water supply, proper sleeping arrangements for Natalie and that Natalie's bed was in poor condition. She further alleged that Mr. Flower continued to have alcohol problems even though in August, 1993 she knew or should have known that by then any such problems had been resolved through court-ordered counseling.

In sum, Mrs. Flower's fears, described as "hyper-vigilance" by the child psychologist, and her animosity toward her ex-husband interfered with and took precedence over the best interest of the child. I have no problem with the stability of the paternal grandmother who lives with her son and with Natalie and who contributes substantially to the proper raising of the child. On the other hand I am concerned about the stability of Natalie's mother. From testimony about her visit to Mrs. Warren, the child's teacher, it almost appears as if she didn't want her child to succeed in pre-school.

Further, the court is now faced with a situation in which the child has been with Mr. Flower and his mother in a healthy environment since May 24, 1993, a little more than eight months. Independent investigations by DCF and Family Relations have found the child to be healthy, well cared for and well adjusted to her present environment. The court is particularly impressed with the father's devotion to his daughter's welfare. He makes breakfast for her in the morning, comes home for lunch and takes her to and from nursery school, and he has agreed to unsupervised visitation with Mrs. Flower. In this case it appears that the father accepts Natalie's need to bond with her mother, while Mrs. Flower's understanding of the child's need to bond with her father appears to be totally lacking.

The court finds, from the totality of the evidence, that the minor child, Natalie, is being well taken care of living with the father, that her needs as to her health, education, welfare and quality of life are being met where she is and that it would be harmful to her as well as disruptive to remove her from this environment.

Additionally, the court cannot ignore the recommendations of Family Relations and DCF that custody remain with the father. Accordingly, in the best interest of the child, custody is awarded to the father, Robert Flower. Visitation is to be agreed upon by the parties. If you cannot reach agreement, come back to me and I will decide visitation. I set certain conditions, such as the number and timing of telephone calls from Mrs. Flower, that certain appliances should be removed from Natalie's bedroom, that Natalie should be regularly examined by a pediatrician with any problems to be promptly addressed, that baths and application of ointment for the child to be done by the grandmother or some other female without participation by the father, and that both parents complete parental education programs and such other counseling as may be recommended by Family Relations.

Family Relations shall also continue supervision of the situation and monitor compliance with the court's orders, and neither parent nor any relatives shall disparage either party or any other relatives in the presence of Natalie."

There were additional conditions including a revaluation by the court in sixty days. The parties seemed to accept the court's decision and were advised that violation of these orders would be considered conduct not in the best interest of the child. The two grandmothers had no choice but to abide by the decision, but if looks could kill, both would be dead.

The Woodley Case. The other example I would like to present was a closer call. A dissolution action had been commenced by the wife, Patricia Woodley against her husband, Kenneth Woodley. The children, Laura and John, ages five and seven respectively, were living with their father at the marital home in a rural area of eastern Connecticut. He made his living by growing and selling trees on the premises as well as using the lumber from some of the trees to do woodworking, creating and selling items of furniture and smaller items to be used for decorative purposes.

The wife was a graduate of the University of Connecticut and worked for an advertising agency in Hartford. She had fallen in love with the owner of the agency and was living with him in his home in a suburb west of Hartford. This appeared to me to be the sort of situation I described earlier in this chapter, of a couple that had married at a young age with one of the parties quickly outdistancing the other in terms of knowledge and sophistication. The husband led a quiet life working with his hands in a rural area while the wife, who in this case was very attractive, entered the glamorous world of advertising in a city and participated in a highly competitive and sophisticated field of business with comparable social activities.

She had announced to her husband that she had fallen in love with someone else, wanted a divorce and was moving in with her intended new husband. She told him that she would get settled in her new home and then, when everything was ready, she would have the children, Laura and John, move in with her and transfer to the local school system. The husband at first agreed, but later, when it came time for the children to move, he changed his mind and refused to give up physical custody of the children.

The wife then moved for custody **pendente lite**, which means temporary custody pending the outcome of the divorce. I was to decide who should have temporary custody while the case was pending with a final decision on custody to be made at the time of the hearing on the divorce itself.

I did not take into account fault in the marriage. Fault is only a consideration in awarding alimony and property and should not affect custody of the children. The *only* consideration is "the best interest of the children".

I fully recognized the benefits that would accrue to the children by moving in with their mother. In addition to motherly supervision, they would be living in a more intellectual and sophisticated environment, the school system being located in an affluent Hartford suburb would presumably provide the children with a better education, and the horizons of their world would be more much more likely to expand. The new husband, a widower, had two children of his own, a little bit older than Laura and John. I looked at this as a plus if they got along and a minus if they did not.

It bothered me a little that the wife had chosen to move without the children despite the understanding that they would join her later. I also believed that the husband who appeared to be suddenly confronted with the situation of his wife wanting a divorce and leaving him for another man might have been in a state of shock when he agreed to the children joining his wife later, and, therefore, I believed that he had a right to change his mind.

The deciding factor in my decision was the fact that the children seemed to be happy and well taken care of where they were, and I was uncertain how they would fare once they moved. Plus, of course, this was only temporary custody that was at issue.

I ordered the Family Relations office to do a thorough investigation of the advantages and disadvantages of the proposed move to help determine what was in the best interest of the children. I realized that the investigation might show that the move would be beneficial to the children, and if so, and after consideration of other factors unknown at this time, it was appropriate to give custody to the mother, then custody would be awarded to her. What I did **not** want was to grant custody to the wife now, move the children and then have a report that indicated the children should be with the father and have to uproot the children and move them back again.

I, therefore, granted temporary custody to the father with liberal visitation to the mother, including a potential for overnight visits which might give an indication of their reaction to moving in permanently with their mother. I believed that it was better to keep the situation stable until the family relations report was finished. There was no harm in keeping the status quo for the three to four months it would take to complete the investigation and report. The mother started to cry when I announced my decision but seemed to understand that it was not a final decision.

VISITATION: I have always believed that there should be liberal visitation afforded to the non-custodial parent. It is bad enough for the children that their mother and father have been divorced and that the non-custodial parent, usually the father, is required to live elsewhere, so every effort should be made to maintain the bond that existed with the non-custodial parent.

Although it will never be the same as living together in the same house as part of a family, the more access and contact with the father (and from hereon in I will consider the father to be the non-custodial parent since that is usually the case) the better in order to retain the bond that existed before the divorce.

Shared custody is sometimes appropriate, a situation in which the parents live near each other so that the children remain in the same school system and can have the same friends, where there are similar bedrooms in both houses and, where possible, sufficient clothing in both locations so that there will be minimal inconvenience when the children live with the father during his periods of shared custody.

That is the ideal, but physical constraints as well as continuing bitterness between the parents may well make that difficult. Next most favorable would be *joint custody* in which there would be only one custodial parent, but both parents would be equally informed and participate together in making decisions as to the children's medical and educational needs. This too could be difficult if there is substantial bitterness between the parents continuing after the divorce.

The next alternative is sole custody awarded to one parent with reasonable rights of visitation in the other parent. This should include liberal visitation with the non-custodial parent, and unless the children are too young, overnight visitation at the father's residence, usually with alternating weekend visitation. Of course, the children's school activities, including sports and extracurricular activities, always take precedence over the visitation schedule, and if the parties are truly concerned about the best interest of the children, they will agree upon a visitation schedule that accommodates both the needs of the children and the proper visitation with the father.

The problem arises when the father, the mother or both still feel angry and/or rejected as a result of the divorce. One ex-spouse may quickly find a significant other and/or remarry very quickly. This often irritates the other ex-spouse because he/she now knows the divorce is final and the relationship will not be renewed factually as well as legally. It may also make the ex-spouse suspicious and jealous that the new person in the other's life had been waiting in the wings while the divorce was pending and in fact may have contributed to the divorce.

The parties are urged to work it out. If they cannot, then the judge refers them to a family relations officer for investigation and evaluation. The officer may discover that the custodial parent is deliberately scheduling the children's activities to conflict with the other spouse's visitation rights or is brainwashing the children by making derogatory remarks or lying about the father so that they turn against the father, and don't want to go with him. She takes the position that "they don't want to go with you. I can't force them to go with you." If her brainwashing has been successful, they might really feel that they don't want to visit the father.

A trained and experienced family relations officer can generally get to the truth. The officer's report is then furnished to the court, and based upon the report and any other evidence the parties wish to present, the court will make a decision as to what is in the best interest of the child.

There was one case in which the father had claimed that the mother was deliberately turning the children against him. I interrupted the proceedings, kept the parties in the courtroom, and instructed a very competent family relations officer to go immediately to the children's school and interview them. I did it quickly so that neither the mother nor the father would be able to "prime" the children in advance of the officer's visit. It turned out that the mother *was* brainwashing the children against their father.

I ordered immediate counseling with Family Relations to try to overcome the damage the mother had done. I also ordered a schedule of visitation to which the parties had to adhere. I warned the mother that if she improperly interfered with the children's relationship with their father, I would consider taking custody away from her. You will note that I did just that in the case of Mr. and Mrs. Flower

There is, of course, often another side to the story. There are cases in which the father either cancels his weekend visitation with the children the day before it is to begin or just doesn't show up. The mother then has to cancel her plans for the weekend. The same is sometimes true of visitation during the week. The children are disappointed in both cases.

Responsible and emotionally stable mothers and fathers should be able to work things out in a fair manner that puts the best interest of the children first, and that happens in the overwhelming majority of cases. When emotions are too high or either or both of the parties are unreasonable, that's when the court steps in as a neutral party, to resolve the matter.

I have had dozens of cases in which I have listened to all the claims, and then made specific schedules in great detail, taking care of every possible contingency, and ordered the parties to abide by them.

CHILD SUPPORT: Child support in Connecticut is generally determined by the Child Support Guidelines which are developed by a committee specially appointed by the Legislature and Governor for this task. Included on this committee are Family Relations officers who have dealt with problems of child support day in and day out, as well as accountants, experienced family lawyers and others who bring sufficient background and experience to make a worthwhile contribution.

The guidelines take into account the gross and net income of the parents, the age and number of children, available benefits, deductions from pay, child care expenses, etc., in arriving at a figure for weekly child support from the non-custodial parent. Judges are required to follow these guidelines in awarding child support, but may, in appropriate circumstances, deviate from the guidelines.

When salaries are fixed, there is generally no problem in arriving at the proper figure. However, problems do arise when someone is self employed, and the judge has to determine the earning capacity of that self employed person. Testimony from the interested party cannot always be relied on. (See the case of <u>Dr. John Doe vs. Dr. Jane Doe</u> in the chapter " **Lying Under Oath**".)

Judicial deviation can be for several reasons, i.e., special needs of the children for which the father has the ability to pay, whether it be educational or health needs, special arrangements for visitation by the father which may further deplete his income.

The assets or income of the new spouse should *not* be taken into consideration since such spouse has no legal obligation toward these children. There are exceptions such as the new spouse paying for the rent and utilities which thereby reduces the amount of money needed to support the children. Sometimes it can be very difficult, such as a situation in which the husband starts a new family and is responsible for the children of his first family yet must also provide for the children of the new family.

The children of his first family have to come first. He should not have had additional children if he could not afford them while still keeping his child support payments for his first family up to date. This sounds reasonable, but what if he does have children in his second family? Often there is just not enough money to go around, and that's when the judge has to make difficult and sometimes creative decisions.

As a general rule, visitation should not be denied the husband simply because he is in arrears in his child support payments. Cutting down on the visitation or eliminating it harms the children who should otherwise be able to maintain their bond with their father. Cutting visitation should never be used as a weapon especially if he has lost his job or suffered a reduction in his income. However, if he has spent money on vacations and entertainment to the extent that he does not have the funds for child support, his failure to pay is considered willful, and there are other steps that can be taken to extract payment.

He can even be held in contempt of court and put in jail. This usually inspires a strong effort to find the money whether through loans or selling of assets and then when he is current in his obligation, he can arrange his expenditures with child support payments assuming more importance than vacations and entertainment. For the father who has legitimately lost his job, allowances have to be made, but the court should continue to closely monitor his efforts to gain new employment. The obligation to support his children must take priority, and only highly unusual circumstances would relieve him of this responsibility.

ALIMONY: Alimony is based primarily on the length of the marriage as well as the wife's ability to be gainfully employed. I can recall one case in which the parties had been married for less than a year when the husband caught the wife having an affair with another man. The wife had not given up her job, and there were no children. Alimony was denied.

When it's a matter of a marriage of ten to twenty years duration, especially when the wife stopped working to take care of the children, alimony is appropriate in addition to child support until the wife can regain the skills she had when she stopped working—that is, when she can be re-employed in the marketplace. Unless there is money for day care, she should receive alimony during the period the children are still at home until they reach the age where they are in school and can be self sufficient after school. In most cases, the alimony should be limited to the amount of time it takes for the wife to become re-employed and earn the money she needs to support herself in the style to which she has become accustomed during the marriage.

For example, if the husband is a top corporate executive and earns a substantial amount of money, the wife is entitled to alimony sufficient to continue the life style she had during the marriage. Of course, every case is different, and the judge should consider all the circumstances in making a decision.

Sometimes, the court will award alimony of $1 per year. The law states that if alimony is not awarded at the time of the divorce, it can never be claimed in the future. The $1 per year enables the wife to seek an increase if the husband suddenly starts earning a lot more money.

Increases are, of course, not automatic, but at least she has the right to apply based upon *"a substantial change of circumstances."* Conditions are usually put into the judgment, such as alimony being cut off upon the remarriage of the wife or continual co-habitation with a male for a significant period of time, and, of course, the alimony is terminated upon the death of either party. This is often accompanied by a requirement that the husband maintain sufficient life insurance in favor of the ex-wife in order to guarantee money to replace the alimony in the event of the ex-husband's premature death.

PROPERTY DISTRIBUTION: Even though there is no community property in Connecticut, generally, in a marriage that is reasonably long, the assets as well as joint liabilities are divided equally. If the wife is awarded custody of the children, the husband transfers his interest in the house to the wife, and the wife gives him a mortgage for half of the equity in the house which must be paid if the wife remarries or cohabitates as described above, the house is sold, upon the wife's death, when the youngest child reaches 18 or 22 or none of the children are residing in the house, whichever comes first. [For more specifics on property division, see Appendix A.]

The Truths of Justice

There is one other asset that deserves special mention, and that is the pension of both parties. The husband is generally the one with the more substantial pension earned during the life of the marriage, and it is definitely an asset of the marriage and should in most cases be divided equally.

In one case I tried, <u>Evans v. Evans</u>, the husband had listed his pension from the U.S. Department of Agriculture as being worth $30,000. Amazingly, the wife's attorney was willing to go along with that estimate. Based upon my belief that the court should not allow someone, the wife in this case, to be cheated because of the incompetence of the attorney, I ordered the husband to obtain all information regarding his pension from his employer, the USDA, and then retain a qualified pension evaluator to determine the real value of the pension. There is a formula with which I was familiar, but I thought it would be better if it were evaluated by a professional.

This was done, and suffice it to say that the value far exceeded the amount estimated by the husband. I, then ordered that such value be divided equally through what is called a QDRO (Qualified Domestic Relations Order) that was acceptable to the USDA which essentially ordered the USDA to pay one half of the pension benefits earned to that date to the wife. The attorney had charged the wife $6,000 for representing her. In view of the attorney's laxity, I did not believe the fee was warranted, but since the arrangement was a private matter, I had no jurisdiction to change it. I recommended to the wife that if she could not resolve the amount of the fee, she should contact a committee of the Bar Association which mediates disputes over attorneys' fees.

CONTEMPT: Contempt of court is a finding that a party has willfully disobeyed a court order, and motions for contempt are common in family matters. Before a finding of contempt is made, the parties usually work out their differences, and that's the end of it.

However, there are some occasions in which the party continues to disobey the court order. Two examples are worth mentioning. During the marriage, the wife had loaned the husband $20,000.

When the divorce was decided, the husband was ordered to pay the wife lump sum alimony of $20,000 in the form of a promissory note with equal monthly payments until the note was paid. The husband failed to do so. When the matter came before me on a contempt motion, I noted that the motion had been continued eighteen times, always with a promise by the ex-husband to bring the payments current. The ex-husband's excuse was that he was a building contractor, we were in a recession and he couldn't get any work. I reviewed the financial affidavits, and questioned his attorney. I concluded that he must have had some work since the first continuance. He was $4,800 in arrears. I told him that based upon the totality of the evidence, he could have made the payments, and, therefore, he was in willful violation of the court order.

"Sir, I find your non-compliance with the order of this court to be willful, and accordingly, I find you in contempt. You may purge yourself of contempt upon payment of the $4,800 to your ex-wife by bank or certified check. Until then, I'm committing you to the custody of the Commissioner of Corrections. Sheriff, take him into custody." (This was at approximately 11:30 A.M.) "You have the keys to the jail, sir. You can open the jail cell upon payment of the $4,800."

At 2:30 p.m. he had come up with the money which he allegedly didn't have and couldn't get. I noticed a person who was apparently his girlfriend sitting in court with him. I don't know her involvement in raising the money, but no doubt his confinement was an incentive to both to obtain the money needed for release.

The second example is of an ex-husband, 65 years old, who had fathered two children with his wife before they were divorced. He had been a pharmacist but was now retired. He claimed he couldn't get a job, had no income etc. However, after reviewing documents from various companies that I had requested, I determined that he was substantially exaggerating his poverty. His attorney had demanded that I dismiss the motion for contempt, that I had no jurisdiction, and that any order would be invalid. That certainly didn't help his client.

The Truths of Justice

I told the attorney: "Counsel, please spare me your histrionics and your so called outrage. Mr. Stevens, I find that since you have willfully failed to pay $3,400 in child support, you are in contempt of court, and I'm sending you to jail. The purge amount is $3,400. Sheriff, take him into custody."

I later learned from the sheriff that as he was being led out, he muttered: "I'll rot in jail before I pay that bitch one more cent." This was Thursday morning. By Friday morning he had paid the clerk the $3,400 and was released. His new attorney subsequently told me that he had called her saying, "Joanne, I'm in trouble. I didn't know I would be put in jail with drug dealers, murderers, rapists. You have to get me out of here."

All these individuals needed was a little incentive to find the money they were obligated to pay. I will close this chapter with a true story from my days as an attorney. At that time I was also a Justice of the Peace authorized to perform marriage ceremonies. One morning, I met the about to be newlyweds in my office at 8:30 a.m. because they had to catch a morning flight for their honeymoon, and I had to be in Family Court by 10:00 a.m.. I watched the bride and groom cooing at each other, holding each other's hands as if they were hanging from a cliff, and expressing their deep love and commitment for each other. I performed the ceremony and sent them on their merry way. Then I went to family court to represent a wife in a rather bitter divorce. I thought back to earlier in the morning and wondered if my client and her soon to be ex-husband had felt the same love and commitment demonstrated by that morning's bride and groom at the time of their marriage. Certainly "for better or worse" is a phrase worthy of more consideration than apparently it gets. What had happened to the "wedded bliss"of the couple before me? The atmosphere of optimism and togetherness from the early morning was missing in family court. I thought: "How sad."

Chapter Nine

STALKING AND THE STRANGE CASE OF KATHY GERARDI

"The fourth is freedom from fear." Franklin D. Roosevelt, from his message to Congress, January 6, 1941 describing a world "founded upon four essential human freedoms."

President Roosevelt was talking, at the time of the quotation above, in terms of every nation living in freedom from fear of physical aggression from any of its neighbors. However, in the United States, every individual is entitled to that same freedom: freedom from fear of attack. This freedom is also found, phrased in different words perhaps, in the Declaration of Independence and the United States Constitution, i.e., *"life, liberty and the pursuit of happiness"*. Because of growing national concern about stalking, and wide reports of such stereotypical police responses as, "He hasn't committed a crime. There's nothing we can do until he actually attacks you", most states (Connecticut included) have adopted criminal laws against stalking, threatening and harassment so that the police can now act before it's too late.

The political parties may differ upon the role of government in the lives of its citizens, but no one will disagree that it is the government's role to protect its citizens from criminal acts. The legislature adopts appropriate laws, and then it is up to the police and the courts to enforce them.

What is the legal/criminal definition of stalking? "A person is guilty of stalking . . . when, with intent to cause another person to fear for his physical safety, he willfully and repeatedly follows or lies in wait for such other person and causes such other person to reasonably fear for his physical safety." Here are some examples:

There was the case of a public official who had an intimate relationship with a female clerk in his office. The relationship broke up at her initiative, and she rejected his efforts to restore the relationship. Unfortunately, he would not take "no" for an answer. He would park across the street from her house, and then follow her to work or wherever else she was going. At other times, he would put roses on the windshield of her car, and would even leave a photograph of them together in an intimate scene on her front porch. He would call her frequently despite her requests not to do so.

At work, he would sit at his desk and, according to her, stare at her. When she went into the "vault" (a floor to ceiling safe,) he would "coincidentally" find some reason to be there at the same time. He typically left the office a few minutes earlier at the end of the day to sit in his car and watch her when she came out. When she drove away, he would follow her in his car for at least part of her ride home. Although he never specifically threatened her, this constant stalking turned her into a nervous wreck.

To say she was in fear of being attacked is an understatement. Criminal charges were brought against him, and in view of his continuing denial of guilt, the case was set to go to trial. The victim was afraid to testify, and at the last minute, an agreement was reached. He was granted accelerated rehabilitation, with the de facto acquiescence of the state's attorney and the victim.

He neither admitted nor denied guilt and was put on probation for the maximum period of two years with the specific condition that he was not to contact her in any way, was not to follow her or do anything that would fit under the definition of stalking. She had obtained another job and moved to a different city. He was specifically prohibited from entering those city limits for any reason. If he violated any of these provisions, the accelerated rehabilitation program would be revoked, the original charges would be reinstated and he would face new charges for the new incidents of stalking. He later lost his job for this and other reasons, but there were no further criminal incidents.

The Truths of Justice

There are dozens of cases in which an ex-husband or an ex-boyfriend doesn't want to be an "ex". Again, they don't understand or don't want to understand the meaning of the word "no". This often takes the course of the first incident I've described. Sometimes, however, the ex-husband or boyfriend follows the victim under the guise of making sure that she does not go out with anyone who might be a danger to their child or children. Sometimes, it is pure jealousy and can result in threats against the new boyfriend or husband.

Can you imagine how a boyfriend or new husband would feel, if the ex-boyfriend or husband continually followed them, for example sitting near them at a restaurant and staring continuously at them. A budding romance may break up because of it, which is just what the stalker wants. On some occasions, it can turn violent.

The victim and the boyfriend pull up in front of her house at the end of a date, and the stalker is right behind them. He gets out of the car, runs up to his ex-girlfriend or wife and begins to berate her for going out with the boyfriend or makes up some excuse to yell at her and threaten her. The new boyfriend, of course, tries to intervene, which is just what the stalker wants. He then turns his wrath on the boyfriend and starts to assault him.

I can recall one specific incident in which the ex-husband just could not get over the fact that his wife had divorced him. He stalked her, and when he saw his wife and a new date go into her house, he worked himself into a rage. He got out of his car, and without bothering to knock broke the door down. He actually found the couple in bed together which really set him off. He grabbed his ex-wife and pulled her out of bed and onto the floor, and then proceeded to beat the boyfriend to a pulp.

There was blood all over the sheets when the police and ambulance arrived. After the ambulance left with the boyfriend barely surviving, and while the police were still taking a statement from the shocked and tearful ex-wife, the telephone rang. It was the ex-husband calling to continue to berate the ex-wife. When the police officer got on the telephone, the ex-husband quickly became even more hostile. Incredibly, he threatened the police officer that he would get his gun and come over to the house and kill the officer if he was still there. The police responded by going over to his parent's house and arresting him.

When he was presented before me the next morning, I ordered him to be held under a $1 million dollar bond and also ordered him to undergo an immediate psychiatric examination. There was no way I was going to let him back into the community. He was either going to end up in prison or a lock down psychiatric institution.

Another incident involved the man who shot at his ex in a Vernon restaurant parking area (this case is described in more detail in the chapter on **Domestic Violence**.) She managed to signal a policeman who became the stalker's next target. Fortunately, he missed, and the officer returned fire wounding the man in the shoulder. He was quickly taken into custody. After a visit to the local hospital, he was presented in court before me later in the day, charged with attempted murder and a number of other charges. I set bail at $2 million.

I recount this incident to illustrate how serious stalking can be and how dangerous it can be to the victim. I don't know whether ex-husbands and boyfriends were always like this or whether this has become a phenomenon of our increasingly complex and emotional society.

Perhaps, people cannot handle rejection as well as they once did. Perhaps, it is a growing disrespect for the rights of others, an outgrowth of an attitude that what is good for *me* is the only thing that matters. I leave that to the psychologists, psychiatrists and sociologists who no doubt have much more expertise in this area than I do. One thing I do know from experience. This is a growing and deadly problem and must be handled with swiftness, severity and consistency in the justice system.

Of course, not all stalkers are men. Some women stalk too, a fact exploited by the film **Fatal Attraction**, but they are in the minority. Stalkers are overwhelmingly male. Also, not all stalkers are ex-boyfriends or ex-husbands. A recent example comes to mind.

The stalker had been convicted of attacking three different teen-age girls in 1982 on Cape Cod. He was found guilty of rape, kidnapping and assault with a dangerous weapon and served ten years in prison in Massachusetts. He was then sent to a prison run mental facility for sex offenders but released in 1998 when a judge concluded that state officials had failed to prove he was still a threat. He next turned up on the University of Connecticut campus in Storrs, Connecticut in early 1999. A rock, handcuffs, rope, and a knife were found in his car, exactly the same type of weapons he had used in the 1982 attacks. There was also a rock filled sock and condoms. On the U-Conn campus, he was reported to have approached several women at different times asking them to baby-sit children, watch dogs or answer telephones. In four different incidents he was charged with stalking and disorderly conduct.

Then, there are the cases of celebrities who have been stalked, many right here in Connecticut. A woman obsessed with David Letterman broke into his house in Greenwich on multiple occasions. Celebrities, of course, can afford security specialists, but even with bodyguards, the victims are living in fear, and particularly for women who live alone, it rises to the level of terror. No one should have to live like that. Stalking laws are now on the books, and they must be enforced.

A vivid example of the emotional impact suffered by the object of a stalker and a bizarre turn of events that turned a victim into a defendant is

"THE STRANGE CASE OF KATHY GERARDI."[1]

It was September of 1979, and another school year was starting in the town of Willington, Connecticut, a small rural town thirty minutes east of Hartford off Interstate 84. Incorporated before the American revolution in 1727, it had a population of about 6,000 people. Its principal activities were agriculture and manufacturing but it also served as a bedroom community to Hartford.

Enter Brian Philbrick, a five year old boy who was starting kindergarten at Center School. Also entering Center School for the first

1 Real names are used in this case.

time as a kindergarten teacher was Kathy Gerardi, age twenty eight, who during the first week was sharing a kindergarten classroom with another kindergarten teacher. It was during that first week that she first met Brian Philbrick. When the week was over she moved her class into another classroom and lost track of him.

By September, 1984, Brian was eleven years old and a student in Mrs. Gerardi's fifth grade class. He was a likable child but somewhat emotional. He needed and received extra help from Mrs. Gerardi both emotionally and academically.

Fast forward approximately ten years to the spring of 1994. At this point Kathy Gerardi had been teaching in Willington for seventeen years. She was considered an excellent teacher who was well respected and well liked. Brian Philbrick, then twenty-one years old, was living in Branford, Conn., on Long Island Sound. She hadn't seen or talked to Brian Philbrick since 1985; that is, not until the early morning hours of a day in May 1994 when her telephone rang, waking her up.

It was Brian Philbrick who proceeded to tell Mrs. Gerardi that he had been thinking about her in the intervening years, that he was in love with her and that he had to have her. He made explicit sexual threats as to what he was going to do with her. She hung up on him. She and her husband, Lenny, told him to stop calling, but the calls continued. They changed their number.

Then, he started showing up in her driveway and at school. The Gerardis did not want an unlisted number because her students often called her at home, and she felt that her two sons in college might need to reach her in an emergency. So the calls continued. Some were sexually explicit, but some were just threatening. "You know who I am and you know what I want" or "You know what I want and I know where to find you".

Mrs. Gerardi learned through a private investigator that Brian had been convicted of sexually harassing two other women by telephone. The state police then became involved. They taped a telephone conversation between Kathy Gerardi and Brian Philbrick in which he admitted making the calls, that he was experiencing many family problems, that he was troubled and con-

111

fused, had attempted suicide and that he had a drug and alcohol problem. Brian, who was then five feet, nine inches tall weighing 240 pounds, was called in by the state police for an interview. He admitted the calls, said he was obsessed with Kathy Gerardi and that he masturbated when looking at her picture from an old yearbook and from talking with her on the telephone. He indicated he wanted to stop harassing her, but he just couldn't control himself.

By this time, Kathy was constantly looking over her shoulder, or expecting her stalker's face to appear at the door of her classroom. She was losing her ability to concentrate, she was losing weight and was constantly tired from the emotional distress. At this point, letters and notes started coming. "You will soon be mine. Look who is laughing now." and "Time is running out for you; look who is laughing now."

At the front door of her house she found a note that said: "Guess who was here? Me! Ha Ha." When she took this latest note to the police, she was informed that Brian had been arrested and was in custody. In his confession he admitted to being at her home on many occasions, that he would masturbate outside while watching her through the window, and that he had been to her school. Meanwhile Kathy had been suffering from nightmares in which Brian had done terrible things to her. She would wake up screaming, shaking and in a cold sweat.

Once he was arrested and in jail awaiting trial, the nightmares were less frequent, but they did not stop. Brian pleaded guilty to charges of harassment and stalking, the case was continued for sentencing, and he remained in jail unable to post bond. At the time of sentencing, Brian had been in jail for six months. Mrs. Gerardi was asked to speak at the sentencing. In what may have been misguided compassion, she urged the judge to grant probation. She believed that counseling would help him to get rid of his obsession more than spending additional time in jail where he would brood about getting even with her. Brian did receive a suspended sentence and probation, and, of course, the six months he had already served was taken into account. Strict conditions were imposed as part of his probation, such as the wearing of an electronic monitor and keeping a curfew, and he was ordered to get counseling.

Changes were also made at her school. Her classroom was changed, construction paper was placed over the door so no one could see in, visitors had to sign in at the office and wear a badge, some outside doors were kept locked, and Brian's picture was distributed to all staff members. All of this was considered a big help in preventing a recurrence of stalking by Brian Philbrick; but it wasn't to be. As soon as Brian was out of prison, Kathy Gerardi's troubles flared up again. According to Kathy, the electronic monitor was removed in a few weeks, and he was not held to his curfew.

Kathy Gerardi was under her doctor's care, and she was seeing a psychiatrist. She was taking Prozac to deal with the stress and AmBieu to help her sleep. She still feared Brian Philbrick, the nightmares returned, and she became unnerved to learn that someone had entered a kindergarten class in Dunblane, Scotland and shot to death 16 children and their teacher.

She and her husband discovered that all the mail had been taken from their mailbox, opened and scattered around the street. Another call was initiated by her to the state police headquarters, but Brian denied everything. Kathy was concerned that he had found her golf league registration and the address of a summer cottage they had rented. The Gerardis took additional security precautions.

The phone calls had not been renewed, but they had a security system installed at their home complete with motion sensors. The blinds were kept down at all times, and Kathy started to take a baseball bat with her wherever she went, including school. On April 24th, her birthday, she received a birthday card at school in a letter postmarked from southern Connecticut which was the same postmark as on a previous letter. She recognized Brian's handwriting on the envelope. The birthday card stated in letters cut out of a newspaper or magazine, similar to the previous letters, the words: "I have two simple wishes for you on your birthday: 1. May your wildest fantasy come true . . . 2. May I be directly involved in #1." "guess who" was glued to the card in cut-out letters. Kathy wondered how he knew it was her birthday if he hadn't opened the mail.

On May 9, 1996 Kathy brought an additional letter to the state police unopened. It stated, again in cut out letters, "Hi Sweetie, I am not who you think I am. Leave Philbrick alone. Stop going to the cops or you will be very sorry. I mean what I say and I know where to find you. One . . . Two . . . Three . . . POW! So long Sweetie." Because of the threatening content of the letter and the fact that it had been released to the media, parents and school officials became concerned for the safety of the students. A state trooper was hired by the school to provide additional security until Brian Philbrick was arrested on May 15, 1996, charged with threatening, harassment and disorderly conduct.

On June 12, 1996 a letter addressed to Kathy Gerardi was received at the Hall Memorial School in Willington, consisting of cut out words taped to paper which stated: "OK Bitch, drop it all now or we shoot the kids. Bang. Bang. No more teacher, no more kids, DOA." Security at the school was once again heightened, and several state troopers were assigned to patrol the school. Extracurricular activities were canceled and a large number of students were kept home from school by their parents.

This letter, however, was postmarked in Willington, and remember, Brian Philbrick had remained in custody since his arrest on May 15th. The envelope which contained the letter had an embossed rose on the back, the same embossed rose that was on the back of several thank you notes Mrs. Gerardi had sent to state troopers. This was hardly the work of a careful or cunning criminal. Then the state police laboratory concluded that the letter inside the envelope of May 9, 1996 contained the fingerprint of Kathy Gerardi. Remember, she had turned it over to the state police with the envelope sealed. It had not been handled by Mrs. Gerardi once she turned it over to the state police unopened.

On June 20, 1996 she admitted writing the letter of May 9,1996. She was arrested and eventually admitted to preparing the June 12th letter and an additional letter on June 5, 1996. She adamantly denied involvement in the birthday card of April 24th. Brian Philbrick also continued to deny involvement in the birthday card incident.

Mrs. Gerardi was charged with 3 counts of making a false statement, 4 counts of filing a false report, 4 counts of breach of peace and 4 counts of tampering with evidence. The last 4 counts are felonies. **Suddenly the victim became the accused.**

Mrs. Gerardi retained Attorney William Collins of Manchester, an experienced criminal lawyer who promptly made an application for Accelerated Rehabilitation. The hearing on what was certain to be a contested application was scheduled for September 4, 1996 at 2 p.m. As the presiding judge of the G.A. (geographical area) criminal court I was to preside over the hearing. Accelerated Rehabilitation is a special program for first time offenders. The defendant pleads neither guilty nor not guilty. It is simply an application which, if granted, means that the defendant would be put on probation for up to two years with or without special conditions. If successfully completed, all charges against the defendant would be automatically dismissed. It is a program which can be granted only once. The criteria to be considered will be described later, but the decision as to whether to grant it is discretionary with the judge.

Because of the bizarre nature of the facts in this case, (it was hardly a routine stalking case) it received national attention. The first issue I had to decide was how to deal with the media. I received a request from NBC's *Dateline* to film or videotape the entire hearing, and a request from a local newspaper to permit photographs to be taken in the courtroom. I rejected both requests. The Connecticut Rules of Practice permit such coverage for *trials* only. For a jury trial, "after the jury has been sworn" and for a non-jury trial "commencing with the swearing in of the first witness" would seem to prohibit coverage in a *pre-trial* diversionary program such as Accelerated Rehabilitation. Mrs. Gerardi was almost sure to be a witness so conceivably this could be interpreted as a non-jury trial.

However, I adhered to a strict interpretation of the rules and stated that such coverage was not permitted for this pre-trial hearing.

There were other reasons as well. I stated in a letter to the Administrative Judge the following:

"In view of the highly sensitive nature of the forthcoming hearing, I believe that the presence of cameras and/or recordings may well have a negative and disruptive effect upon the hearing. No matter how unobtrusive the cameras and recordings may be and no matter how good the intentions of such media may be, the participants and the audience will know they are present. Their presence could easily inhibit some of the participants or even discourage their potential participation entirely. Also, the presence of cameras and/or recording equipment may have the opposite effect with some, inspiring them to seek and/or take advantage of the limelight".

Perhaps I had been sensitized by the proceedings of the O. J. Simpson trial. I was determined not to allow this hearing to turn into a circus. Some of my reasoning turned out to be prophetic. The large courtroom was filled to capacity, including members of the media. At one point Attorney Collins turned his back to me and continued to make his argument directly to the audience. I interrupted him with a reminder that I was the one he had to convince, not the audience. I suggested to him that he might want to stand to my right in a position in which he would be facing both me and the audience. He adopted my suggestion, and after an apology to the court, he continued. I'm sure he just got carried away.

Except for the media, the courtroom seemed evenly divided between those who favored the granting of the application and those who opposed it. I had received directly and through Attorney Collins and Assistant State's Attorney Sandra Tulius hundreds of letters on the subject. Including petitions, there were approximately 100 in favor of the application and the same number in opposition. I read every word of all of them as well as several psychiatric reports concerning Mrs. Gerardi.

The atmosphere was tense as the hearing began. Attorney Collins went first since it was the defendant's application. He pre-

The Truths of Justice

sented testimony from Mrs. Gerardi's mother and from Mrs. Gerardi herself. This was the first time I had seen Mrs. Gerardi. She was about 5 feet 3 inches tall, and she looked frail and gaunt. As she testified later she had lost 37 pounds, dropping from 125 to 88 pounds. What struck me immediately as she took the witness stand immediately to my right was that she was partially bald. My first reaction was that parts of her head had been shaved for a surgical operation. Once she started testifying I quickly realized that large patches of her hair had fallen out as a result of her emotional trauma.

She described her ordeal stemming both from Brian Philbrick's stalking and her falsifying the subsequent letters. She explained her reasons for her actions, among them that if one of the letters threatened the children, more police protection would be provided for both her and the children. She did achieve her goal. Additional state troopers were added to the school for increased security. Of course, this was the main sticking point with those who opposed the application, namely, that they thought the letter threatening the children was horrible. It was clear that the residents of the town of Willington were equally divided between those who sympathized with her and those who opposed her. Attorney Collins described her exemplary record as a teacher, her mental and emotional breakdown, and ended with an impassioned plea to grant the application. He was effective.

However, at least equally effective was State's Attorney Sandra Tulius who presented the prosecution's opposition. "Sandy" Tulius is an experienced prosecutor who has seen it all. She was thoroughly prepared, and made a strong and effective argument against granting the application. She focused on the seriousness of the crime and whether Mrs. Gerardi would likely offend again. She attempted to convince me that Mrs. Gerardi was in control of her actions when she fabricated the evidence. "The details of fabricating the evidence took a concentrated effort by someone who was not in a fog as she described. This was someone who knew absolutely what they were doing".

117

She criticized Mrs. Gerardi for creating fear in the community. "She scared the hell out of them" she said. Attorney Tulius said that Mrs. Gerardi didn't merely "make a mistake" as she had claimed. "She committed crimes that are against the laws of the State of Connecticut". Her voice rose as she became more impassioned in her argument. It was impressive.

The state police also objected to the application, and then Willington's First Selectman, John Patton, rose to speak, saying that her actions had caused too much damage in the community to be dismissed. Brian Philbrick's attorney, Arthur Meisler, said that Mrs. Gerardi's actions brought his client a lot of trouble he didn't deserve, forcing him to spend an extra six weeks in jail until Mrs. Gerardi confessed. I pointed out to him that Philbrick was the one who caused all the trauma to the defendant. "I have a hard time feeling sorry for Mr. Philbrick."

The testimony had been heard and the arguments made. It was getting close to 5 p.m. It was decision time, and it was up to me to make it. First, I touched upon two other areas

the court had to consider when deciding upon an AR application. One was the defendant's background. That was easy. Up until this situation she had a superb background and a superb record as a teacher. Next was to consider the opposition to the application, and then the two other considerations mentioned by Attorney Tulius, the seriousness of the crimes and the likelihood of the defendant offending again.

"I think we're missing the point here." I said. "***This was all started by Mr. Philbrick. He*** is the one who caused the trauma to the defendant . . . the terror and the fear and the emotional trauma".

As for the opposition, I rejected the state's contention that Mrs. Gerardi was seeking attention. There was no psychiatric evidence to support that. As for the first selectman's opposition, I reminded him that Mrs. Gerardi had been a teacher in Willington for 17 years and had served her community well, that it was because she was a teacher in Willington this entire situation started. She was Brian Philbrick' teacher, and as a result of her employment by the Town in that capacity she became subjected to harassment and stalking by a former student.

As for threatening the children, I pointed out that these children are more resilient than they are given credit for. Sure, she lied and as such would not be a shining example or role model for them. The children should be told that Mrs. Gerardi was suffering from a mental illness. This is no longer the shame it used to be. Mental illness is out of the closet. The children should be taught about mental illness, and Mrs. Gerardi's action could be used as an example to help them understand how mental illness might occur. They should learn at some point that mental illness is a serious problem in our society. "By the time we get into the next century, it's going to be increasingly widespread. It's not going to go away, and it will increase as the pressure to succeed grows in our increasingly complex society . . . . They should be told that up until this incident she was a shining example of integrity, but the lack of integrity came from a mental illness, and they should learn what that is."

I then turned to the seriousness of the crimes. "There are felony charges, but the seriousness of the crime has to be considered along with her mental illness. It makes the crime less serious than it would otherwise be . . . . The main consideration here has to be the psychiatric reports. There is no question that her actions were totally out of character for her. Dr. Kenneth Schooff of Professional Resource Group states: "The symptoms this patient developed were a direct result of the stalking behavior exhibited by a former student. She developed classic post traumatic stress disorder symptoms as well as depressive symptoms".

Dr. Richard Bridburg of the Institute for Living states: "I believe that Mrs. Gerardi began to suffer from an Adjustment Disorder with Anxiety and Depressed Mood which gradually crossed over into a severe depression. Thus, by the time she was hospitalized at the Institute of Living, she was suffering from a Major Depression, Single Episode."

Natchaug Hospital states: "The diagnosis is Major Depression; single episode and Post Traumatic Stress Disorder . . . . The above

Post Traumatic Stress Disorder symptoms are the result of stalking behavior of a previous student . . . ."

An unsolicited letter came to me directly from the director of the out-patient psychiatric clinic at Charlotte-Hungerford Hospital, who admittedly had not seen Mrs. Gerardi. He states: ". . . post traumatic stress disorder, shortened to PTSD . . . results from being the victim of a traumatic event: Rape, physical assault, being stalked, fearing for one's well being over time. . . The fact that the defendant (Brian Philbrick) admitted to stalking Mrs. Gerardi for . . . about a year and a half, makes it very likely that she is experiencing PTSD". Here is the most important part. *"Individuals experiencing PTSD often act out of character or behave in ways intended to cope with excessive degrees of stress.* They are capable of understanding the inappropriateness of their behavior *after* the fact and learning more appropriate coping behaviors."

After reading these letters into the record, I also commented that all of these psychiatrists believed that with proper treatment, she would recover fully and would not offend again. Then I continued as to the mental illness: "Now, did she overreact. I don't think so . . . She clearly has suffered. She has lost thirty-eight pounds. From one hundred and twenty-five to eighty-seven pounds all as a result of this traumatic syndrome, and *I don't know how I or any man can look into the mind of a woman who has been harassed and stalked sexually for nearly a year and a half.* I can listen to her and I can try to understand what a horrible experience that she went through, but I have never been stalked sexually or otherwise and I don't expect I will . . . but I find this woman to have been in a desperate situation, so desperate that she included the children in her threatening letter. Now, it was the wrong thing to do. No question about it. But if you look at her mental condition, whether brought on by the medication (Prozac, Xanax and AmBieu) which she admittedly says that tended to have a negative effect on her in certain ways, whether it's because of the post-traumatic syndrome itself, it was her mental illness that caused her to do what she did . . . ."

The Truths of Justice

Finally, I turned to examples of the compassion she had shown in various situations, some of which information was taken from the letters I had received. First, of course, was when she asked for probation and counseling for Mr. Philbrick when the State was seeking more jail time. I quoted from some of the letters: "Kathy Gerardi went to extraordinary effort to help a young female student who had been sexually abused by her father. She went to the emergency room and comforted her during the examination. It was Kathy who stayed by her side after school hours. It was Kathy who brought her an outfit to wear on the class trip . . . and it was Kathy who kept in touch with this girl throughout the many foster home placements . . . ." Another letter described how Kathy Gerardi had organized fund-raisers and obtained meals for a teacher with terminal cancer and helped another Willington family of cancer victims. Another letter described how hard she had worked to help a significantly retarded boy. There were other examples as well. I concluded with these remarks: ". . . what I'm trying to say here is that there are many ways in which Mrs. Gerardi has shown compassion for the people in Willington, whether it's students, teachers or just plain citizens, *and I think it's time to show some compassion for her*".

I then entered the following order: "So based upon all of that, the application is *granted*, and the probationary period is two years . . . . Now, there are two conditions for the accelerated rehabilitation. One is that she shall submit to such assessment, evaluation, treatment and counseling as may be directed by the Office of Adult Probation . . . . And finally, I believe under all the circumstances she should reimburse the Town of Willington for their expenditures for the extra police protection. I'm putting a four thousand dollar cap on that. The bill to date is $2,000. It is to be paid in equal payments over the next twenty-three months."

I recognized that this decision would not be popular with those opposing the application, but I urged the town to move on: ". . . it is also time for a town that is split to begin the healing process and get all of this behind you".

The Truths of Justice
AFTERMATH

Alas, it was not to be. The town remained divided. Two years later, Kathy Gerardi applied for reinstatement as a teacher in Willington. The Board of Education rejected her application. A court appeal was filed. Also, she instituted a separate suit against the Board and the Town claiming, among other things, that she suffered discrimination because of her mental illness from which she had recovered by the time of the rejection.[2]

Kathy Gerardi subsequently was interviewed on NBC *Dateline*. *Good Morning America* called me shortly after the decision seeking an interview. I declined citing the Judicial Code which prohibits judges from commenting upon a pending case. (The 2 year probation was still pending.) I received several cards and some phone calls from people I knew thanking me or praising my "compassion". Mrs. Gerardi, in a lengthy article in the Sunday Northeast Magazine of the *Hartford Courant* of August 30, 1998 thanked me indirectly by stating: "I believe that God was looking out for me the afternoon of my hearing in the person of the Honorable Judge Richard Rittenband."

There were no letters to me criticizing my decision. People generally don't write to judges criticizing them. The notable exception was the *Hartford Courant*, the nation's oldest continually published newspaper. In an editorial titled "Reprieve from a living hell", dated September 9, 1996, the *Courant* stated that ". . . compassion won out over retribution last week", but then went on to say: "While we disagree with the judge's granting of probation . . . ."

Ironically, in another editorial two years later, the *Courant* urged that Mrs. Gerardi be *rehired* as a teacher in Willington. If accelerated rehabilitation had not been granted and Mrs. Gerardi had been convicted of a felony, her application for reinstatement would have been further undermined, contrary to the *Courant's* goal of having her rehired.

---

[2] Her law suits were eventually settled, but she did not regain her teaching position in Willington. That's unfortunate, because she had been an outstanding teacher and what she did was not her fault. However, life goes on and she did secure a teaching position in another town. It is that town's gain. I wish her well.

Finally, with the benefit of hindsight, would I do it again? Absolutely! It was the right thing to do.[11]

Note: Brian Philbrick was subsequently arrested for stalking two other women. He was sentenced to ten months in prison for each charge, to run consecutively, for a total sentence of twenty months.

Chapter Ten

THE COURT VS. THE PROSECUTION

In the fall of 1993, Adrian Santiago was arrested for a murder that took place in eastern Connecticut not too far from the location of the Superior Court building. It was alleged that Santiago had come up from Puerto Rico as a "hit man" by the NIETA gang to kill a 17 year old boy because he had left or was about to leave the gang. He and Santiago were riding bicycles in the late evening when Santiago pulled out a gun and shot the victim.

Santiago had waived a probable cause hearing, and the case was at a stage in which the parties were seeking discovery of important information from each other. Santiago was represented by Attorney Fran Parton of the Public Defender's office. The state was represented by the Chief State's Attorney for that Judicial District. Two of his assistants, Martin Smith and Ralph Jones were handling this particular case.[1]

I became initially involved in the case when the state sought a protective order to protect the names, addresses and/or location of two witnesses for the state. After a hearing in which the state presented two police officers to testify, one of whom was an expert on gangs, I ordered the defense not to disclose the names to anyone but its own staff and the same as to the address or location of these witnesses.

Next a hearing was held on what appeared to be the state's refusal or neglect to turn over certain material to the defense. After deciding what materials in dispute were to be turned over to the defense, I ordered that all materials due the defense were to be given to the defense at the public defender's office at 10 a.m. on a specified date; otherwise, such materials could not be used at trial by the state. That was the easy part.

---

[1] Real names of the attorneys are not used in order to protect their privacy.

The Truths of Justice

Subsequently, Attorney Parton asked for a hearing claiming that the state had not turned over to her all of the exculpatory material and information it had in its possession. It has long been the law that under the United States Constitution as interpreted by the U. S. Supreme Court in the famous case of <u>Brady v. Maryland</u>, the government in a criminal trial is obligated to give to the defense all material and information it has or has available to it that would be or tend to be favorable to the defendant's claim of innocence. This is called "Brady material." The rationale behind this ruling is that the government, whether federal or state, has the obligation not just to convict defendants but *to ensure that justice is done*. Therefore, any evidence that would exculpate the defendant, that is any evidence that might show his innocence rather than his guilt, must be turned over to him to make sure that the entire truth is presented at the trial.

Attorney Parton presented me with affidavits from two witnesses who stated under oath that they had been interviewed by the state police and had told the police about two other individuals who, according to the word on the street, were suspects in the murder. These names had been given to the police as well as additional information about them and the source of this information. Attorney Parton stated that this information had not been given to her by the state, and that, therefore, the state had withheld exculpatory or potentially exculpatory information from the defense in violation of the ruling in <u>Brady v. Maryland</u>. Assistant State's Attorney Jones was then given the affidavits for review and expressed surprise. "This is the first time I've seen these, the first time I've been made aware of this information, your honor." he stated. "I'll get right on it ." he promised.

"Attorney Jones, no one is questioning your honesty in this matter. I have always known you to be a man of integrity and honor, and I continue to believe that. However, as you well know, the police are considered an arm of the prosecution, and their knowledge is imputed to you. Therefore, their failure to present you with this information becomes a failure on the part of the state to promptly turn over Brady material to the defense."

"Your honor," Jones replied. "I don't understand how this happened, and I will get right on it."

"I'm afraid you're not getting the message, counsel. The public defender doesn't trust your office, and I can see why." I said. "Here's what I'm going to do to resolve all of this. There does seem to be a conflict between your office and the public defender's office concerning discovery. There have been delays, each side claiming the other is responsible for them, and this latest incident, it seems to me, further compounds the problem. So, to clear all of this up, the state is hereby ordered to turn over to this court all of its evidence in this case for the court to review same in camera (privately in chambers). I will determine what is exculpatory and what is not. The evidence is to be turned over to me in my chambers at 10 a.m. on Thursday, August 24, 1994; and that is to include any evidence that is developed between now and then. You have a continuing duty to disclose."

"With all due respect, your honor, you don't have the authority to do this. I've never heard of this being done anywhere else. It is the prosecution that is permitted to determine what is exculpatory." Jones replied.

"With all due respect to you, Attorney Jones, I *do* have the authority under Section 745 of the Connecticut Practice Book.[2] I will grant you that this is a little unusual. However, this is a murder case, and in view of the difficulties between the parties so far, I intend to fully exercise that authority. Sheriff, you may adjourn court."

That, of course, was not the end if it. Attorney Smith, who was supervising state's attorney and also an honest and straightforward individual, came into my chambers a day or two later. "You're questioning our integrity." he said.

"No, I'm not." I replied. "There is a basic problem with the system. What would have happened if Attorney Parton hadn't developed this information on her own? If the state police had never turned this

---

[2] Sec. 745: "In addition to any other disclosure or inspection permitted by these rules, the judicial authority may, upon motion of the defendant and a showing of good cause, order such other disclosure, inspection, testing or copying of specific information and materials as the interests of justice may require."

information over to you? It's likely that she would never have obtained this information. It may have never come to light.

I'll concede that it may have been a mistake on the part of the police, that somehow the information slipped through the cracks, or that the officer checked out the lead and found it to be useless. But, it's not up to him to decide that. It's initially up to you to decide whether it's exculpatory, and if in doubt, turn it over. ***The problem then is what if you don't think it's exculpatory?*** Then, it never sees the light of day; and if you're wrong, honestly wrong, the defendant never obtains the information to which he is entitled under the constitution. The State Supreme Court has held that it is error not to turn this information over promptly. It must be turned over in time to do the defendant some good. The case I'm thinking of is where the identity of two witnesses didn't surface until the trial. By that time, they had left for parts unknown so the defense couldn't even talk to them. Under normal circumstances, you are invested with tremendous power and discretion in determining what is exculpatory. But what if you make a mistake, and the exculpatory information is never disclosed late or otherwise? An innocent person can be convicted. That's why there should be some general safeguards. That's the province of the legislature.

However, in a case like this in which I learn that some exculpatory information has been withheld no matter how innocently it may have been, a warning bell goes off, and I believe it is my duty to act to protect the defendant's constitutional rights and make sure he has a fair trial. Besides, how have you been harmed? If there is nothing exculpatory, you haven't lost anything, and if there is, you haven't lost anything. You're guaranteeing a fair trial and eliminating a possible grounds for appeal in the event you secure a conviction."

On August 24th the state moved to reconsider my ruling. I listened to the same arguments that I had heard before, and did not change my ruling. I scheduled the in camera review for September 1st. I was concerned that there might be another delay, and I was due to be assigned to another court later in September, so I added to my order the following: "I want the state to know that if you fail to comply with my order, I will dismiss the murder charge and release the defendant. He will probably be on the next plane back to Puerto Rico, and you may never find him again. Is that what you really want? A dismissal? It's your choice. Either comply with the court's order or have a murder charge dismissed."

By now it had become a test of wills between the court and the state. I felt confident in my position on the issue, and I strongly believed that the court, the impartial arbiter who must make sure that justice be done, must prevail. Nevertheless, I offered the state a way out. "I know that you think I'm wrong on this," I said, "so I will be willing to stay my order dismissing the charge to give you the opportunity to appeal to the Appellate Court. During the stay and the appeal the defendant will remain in custody."

The state chose not to appeal. I believe I know the reason. Either underneath it all, they believed that I ***did*** have the authority to make the ruling, or, more likely, they were concerned that I might be upheld. By not appealing, my decision could not be viewed as binding precedent.

I'm merely a Superior Court judge who made a decision, and my decision is not binding upon any other superior court judge. Since the decision was orally from the bench and not in writing, it would not be published in the **Connecticut Law Tribune** or the **Connecticut Law Reporter** and, therefore, no other superior court judge would even become aware of it. Since the state's attorney was probably correct that such a decision had never been made before, and my own research had revealed none, it was probably a "case of first impression." However, ***if the Appellate Court were to uphold my decision, then it would be precedent, thus permitting all superior court judges to make a similar ruling.***

On the evening before the deadline, the states' attorneys' office was still insisting that it would not turn over the evidence to me. However, at 10 a.m. the next day, Attorney Jones did come to my chambers and release all of the evidence to me. I reviewed it, and found only two or three items that I believed to be exculpatory material and ordered the state to give that evidence to the defense. The state complied with the order, and that ended that conflict. The exculpatory material apparently didn't do Mr. Santiago much good. He was subsequently convicted by a jury. Would I have dismissed the murder charge? Yes, if only to let the state know that the court was in charge and that its orders had to be obeyed. I might have dismissed it without prejudice, thereby allowing the state to have the defendant rearrested and held on bond, or, more likely, I would have stayed the order without any request from the state still allowing the state to appeal. Under those circumstances, the state probably would have appealed. But, who knows? Fortunately, the state complied with my order, thereby reaffirming the rule of law. Thus, those decisions never had to be made.

Chapter Eleven

ILLEGAL DRUGS

The sale and use of illegal drugs has been, perhaps, the biggest scourge in this country during the last half of the twentieth century. If we can eliminate the use of illegal drugs in this country, the nation's crime rate will be drastically reduced.

How did it all start? It seems to have first become more prevalent in parts of western Europe. Then, came the counter-culture in the United States in the early sixties with its rejection of authority and self-discipline and the adoption of promiscuous sex and a "What's in it for me?" attitude. The younger generation began to use marijuana, then cocaine and heroin, LSD and amphetamines. By 1965 it had become a major problem across America. It was a generation that had lost their idol, John F. Kennedy, by assassination and his replacement as their idol, his brother, Robert F. Kennedy, also by assassination. It was the time of the explosion of the civil rights movement when young people, both black and white, rallied against the evil of racial discrimination, with brave individuals traveling to the south to register black voters and to join in protests.

Violence erupted and some of them lost their lives, their killers not brought to justice until many years later. The civil rights movement suffered a tremendous blow with the assassination of the Reverend Martin Luther King, Jr. on April 4, 1968, almost two months before the assassination of Robert F. Kennedy on June 5, 1968. Three of the leaders of this young idealistic generation had been taken away from them by violence in a short span of time. What these young people had considered good for America had suddenly been taken from them. Violence abounded with the urban riots that occurred following King's assassination in April, 1968 and re-emerged during the protest at the Democratic National Convention in the summer of 1968 which turned into a "police riot" in Chicago. Much of this the young, spurred on by eloquent speakers and charismatic leaders, blamed on the "establishment", a term used interchangeably with "the government."

And if you think this produced frustration, imagine the frustration of the young with what they considered illegal involvement of the United States in the Vietnam War. In many ways their concern about the Vietnam War struck closer to home. Not only did they think U.S. troops shouldn't be there, but they also didn't want to be part of those U.S. troops; that is they didn't want to risk their lives in a war they considered both illegal and unjust. This was not World War II in which the cause and the motives were clear, nor Korea where the reason may have been less clear than World War II, but was certainly clearer than Vietnam.

I served in the Air Force as a counter-intelligence agent and criminal investigator during the Korean War. There was no big uproar or criticism of that war, although Americans suffered approximately the same number of casualties in Korea as they did in Vietnam. Ten years after the Korean war the media had developed the technology that enabled it to bring horrifying scenes of battle, casualties and body bags into everyone's living room, and the more widespread coverage of the Vietnam war and the resulting protests threatened to tear our nation apart.

Our involvement lasted nearly eleven years, and it was always surrounded by huge controversy at home. Ultimately we lost the Vietnam War. So, with the frustrations of losses in the civil rights movement and those produced by the Vietnam War, young people not only distrusted government but developed a general disrespect for any kind of authority. Pledges by presidents in that era proved to be false although not too many of us knew it at the time. Then came Watergate, Iran-Contra and the Clinton presidency during all of which government officials lied, and these lies were discovered. Is it any wonder that many Americans grew to distrust their government and still do?

In the sixties, faced with what they considered the hopelessness of the future, young people, led by such drug icons as Timothy Leary, decided to "drop out", "tune out", "do it now because we may never get the chance later," and generally experiment with an exploding pharmacopoeia that was over the counter, under the counter, black market and "grow-your-own.". The result was that the drug problem became rampant in our society.

How did this affect America? Now that there was a serious demand for illegal drugs, enter the sellers of illegal drugs to provide the supplies necessary to meet that demand. As the demand expanded so did the number of sellers and the importation and manufacture of more drugs. Everyone seemed to be doing it or at least experimenting with it. It was the hip, the cool thing to do, and once people became addicted the demand continued to grow. The demand didn't just come from the young people of the protest movements who by the eighties and nineties had become or were approaching middle age. Many of those who had served in Vietnam had become hooked on drugs there and remained so when they came home.

Following the end of the Vietnam War, the protest movements seemed to die out. Much was accomplished in the civil rights movement so there were few marches led by charismatic figures. Racism remained alive in America and it still is, but blacks and other minorities have made strides that eliminated the urgency marked by the civil rights movement. We still have much to do to stamp out racism (see the two examples in the chapter *"You Be the Judge"*), but the frustrations of the sixties have lessened and been replaced by the frustration of not being able to get a job during recessionary periods, and even in the late nineties when the economy was booming, people at the low end of the economic ladder still lacked the skills to obtain good jobs.

We have seen the advent of corporate downsizing, and as our society has become increasingly complex, the pressure to succeed has become more intense. Road rage and random shootings are signs of growing frustration and pressure. Well to do people from the suburbs drive into the cities to buy drugs. They seek drugs either because of some frustration in their lives or to experiment with them so that the highs they receive allow them to forget about their otherwise boring or unsatisfying lives. Then, they become addicted, and the increased demand is fulfilled by more drug dealers and more sales.

The Truths of Justice

Drugs affect Americans in at least two ways. First, they become addicted, and when they run out of money to buy more drugs, they have to commit burglaries, larcenies and sometimes embezzlement to get the money to feed their habits. Burglaries and robberies often lead to violence. The burglars are sometimes surprised by the home-owner who may try to resist and end up being shot. I have had dozens of guilty pleas before me to such crimes, and very often the reason for the crime is to obtain the money to buy drugs. Just last week as this is being written, I signed two arrest warrants for burglaries by individuals who were not only high on cocaine but needed the money to buy more drugs.

The second effect on Americans is that those who use these drugs and become addicted bring serious trouble into their lives, their families' lives and public life. The drug addict loses his/her job because he/she cannot perform his/her duties. Unemployment results putting a strain on the family and continued use, such as with an alcoholic, makes the addict impossible to live with. Then too, there is danger from addiction. Not only does the addiction scramble brains (sometimes permanently), but people high on drugs have lost their inhibitions.

Some people believe marijuana is harmless and should even be legalized. Not in this judge's experience. David Copas, the man who murdered a sixteen year old girl mentioned in the chapter entitled *"Murder in the Connecticut Woods"*, was, according to his written confession, smoking pot all day, and when he and his victim were together for approximately six hours before he killed her, they had both smoked a lot of marijuana. As you may recall, he was caught lying in his confession, but the part about *his* smoking pot all day and night I believed to be true. The man charged with burglary of his neighbor's home with the intent to commit sexual assault (described in the chapter on *Sexual Assault and Pedophiles*) claims to have been high on cocaine.

In May of 1999, the driver of a pickup truck killed in an Interstate 91 crash in Meriden, Connecticut that also claimed the lives of four others was high on cocaine at the time of the accident. The autopsy report said that he had "acute cocaine intoxication." For those who think marijuana is harmless, recall the worst motor vehicle accident in New Orleans history on Mother's Day, 1999 in which twenty two people died. Police reported that marijuana ingested by the driver of a charter bus between two and six hours before the accident was the main cause of the crash. Further, marijuana is considered a "gateway drug" often leading to addiction to the more serious drugs of cocaine and heroin.

The cases of people dying from an overdose of heroin are too numerous to mention. Heroin can be even more devastating than cocaine, because once you become addicted to heroin, you have to have it every day. That takes a lot of money, and the need for it leads to crime as a means of getting it. You can become addicted by snorting it just once. The needles come later. Between 1992 and 1997 the number of Americans entering treatment centers for heroin surged 29%, from 180,000 to 232,000 even surpassing cocaine; and that doesn't include heroin addicts who don't enter a treatment center. An example from my experience is a nurse who got hooked on heroin 14 years ago, starting a tailspin into joblessness, despair and the brink of suicide.

The dead end street that is the life of an addict is one that is traveled by more and more Americans, according to a September, 1999 report of the Substance Abuse and Mental Health Services Administration of the U.S. Department of Health and Human Services. Certainly, drug addiction is a disease just like alcohol addiction, and the consequences are often more serious than alcohol addiction.

If it's a disease, why is possession of it considered a crime? The answer is the devastating effects on society of addiction I've just described. Hopefully a prison term for possession will deter first time use. Also, the demand for these drugs by addicts creates networks of drug suppliers and sellers. This has led to violence between dealers with innocent people being hurt as well, violence against addicts who do not pay for the drugs, crimes by addicts to obtain the money they need to buy the drugs, and finally, further demand for drugs and the increase in sellers have produced the "gangs" that roam the streets of our major cities, frequently making downtown a very unsafe place to be. It was the gangs that were responsible for the "drive by shootings" in which many innocent people including small children lost their lives.

What to do about it? In Connecticut, through an aggressive and coordinated effort by the United States Attorney and the F.B.I., the Chief State's Attorney and state and local police as well as local prosecutors, gang members were hunted down, prosecuted and given substantial prison terms. Local law enforcement has proven effective, at least in some areas in which I have been assigned as a judge.

Vernon, Connecticut with a population of approximately thirty thousand people is probably the largest town in Tolland County. It is located about fifteen miles east of Hartford on Interstate 84. When I was sitting there as a criminal court judge in the mid nineties, Vernon had a serious problem with the sale of illegal drugs, including the problem of gangs dealing in drugs.

Under the overall direction of Assistant State's Attorney Matthew Gedansky, the Vernon police with help from the state police and the Tri-Town Narcotics Task Force, embarked upon a concerted effort to eliminate the drug trade in Vernon. They used confidential informants, undercover police officers and various surveillance techniques that led to the arrest of dozens of drug sellers which also led to the break up of the gangs.

They had solid cases so most defendants pleaded guilty. My colleagues and I handed down sentences ranging from a low of four years to a high of twenty-eight years. Not only were the dealers put away for long periods of time, but word traveled that the police, the prosecutors and the judges in Vernon were serious about cracking down on illegal drug sales.

Sure, the prison population has gone up, but the crime rate is down. That is due, at least in part, to locking up the drug dealers. Admittedly, these are not large urban centers, and the dealers were small time, but it does show that with a strong effort by law enforcement officials and serious prison time for dealers, a dent can be made in the drug trade.

It should be noted that the strengthening of drug laws by the

The Truths of Justice

Connecticut Legislature has been helpful as well. Recognizing that drug addicts have a disease, whereas many drug sellers are not addicts, the legislature, several years ago changed the criminal law on this subject.[3]

Although possession of cocaine or heroin is still a serious offense that can carry substantial jail time, *sale of drugs by a person who is not dependent upon drugs (i.e. not an addict)* is a much more serious offense. The General Assembly recognized that drug addicts sell drugs to get more money to buy the drugs needed to feed their habit, but non addicts sell drugs strictly for the profit. Therefore, if an individual is convicted of the sale of drugs, and such seller is not drug dependent, he/she faces a five-year mandatory minimum sentence.

In the first drug case that I tried, *State vs. Frankie Jenkins*, Mr. Jenkins was observed by police selling drugs in front of his apartment building. He claimed that he was drug dependent. His attorney produced a doctor who testified that Jenkins was drug dependent. However, the sale was in July, and the doctor did not examine him until the following February. The doctor admitted that his opinion was based solely on what Jenkins had told him in February about his condition the previous July. There was no one else who knew him at the time of the sale who could testify that he was drug dependent at the time of the sale.

I sentenced him to ten years in prison, suspended after he served the mandatory minimum of five years. His appeal to the Appellate

---

[3] In November, 1994, Superior Court Judge Arthur L. Spada (now retired from the bench and serving as Connecticut's Commissioner of Public Safety) issued his report as a one judge Grand Juror concerning his investigation of police corruption in the City of Hartford. This report was based upon an exhaustive eighteen-month probe which included testimony of 148 witnesses. The report resulted in the arrest of several police officers. What is particularly interesting is Judge Spada's finding that Hartford's illegal drug trade was being fueled by public money. Drug sales doubled just after welfare recipients received their checks twice a month. In a thorough and comprehensive 40-page report Judge Spada did not pull any punches. He strongly criticized welfare fraud as a major factor in the drug business. He found teenagers living in subsidized housing making up to $50,000 a year from drug sales and people working full-time and collecting public assistance. A major drug dealer overseeing a four-block neighborhood grossed $9 million a year from sales while a casual seller takes in $100,000 a year. Many of these dealers were also receiving welfare checks. Gov. John Rowland appointed a blue ribbon commission to review Judge Spada's report and consider his recommendations. The Commission's findings echoed the Spada report and added some recommendations. All of this resulted in the Legislature's adoption of welfare reform described as among the toughest in the nation. This is a major step forward in the war on drugs; but more is needed. This legislation does not reach the root problem of how people get addicted to drugs in the first place. The demand for drugs must dry up, and that requires education on the subject as described elsewhere in this chapter.

Court was denied, and as far as I know, he served the full five years (perhaps, with some time off for good behavior under a program that is no longer available). At least he was off the streets for the bulk of the five years. (This case is also mentioned in the chapter entitled *The First Amendment and Freedom of the Press* in which a newspaper reporter who witnessed the sale refused to testify.)

What about treatment? Drug addicts *must* receive proper treatment for their addiction even though they have no one else to blame for it, if they are ever going to "kick the habit". It is important to society that they receive effective treatment. If they do, they will no longer be buyers for those who sell drugs, they will be able to have a normal life free from drugs, they will no longer commit crimes to obtain the money to feed their habit, and they will no longer be at risk of losing their job, or if they've already lost it, being drug free should help them to become re-employed.

There are two kinds of treatment, outpatient and inpatient. The tendency towards reduction in the number of available treatment beds should be halted. If addicts don't get treatment, they will eventually be arrested for possession of drugs or for the crime they had to commit to get the money they needed to continue to satisfy their habit.

That is usually where the courts enter the picture. I have sentenced hundreds of people to probation, either after they serve a prison term, or often if it is not a serious offense for which they have been convicted and they do not have a criminal record, I have given them a suspended sentence and put them on probation.

A special condition of probation in nearly all the cases in which drugs were involved in some manner, is usually expressed in the following terms: *"You are to submit to such substance abuse evaluation, treatment and counseling, either outpatient or inpatient as may be directed by the Office of Adult Probation".* Outpatient treatment does not always work. The individual may spend time receiving counseling for an hour or two, but then, when he returns home, he will be subject to the pressures and temptations offered by drug sellers in his own neighborhood.

Inpatient is more effective, and when some one does not succeed with outpatient treatment, I generally order him/her to go to inpatient treatment. However, even inpatient treatment is not always effective. There are few, if any, lock down facilities so usually the patient can leave at any time and not return. Note the case described in the chapter *"Lying Under Oath"* in which the defendant had failed three inpatient treatment opportunities. I had no choice but to send him to prison. My recommendation is that inpatient treatment be given while the defendant is incarcerated in prison. He/she is a "captive" patient, and the treatment must be mandatory.

Education is by far the most important means we have of dealing with the drug problem. We must dry up the demand for illegal drugs. If we do, the sellers will go out of business, and we can have an essentially drug free America. The rewards will be tremendous.

The crime rate will drop drastically, we will have to spend much less money on law enforcement, prisons, rehabilitation centers and lost work productivity. First a commission should be appointed to develop an educational campaign on a national level. Ideally this commission should be composed of educators, experts in both child and adult psychology, and the most creative people from the worlds of advertising and film.

Television commercials should be developed with the same creativity that is used to sell automobiles, cereal, hamburgers, etc. The commercials that are already on the Saturday morning cartoon shows must be effective or they wouldn't be used. Advertising geniuses can be successful in selling a product to young people. Why can't they develop commercials that will sell to young people the dangers of drugs. They should be shown to children in kindergarten right up into adulthood. It will take creativity and, of course, money, but the rewards would be worth the effort.

I will close this chapter with the true story of a former client of mine. Roy was eighteen when I first represented him as his attorney. He had been caught by police surveillance selling drugs to people who drove up to his house and bought drugs from him as he was standing on the sidewalk. He was arrested and presented in court.

The Truths of Justice

I cited his age, the pressures of his life, his limited opportunities, etc., and persuaded the judge to give him a light sentence. He served fourteen days. The pressures were these: Roy was black, he lived in Hartford's north end, he was a senior struggling to complete high school, and at night he worked at a downtown bank vacuuming rugs. He had no hope of going to college, and he was not likely to get a good paying job when he graduated.

At the same time, the *Hartford Courant* printed an extensive story on the sale of drugs in Roy's neighborhood. The article described how young men in their late teens or early twenties were making a thousand dollars a week profit selling drugs. There was no overhead, and I doubt very much if the profits were reported to the IRS. Here you have Roy about to enter the lowest level of the work place without much prospect of rising higher, and there you have men slightly older than he making approximately $52,000 a year tax free. Wouldn't you be tempted in that situation, particularly knowing that at that time offenders were serving no more than fifty percent of their sentences, and often only ten percent due to prison overcrowding?

Nowadays, those who commit crimes of violence serve 85% of their sentence with no time off for good behavior. Of course, if there were no demand for drugs, there would be no sales, and Roy could not go into the business of selling drugs. Despite my warnings to Roy, a year or two later he was arrested again, this time in a white suburb west of Hartford. He had stopped at a condominium in Canton at 6 A.M., and was knocking on the front door. Apparently no one was home, but a neighbor had called police. By the time police arrived, Roy had returned to his car and was preparing to leave. At that point he had committed no crime, although he had probably been "racially profiled by" the neighbor and the police officer. It's called *DWB*, "driving while black," or in this case, perhaps BTB, "being there black".

The officer pulled his cruiser on an angle in front of Roy's car effectively blocking him. This was stopping him without probable cause. The officer went up to Roy who was sitting in his car, and asked him for his license and registration, which Roy gave to him. At that point the officer noticed a few cans of beer in the back seat, one of them open, which was illegal.

Finally he had found a violation, so he ordered Roy out of the car. Unfortunately for Roy, the officer then found packets of drugs on his person as well as a .38 caliber pistol. When his case came up in court, I filed a motion to suppress the evidence claiming that the original stop was without probable cause that a crime had been committed, and, therefore, the search was illegal. The prosecutor agreed, and Roy was sentenced on a lesser charge to the time he had already served, namely thirty days since his arrest. Of course, the gun and the drugs were confiscated as they should have been.

I talked to Roy afterwards. The conversation went something like this. "Roy, are you crazy? Carrying a gun and drugs and a list of buyers! The cop made a mistake, and it probably wouldn't have happened to you if you were white, but we both know you committed serious crimes. Roy, I'm not a miracle man. I can't get you off every time. If the cop hadn't made a mistake, you'd be facing up to twenty years in prison. If it happens again, you *will* go to prison. This is your wake up call. *Get out of the drug business*."

I can't repeat my gestures on paper, but suffice it to say I must have made an impression on him. Although this was many years ago, before I became a judge, I hear from Roy from time to time. He stopped selling drugs, and became a law abiding citizen. I certainly don't excuse what Roy did. Fortunately, he was stopped before he got into further trouble. The point is that there would have been no involvement by Roy in the sale of drugs if there was no demand, and there was no longer money to be made by selling drugs. We must create a drug-free generation, and it is my belief an effective program of education is the best way to do it.

Chapter Twelve

SEXUAL ASSAULT AND PEDOPHILES

Sexual assault by adults against adults is generally considered a crime of violence rather than a crime of sex. That is to say, a sexual assault, generally by a male upon a female, is more an expression of violence than a desire for sexual relations. Where it is harder to draw the line on this, is the cases of "date rape" in which the foreplay begins between two consenting adults but then, just prior to intercourse, the woman says no. The male doesn't think she means "no" when she does, or he is so sexually aroused that he ignores the "no" in order to reach climax and satisfaction. If the latter happens, there may be violence, but it does not match the common definition of rape which is a stranger breaking into a house or leaping out of the bushes to grab a female he does not know, and forcing sexual relations upon her with violence and/or the threat of violence. From my experience as a judge both types of sexual assault are very prevalent in today's society. Here are a few cases:

Kerwin Sands is one of the most frightening individuals who has ever stood before me. He committed vicious sexual assaults on two different victims within seven weeks of each other. He had a long criminal record which included two instances of sexual assault one (first degree) and one instance of attempted sexual assault. At age thirty six when presented before me, his record stretched back over a twenty year period much of which time was spent in prison.

He was white, five feet ten inches tall weighing one hundred sixty-five pounds with multiple tattoos on both arms. The first offense for which he appeared before me for sentencing took place in the middle of July, 1992. Sands had broken into the basement of a private residence at about 2:30 a.m. where the fifteen year old female victim's bedroom was located.

The Truths of Justice

Wearing a nylon stocking on his head, he awakened the girl by shining a flashlight into her face, clamping his hand over her mouth and saying "don't scream or I'll gag you." He straddled her body, pinning her arms with his knees. She attempted to scream, but he told her that if she screamed, he would kill her. When she asked if he was going to rape her, he said no, that he was only going to look at her. He then took off her clothes and began to fondle her. He forced her to pose in a variety of provocative positions while he took Polaroid pictures of her, one of which included his ejaculating on her face. He threatened her again by showing her the photographs telling her that if she talked, he would show the pictures to everyone. He then penetrated her with his penis.

This information as well as other graphic descriptions were included in a PSI, a pre-sentence investigation report given to the judge as well as counsel for the state and the defendant, to give the parties a clear picture of what happened and a basis for oral argument by counsel. Included also was his criminal record and a narrative describing his family background, education, and interviews with him and the victims all prepared by an Adult Probation officer.

He had very little work history since he was at liberty for only two and a half years of the previous nineteen years. Sands' father had been an alcoholic, both parents were physically abusive to him, and he witnessed his father sexually molest one of his sisters. He quit high school in his senior year at a technical school but obtained his GED (high school equivalency) while incarcerated. During his life he frequently abused alcohol and drugs but denied such abuse at the time he committed the offenses.

While he was on probation, he received sexual offender treatment. He believed he was not in need of therapy, and, therefore, it is not surprising that the treatment had no impact upon him. It should also be noted that he continued to commit crimes following these two incidents until he was caught.

At the end of August, 1992, approximately seven weeks after his assault on the fifteen year old girl, Sands, dressed entirely in black and wearing a ski mask, entered a private residence about midnight.

The Truths of Justice

The victim, in her forties, awoke as he approached her bed. He ordered her to lie down, but she was so terrorized by him that she was unable to comply. His response was to choke her, and before she lost consciousness, he tied her up and ordered her to go outside. She tried unsuccessfully to escape, he caught her and then used his knife to cut the straps on her nightgown leaving her naked. He took Polaroid pictures of her on the grass and then on the diving board of the swimming pool forcing her to pose in a provocative manner.

He further terrorized her by blindfolding her and leading her back to the bedroom where he forced her to her knees and then forced vaginal intercourse on her. At her request he did use a condom which he found in the house. He threatened to exhibit the photos if she disclosed what had transpired.

The woman reported that although she had tried to put this incident behind her, it remained a horrifying event. Surprisingly, at least to this writer, the fifteen year old girl was reported doing well after a year of counseling. I say surprisingly because she seemed to be much more vulnerable considering her young age.

How did they catch Mr. Sands? In December of the same year he was arrested as he was attempting to burglarize another residence. When the police searched his automobile, they found the Polaroid pictures he had taken of the two victims hidden up behind the glove compartment of the car.

In April, 1993, he was being led out of the sheriff's van for an appearance in court when he used a plastic key to unlock his handcuffs and fled the scene. He was recaptured about forty minutes later and charged with escape from custody.

Interviewed by the probation officer Sands agreed with the facts as described and said generally about his actions, ". . . it's like a nightmare . . . I'm not sure what happened."

Based upon a plea bargain agreement between Sands and the state, I sentenced him to forty years in prison with execution suspended after twenty four years. It was clearly insufficient for what he had done and the threat he would still pose to society when released. However, it was done for a very good reason. The victims did not want to testify. They were so traumatized that they did not want to relive this horrible experience. They did not want their names mentioned. I don't even know whether they were in the courtroom at the time of sentencing.

Although frustrating to both the state's attorney and me, this attitude was perfectly understandable. Their names as victims were not generally known, and they wanted it to remain that way. Based upon all of the charges, including kidnapping (they were forcibly restrained), the burglaries, the attempted burglary and the escape, I could have sentenced him to one hundred and fifty years in prison, which I would have done if it were not for the plea bargain. I found no redeeming quality in him, and based upon the viciousness of the crimes and the failed attempts at rehabilitation, I believed that he would always be a threat to society.

It was small comfort that the law had recently changed so that he would have to serve a minimum of eighty-five percent of his sentence. I put him on probation for the maximum of five years, the conditions of which were that he undergo sex offender evaluation and treatment as directed by the Office of Adult Probation, that he admit the offenses, (sex offender treatment is ineffective if the patient does not recognize what he has done) and that he initiate no contact with the victims or their families. I strongly recommended to the Department of Corrections (I had no power to order the DOC how to handle him) that Sands receive sex offender treatment while in prison.

There are, of course, other instances of sexual assault, including sexual assault on a spouse which I describe in the chapter on *"Domestic Violence"*. Some were not as blatant as the Sands' scenario. There was the case of a man who would call realtors ostensibly to sell his house, but when they arrived to view the house and they were female, he would manage to slip a drug into their drink which would make them more susceptible to sexual relations. Fortunately, the drug was not sufficiently potent or long lasting to enable him to achieve his objective. At this writing, this man is still in prison for what he did.

The Truths of Justice

Then, there is the case described in the chapter on "*Stalking and the Strange Case of Kathy Gerardi*" of the man who was released from prison after serving time for sexual assault in Massachusetts and was then caught on the University of Connecticut main campus after attempts to lure dozens of women to one of two vacant houses he had selected where he planned to sexually assault them. Before he could succeed he was caught with these items in his car: a rock-filled sock, rope, condoms and handcuffs. The sexual offender treatment he had received in Massachusetts was obviously not successful.

More recent is the case of a man who had exhibited no symptoms indicative of potential sexual assault. He had broken into a neighbor's house and waited for her under her bed. When she returned home late at night with her young son, she found their dog acting strangely. In checking the house the boy found the man under the bed. When police arrived after the man had fled, they found several items he had left behind, including women's clothing, latex gloves, a seventeen inch long log, a pornographic video tape, a roll of four inch wide adhesive tape and two empty beer cans. His defense attorney called him a "typical suburban guy with no criminal record, married with two children and active in Little League and the Boy Scouts". He had however, a problem with cocaine, was emotionally debilitated and had used cocaine, Prozac and beer earlier that evening. All of this may have been true, but why commit burglary with a potential for sexual assault with a woman who would recognize him?

More difficult to assess is what is commonly known as "date rape". This is the situation in which two consenting adults (although there are times when the participants are under eighteen or even sixteen the age of consent) engage in foreplay. Just prior to intercourse the female says "no". The male either believes she doesn't mean it or he is too excited to stop. This often becomes a "she said, he said" situation with conflicting testimony. The male is generally charged with sexual assault in the first degree. He is then faced with the prospect of pleading guilty to a lesser charge and receiving a light sentence with or without jail time and having to register as a sexual offender, or going to trial and hoping the jury believes him, but facing the prospect of a long prison term if the jury chooses to believe the female.

Sometimes, the police become suspicious when there are inconsistencies in the female's account of what happened, a situation described in the chapter *"You Be the Judge"*, and the charges are dropped. The only advice I can give to the male in these situations, which I concede is easier said than done, is: Stop immediately when the female says "no" or gives any other indication that she does not want to continue. Do not take the attitude that the "no" is only preliminary to an eventual consent. Assume that "no" means "no". As for the female, make your "no" in clear and unequivocal terms and to both male and female, stop the foreplay before it starts to get out of control.

PEDOPHILES

Sexual assault on minors has become an increasingly frequent and alarming occurrence. Perhaps in the past it took place just as much but was rarely reported. Many might remember the case of Polly Klaas, a teenager in California who was abducted from a sleepover party, sexually assaulted and murdered. There are dozens of similar cases across America. This has led to the enactment of *Megan's Law* in which sexual offenders are required to register in those states which have adopted such legislation. This law resulted from the abduction, rape and murder of a young girl named Megan in New Jersey.

Pedophiles generally fit into two categories. There is violation by a stranger, as in the New Jersey and California cases, where the end result is often murder, and there is sexual abuse of minors by a relative.

In the first category is the case of the man from Willimantic, Conn., who shortly after he was released from prison lured a young teenage girl into the woods where he sexually assaulted and murdered her. The second category usually does not result in murder, is often ongoing, and can be perpetrated by those who are accepted and even admired by their community. This can be difficult to explain or even understand.

Sexual abuse of a minor relative often is committed by someone who himself has been sexually abused as a child or who, as a child, has witnessed sexual abuse of his sister or other female relative. In many families this was considered either common and normal, or an isolated event not worth making a fuss over. However, it has a lasting effect upon the minors, traumatizing them for life and sometimes leading them to sexual abuse of their own children.

I was involved as a judge in several cases of pedophiles. Although the cases did not result in death, they were, nonetheless, very serious. One case involved a fifty year old man who had sexually abused his daughter from age twelve or thirteen to age seventeen or eighteen when she finally rebelled and moved out of the home. He would require his daughter to take off all of her clothes. He would then do the same and masturbate on her breasts.

His initial defense was that she had consented, and it took substantial effort to make him realize that anyone under the age of sixteen could not legally "consent". Additionally, he was a very stern disciplinarian as a father, so even when the girl reached sixteen she was afraid to disobey him. She did not speak at the sentencing. His attorney pleaded with me not to send him to jail because of what the other prisoners might do to him. (Pedophiles are often beaten by the other prisoners.) I was not persuaded.

I sent him to jail knowing that possibility, and that his incarceration would further disrupt the family; but I could not let this offense go unpunished. "What kind of a message would I be sending to society if I gave him a suspended sentence?" I asked his attorney. I could not send a message that this type of activity would not have serious consequences. I felt comfortable with my decision then, and I still do.

Another case that can only be described as bizarre was the father who had a fetish about shoes. He would go to the basement with one of his children, place his penis on a flat surface, usually a wooden bench or box. He would then have his child stand on the bench or box and direct him to bring the heel of the youngster's shoe down hard on his penis, which caused him to ejaculate. I'm quite sure the mother knew about this activity just as the mother in the previous example did, but neither of them did anything to stop it.

Finally, there is the case of the grandfather who stayed overnight with his daughter and his young granddaughter. He slept on the couch and for some reason the daughter and granddaughter slept on the floor. The daughter woke up and found her child on the couch with her hand on the grandfather's penis. He claimed that she was a "precocious" child who, on her own, had climbed up onto the couch and placed her hand on him while he was sleeping. He was presented before me on an application for accelerated rehabilitation. I didn't know who was telling the truth, but I denied the application because I believed the matter to be too serious to justify AR. Subsequently, a jury found him guilty, and he was sentenced to two years in prison. (For another case involving pedophilia, see *The First Amendment and the Catholic Church*.)

WHAT TO DO ABOUT IT

More has to be done to keep sexual predators at bay. However, careful distinctions have to be made as to the type of sexual abuser. Those who commit "date rape" probably do not need sexual abuse treatment. Their arrest and conviction should be a sufficient wake up call, but some form of counseling may still be necessary to make sure they understand the word "no", and they have the impulse control to respond appropriately.

As for pedophiles whose sexual crimes are limited to their relatives, even when there does not seem to be any evidence that they will commit these acts with strangers, they should not be allowed to be alone with anyone under eighteen years old. That condition should be part of their probation, and I have ordered that several times. Beyond that the knowledge by their relatives that perpetrators have been found criminally liable should be enough to convince them that any type of incest is wrong and they should take precautions to protect minors in their care.

As for the offenders like Kerwin Sands, the convicted kidnapper and rapist from Massachusetts, the killer who was charged with luring the young girl from Willimantic into the woods, and pedophiles with a pattern of sexually assault, I hold out little hope that sexual abuse treatment will do any good.

My experience as a judge tells me that sexual abuse treatment does not work in such cases. Therefore, more drastic steps must be taken to prevent them from striking again. *This would include committing them to mental institutions when they are released from prison and keeping them there until they no longer pose a threat to society just as in the case of other committed mental patients.* In Connecticut there is a *Psychiatric Security Review Board* which has the final say on release of mental patients. Whether such a Board, or some other body, or perhaps a judge, should have the final say can be up for discussion. Whoever it is, these sexual offenders must not be released until there is credible medical evidence that they no longer pose a threat to society. Based upon the lack of success with today's treatment, it is unlikely that day will ever come. If that means that they remain locked up for the rest of their lives, so be it. The protection of society must take precedence over the rights of these predators who have shown that they are not fit to live in a civilized world.

Chapter Thirteen

THE CATHOLIC CHURCH: SOMETHING TO HIDE

"Congress shall make no law respecting an establishment of religion, or prohibiting the free exercise thereof," **First Amendment to the United States Constitution.**

The interpretation of this portion of the First Amendment presented itself before me in the case of *John Doe v. The Bridgeport Roman Catholic Diocese Corporation, Et Als.*. The other defendants were Roman Catholic parishes and churches within its jurisdiction, namely, St. Joseph's Church in Shelton, St. Edward the Confessor Church and Parish Center of New Fairfield, St. Maurice's Church of Stamford and St. Peter's Church of Danbury, their agents, servants and employees, as well as former Roman Catholic priest Gavin O'Connor who had been ordained in Bridgeport in 1977 and whose last known address was San Diego, Calif.

The allegations (and, of course, at this point they were *only* allegations) against former priest Gavin O'Connor were certainly serious. The plaintiff had alleged that then-Father O'Connor had sexually molested him from 1977 to 1984, from age twelve to age eighteen. The plaintiff was an altar boy who, primarily on weekends, would help with chores such as washing the cars of the different priests, changing the oil in their cars, cleaning out the basement of the rectory and painting tables at the rectory. O'Connor occupied the entire third floor of the rectory consisting of several rooms. O'Connor offered the plaintiff and his brothers the opportunity to watch an "R" rated movie when the plaintiff was either twelve or thirteen, and then the plaintiff would spend the night there. The sexual abuse regarding the plaintiff came to light when one of his brothers attempted suicide allegedly as a result of similar sexual abuse.

It was further alleged that while at St. Joseph's Church rectory, O'Connor sexually abused the plaintiff on numerous occasions. The plaintiff continued to visit O'Connor after he was transferred to St. Edward's Church where O'Connor's sexual abuse intensified to include oral sex and digital anal penetration. The plaintiff and O'Connor also engaged in drinking alcohol and smoking marijuana supplied by O'Connor. It was also alleged that during this period of time ". . . O'Connor would sometimes say a private Mass for himself and plaintiff and would give plaintiff absolution immediately prior to and/or following the sexually abusive acts."

As for the Bridgeport Diocese and the churches over which it had jurisdiction, the plaintiff alleged that at the time of the acts described, O'Connor was within the scope of his duties and within the scope of his employment—or if it was beyond the scope of his employment, the diocese and its churches ratified his unauthorized acts in various ways after they had occurred. The plaintiff also claimed that the diocese and its churches failed to screen or evaluate O'Connor to determine his fitness for the priesthood prior to his ordination and assignments; that they failed to investigate O'Connor's activities prior to his assignment to the Bridgeport Diocese; and that they failed to properly supervise and investigate O'Connor's activities when he was assigned within their jurisdiction. There were several other allegations, but the ones mentioned are sufficient to set the stage for the defendants' motions that were presented to me and on which I had to rule.

The parties were represented by four outstanding, experienced and able attorneys in the state of Connecticut. The plaintiff was represented by Santos & Seeley. Attorney Hubert Santos was considered an excellent criminal defense attorney, probably one of the top three in Connecticut, who had successfully represented defendants in several high profile criminal cases in state and federal courts. His partner, Hope Seeley, was younger and, therefore, with less experience, but one who also had developed a well deserved reputation as a highly competent trial attorney. The defendants were represented by the law firm of Halloran and Sage, one of the more prestigious and older law firms in Connecticut. The lead attorney was Joseph Sweeney, a veteran and highly competent trial attorney who specialized in the defense of civil cases. He was assisted by Attorney James Alissi of the same firm, a younger attorney but also one with a lot of experience and with a deserved reputation as being very competent. Attorneys Santos and Sweeney were the main protagonists and, therefore, I looked forward to a stimulating, competitive, intellectual and dramatic battle between them.

Attorney Santos was tall with a dark complexion while Attorney Sweeney was shorter with a light complexion. They were both considered intellectual heavyweights in the arena of the courtroom, Sweeney being more of a fiery, passionate speaker who moved around in the courtroom for further emphasis, Santos using his height to his advantage but essentially remaining in place. Both proved to be eloquent and passionate in their arguments before the court.

KEEPING THINGS QUIET

The primary motions to be heard were motions in limine (requests for legal rulings just prior to the commencement of trial) and motions to quash subpoenas. The plaintiff's attorney had issued a subpoena for the files of twelve other priests in the Bridgeport diocese, and the defendants' motion was to have the court order that these files did not have to be produced.

These motions were all directed at the potential liability of the diocese and its churches.

Although these defendants had not admitted the allegations of sexual abuse by O'Connor, the plaintiff was present and ready to testify. O'Connor was assumed to be in the San Diego area. His specific address was apparently unknown, so it was unlikely that he would be contacted to attend the trial, and if contacted, it was unlikely he would appear to contest the allegations against him. It was, therefore, probable that with the plaintiff being the only person to testify as to the sexual abuse, the jury would find that the abuse did occur in the manner described by the plaintiff. The real issue before me was whether the diocese and its churches could be held legally liable for what O'Connor had done.

The first motion in limine claimed that the allegations called for the court to examine and interpret or to weigh internal policies and practices of the diocese and its churches, which policies and practices are controlled and mandated to a great extent by the internal doctrines, laws and practices of the Roman Catholic Church, and that such interpretation, examination and weighing are barred by the First Amendment. Each party had submitted extensive memoranda of law including copies of 25 cases decided by various courts throughout the country allegedly on the issues before me for consideration. Some of them were submitted by both parties, so there were approximately forty cases for me to read over the weekend. I read every one of them as well as the arguments of both sides contained in their respective memoranda in preparation for the oral argument the following Tuesday. These issues were ones of great importance important, of course, for the plaintiff, who had allegedly suffered considerably and important for the diocese because my court was going to decide the application of the First Amendment to it. What made this decision particularly important is that it was a case of " first impression" in Connecticut; that is neither the Appellate nor Supreme courts of Connecticut had decided these issues.

I indicated that the first motion was to preclude testimony interpreting or weighing the internal doctrines, laws and practices of the Roman Catholic Church and noted that the First Amendment forbids any law respecting the establishment of religion or prohibiting the free exercise thereof. "The free exercise clause prohibits excessive state entanglement with religion."

I began by citing a U.S. District Court for Connecticut decision by Judge Alfred V. Covello in the case of *Matthew J. Nutt et al. v. The*

Norwich Roman Catholic Diocese et al., a 1995 case. I had known Judge Covello personally for more than 25 years and respected his legal judgment. In his decision he stated that ". . . the United States Supreme Court has held that the first amendment does not create blanket tort immunity for religious institutions or their clergy, thus allowing clergy and clerical institutions to be sued for the torts they commit."

A tort is a civil wrong most commonly used in terms of negligence. Negligence that causes an accident is a civil wrong or tort against the victim. Sexual molestation, although also a criminal offense, is a civil wrong or tort committed against a victim. (In this case, the statute of limitations on the criminal offenses had expired.) In this case it was alleged that former Father O'Connor had committed an intentional tort against the plaintiff by intentionally sexually molesting him. Even if the acts had, for some reason, been negligent acts by O'Connor against the plaintiff, they would still be tortious.

Judge Covello went on to say ". . . the court has never held that an individual's religious beliefs excuse him from compliance with an otherwise valid law prohibiting conduct that the state is free to regulate." "The common law doctrine of negligence does not intrude upon the free exercise of religion as it does not 'discriminate against religious belief or regulate or prohibit conduct because it is undertaken for religious reasons'. "

"The court's determination of an action against the defendants based upon their alleged negligent supervision of the priest involved here in the case at bar would not prejudice or impose upon any of the religious tenets or practices of Catholicism. Rather, such a determination would involve an examination of the defendants' possible role in allowing one of its own employees to engage in conduct which they, as the employer, as well as society in general, expressly prohibit."

"Since the Supreme Court has consistently failed to allow the free exercise clause to relieve an individual from obedience to a general law not aimed at the promotion or restriction of religious beliefs, the defendants cannot appropriately implicate the first amendment as a defense to their alleged negligent conduct."

The Truths of Justice

Defendants in the case before me countered with the case of *Gibson v. Brewer* of the Supreme Court of Missouri which stated: "Adjudicating the reasonableness of the church's supervision of a cleric, what the church should know, requires inquiry into religious doctrine. This would create an excessive entanglement, inhibit religion and result in the endorsement of one model of supervision". The Missouri case held that the ordination of a priest is a quintessentially religious matter which is protected by the First Amendment.

I decided in favor of the reasoning of Judge Covello. "This court, in the case at bar, respectfully disagrees with the ruling of the Missouri Supreme Court in *Gibson v. Brewer* and instead adopts the approach cited in *Nutt v. Norwich Roman Catholic Diocese*."

I distinguished between the hiring of a priest and the ordination of a priest. (Gavin O'Connor was laicized in 1989, a nicer way of saying defrocked.) "The court does not inquire into the employer's broad reasons for choosing this particular employee for the position, but instead looks to whether the specific danger which ultimately manifested itself could have been reasonably foreseen at the time of hiring. This inquiry, even when applied to a priest employee, is so limited and factually based that it can be accomplished with no factual inquiry into religious beliefs." The *Nutt v. Norwich* case did not rest upon the internal doctrine of the church as to why the priest took a vow of celibacy. Rather, the case was considering an illegal act regardless of what the church doctrine was.

Earlier in the debate between the attorneys I posed this hypothetical example: "Supposing a south sea tribe that practiced offering up human sacrifices suddenly moved to Bridgeport, and I am not suggesting for a moment that the Catholic Church bears any similarity to a south sea tribe, wouldn't the state have a right to intervene to stop what, in this state, would be an illegal killing of a human being?"

I further stated "Negligent supervision can be resolved based upon neutral principles of law. They do not require the court to examine the religious laws of the church. Whether the institutional defendants here exercised reasonable care in supervising the

155

priests subject to their authority can be made solely in accordance with well established tort law principles . . . . The church certainly doesn't condone the crime of sexual abuse. If the courts were to preclude questions on the foreseeability of sexual abuse, it would be using the first amendment to prohibit enforcing neutral laws of general applicability."

"It is clear to this court that the First Amendment does not preclude inquiry into acts that are explicitly prohibited by the state . . . . The inquiry in the case at bar that plaintiff seeks, in any event, is not an excessive entanglement in religion. The motion in limine is denied."

SAME DESTINATION, DIFFERENT TACK

The second motion in limine was essentially the same except that the defendants were attempting to preclude any evidence on the issue of ratification. You may recall that the plaintiff alleged that former Father O'Connor was an employee acting within the scope of his employment when he committed the alleged acts. It is clear that the diocese did not authorize these acts nor were they within the scope of his employment. As an alternative, the plaintiff alleged that once these acts came to the attention of the diocese, it took certain steps that ratified what O'Connor had done, and by ratifying what he had done, the diocese was still liable for what he had done.

The plaintiff claimed, among other things, that the diocese had paid O'Connor a substantial amount of money after he was transferred to a parish in Belleville, Ill., and after he was again transferred. The plaintiff claimed that the money was a payoff for O'Connor's unavailability to testify, his silence and/or false testimony to be given.

The defendants countered that under Church law, the diocese was obligated to make sure he was financially able to support himself while he was going through the process of prayer and meditation and seeking forgiveness. The plaintiff, on the other hand, claimed that when O'Connor was serving as a chaplain at the federal prison in Marion, Ill., he was making a good salary adequate to support himself. The plaintiff also claimed that transferring him to the parish in Belleville, where he would be ministering to children, was a ratification of his prior conduct.

The charges of a payoff were too serious to permit a blanket preclusion of testimony. I gave what I described as a preliminary ruling and said I would take up this issue again before any testimony was actually offered. It appeared as if the plaintiff would get into the issue of the payoff, and then it would be the defendants who would have to describe church rules and regulations as to how the Diocese was required to deal with O'Connor in this situation. I warned the plaintiff's attorneys that it appeared they had a weak case on the issue of ratification and that, therefore, I would consider directing a verdict for the defendants at the end of the plaintiff's case in chief, "if the court feels that there is no credible evidence of ratification." However, since the issue of ratification is normally a question for the jury, and it did not appear at this time that the plaintiff would be getting into church doctrine, I denied this motion in limine with a promise to take it up again when the plaintiff would make an offer of proof as to what he proposed to introduce in the way of evidence on this subject.

The plaintiff had provided information as to the testimony and other evidence he intended to introduce. Although I had denied the motions in limine, I said I would rule on some of the proposed testimony, in particular, that of the plaintiffs' expert witness, Father Doyle. I granted the motion in limine on the following, thereby precluding the testimony:

1. Father Doyle's opinion as to what constitutes an ecclesiastical crime under the Code of Canon Law of the Roman Catholic Church. O'Connor is not being charged with violating canon law.

2. Father Doyle's opinions as to violation by Gavin O'Connor of the Code of Canon Law. This is not a violation of canon law that is before us. It's a violation of state law.

3. Father Doyle's opinion or research as to historical sources of the Code of Canon Law of the Roman Catholic Church.

4. Father Doyle's opinion and research as to the provisions of the Code of Canon Law of the Roman Catholic Church dealing with child sexual abuse.

5. Father Doyle's opinion or research dealing with the Code of Canon Law of the Roman Catholic Church regarding the laicization process.

6. Father Doyle's opinions and interpretation of the Roman Catholic Church's doctrine of theology, his interpretations and opinion of theological and administrative tenets of the Roman Catholic Church regarding pastoral counseling and priestly life and as to the Roman Catholic Church's view of celibacy regarding or relating to its ordained clergy."

"However, I am going to allow these questions: Internal church procedures for preordination screening and training of candidates for ordination into the priesthood of the Roman Catholic Church, but it will be limited as to how much investigation is done and it will be limited to the issue of sexual abuse and anything that's attendant to that. I think you can probably get into the issue of checking out whether he was an alcoholic or he used drugs. According to the allegations, 'he used the alcohol and drugs to relax the plaintiff and induce him into the acts described.'"

Other areas of proposed testimony were described, and I found them to be vague or general and said I would rule on them at trial when the specific questions were posed as an offer of proof outside the presence of the jury. I also stated that "what the church knew or should have known is the tort law involved . . . . And I am basing it primarily on negligence law since under tort law, in order to find liability for negligence, there has to be a foreseeability factor."

During the oral argument on the motions in limine, Attorney Sweeney repeatedly told me that I would be determining or the jury would be determining what a reasonable diocese would do in checking the background, including any psychological problems the proposed priest might have, to determine whether he was a suitable candidate for the priesthood. I rejected that argument with the statement "No, I'm not. I and/or the jury would be determining what a reasonable employer would do in this situation, and that can be determined without getting into the internal religious practices and procedures of the Church. Therefore, with the limitations I've described, such an inquiry is not excessive state entanglement with religion."

MOTIONS TO QUASH SUBPOENAS

Following the luncheon recess we took up the defendants' motions to quash the subpoenas that had been issued by Attorney Santos. The primary subpoena to which objection was made was for the defendants to produce the complete personnel files in regard to twelve specifically named priests of the diocese including complaints made against them. The objection was based upon the same First Amendment grounds previously discussed, as well as the objection that revealing this information would be an unwarranted invasion of the privacy of the twelve priests.

Apparently, Attorney Santos had received information from attorneys for the plaintiff in another similar case against the diocese in which a federal jury had found the defendants liable and assessed damages of $750,000. From that case and other sources, Attorney Santos had been furnished the names of twelve other priests against whom complaints of sexual abuse had been made. Attorney Sweeney made the same argument that it was improper to get into such issues "as setting up a standard of what would a reasonable diocese or bishop would have done dealing with this issue." I interrupted him. "Excuse me. I don't think we're talking about what a reasonable bishop or diocese would do. We're talking about what a reasonable employer, whether it's a church, or UTC or the Superior Court, would have done. We're looking strictly at the diocese as an employer."

After lengthy further argument, I made my decision. "The cases that have been cited by the defendants get into the issue of punishment and whether or not the priests involved were subsequently punished and by what means. That's not what we're talking about here. We're talking about the issue of notice, notice to the diocese, notice to the churches. And I don't see where that gets into the internal regulations, procedures, etc, of the diocese. We're talking about notice that the defendants had that there was sexual abuse . . . . If in fact there was a pattern of this happening within the diocese, then it was on notice that this thing was likely to happen again. The motion to quash the subpoena is denied as to these twelve files. As to complaints, I'm ordering compliance with the subpoena. I'm ordering compliance as to all complaints received on or before December 31,1984. I'm issuing a protective order that Attorney Santos, his partners and staff and his client are the only individuals to be privy to these files. They are to be produced tomorrow prior to the commencement of trial."

The taking of evidence was to commence the next day, but in the morning I received telephone calls from both Attorney Sweeney and Attorney Santos telling me that the case had been settled and would be withdrawn, on which basis I vacated the decisions.

Note: Since my decision a three judge panel of the U.S. Court of Appeals for the 9th Circuit ruled for the first time by a federal court that churches are subject to the sexual harassment provisions of the United States Civil Rights Act that governs other employers. Also since my decision, the issue of pedophile priests exploded in the Boston and Bridgeport dioceses, as well as others across the nation. The case I heard was apparently only the tip of the iceberg.

Chapter Fourteen

THE FIRST AMENDMENT AND THE PRESS

*"The basis of our government being the opinion of the people, the very first object should be to keep that right; and were it left to me to decide **whether we should have a government without newspapers, or newspapers without a government, I should not hesitate a moment to prefer the latter.** Thomas Jefferson in a letter to Edward Carrington dated January 16, 1787.*

Although it has been said that President Thomas Jefferson had newspaper reporters, editors and/or publishers arrested for violations of the Sedition Act, a law which provided criminal penalties for persons who, by writing, speaking, or in other ways tried to arouse discontent with the government, this allegation has been proven false. The Sedition Act expired in 1801, before Jefferson became the third president of the United States.

As a matter of fact, Jefferson and his friend, James Madison, authored the Kentucky and Virginia resolutions which declared the Alien and Sedition Acts unconstitutional. Jefferson was the subject of vicious, blatant and scurrilous attacks by the press as were many other politicians. These attacks were much worse than the ones today's politicians undergo. They would make today's criticism and attacks by the media look like harmless nursery rhymes in comparison.

Nonetheless, Jefferson adhered to a free press as an absolute necessity for a free nation.[1] And with good reason. A free press that criticizes the government and its leaders is, perhaps, the first free-

---

1 However, this did not preclude President Jefferson from suing The Hartford Courant for libel. He lost.

161

dom to be lost under a dictatorship. The Fascists in Italy and the Nazis in Germany abolished press freedom and used the press for their own purposes. The Communist regimes in the Soviet Union allowed only one newspaper, **the government-owned Pravda**.

A free press despite its excesses is essential to open government and the accountability of those who conduct it. It was the *Times* and the *Post* that successfully fought the Nixon Administration's attempt to obtain an injunction preventing the publication of the *Pentagon Papers.* The United States Supreme Court ruled in the newspapers' favor calling the application for the injunction an attempt at prior restraint of the press and unconstitutional.

So, how do you deal with the excesses of the press? You hope that the members of the media are all responsible people who genuinely seek fairness and accuracy in what they do; that is, you hope that the media will police itself just as the medical and legal professions try to do.

However, the reality is that self restraint does not always occur. That leaves the individual who has been wrongly accused or wrongly portrayed to the point where his or her reputation has been harmed unjustly, with only one avenue, namely to resort to the courts and bring a lawsuit for libel.

Libel and slander laws are on the books for the very purpose of protecting parties against the excesses of the media which lead to the harming and even the destruction of one's reputation with often dire financial consequences. Destruction of one's business or one's ability to obtain employment are two examples that come to mind.

Libel suits against newspapers are, however, rarely successful. Many years ago Paul "Bear" Bryant, the football coach at the University of Alabama, successfully sued the *Saturday Evening Post,* a popular national magazine which subsequently went out of business. Contrast that with the unsuccessful libel/slander suits brought by Israeli Defense Minister Ariel Sharon against *Time* magazine and by General William Westmoreland, former commander of U.S. forces in Vietnam, against *CBS* and *60 Minutes*.

The Truths of Justice

A major change in libel law developed as a result of the United States Supreme Court decision in the landmark case of The New York Times vs. Sullivan, a 1964 case in which the court held that in order for a public figure to sue successfully for libel, the public figure must prove not only that the allegedly libelous statements were false but that they were made with *"actual malice."* In New York Times vs. Sullivan (the party appealing is listed first), L. B. Sullivan was one of three elected Commissioners of Montgomery County, Alabama including being Police Commissioner. Some of the offending and allegedly false words were "Truckloads of police armed with shotguns ringed the Alabama State College Campus."

The court found that even if this statement was false, the *Times* had to be guilty of actual malice because Sullivan was a public figure. The term public figure has been defined by the high court as ". . . those classified as public figures have thrust themselves to the forefront of particular controversies in order to influence the resolution of the issues involved . . . they invite attention and comment." *"Actual malice"* does not rest upon the *motive* of the person making the statement, such as personal dislike of the person being criticized. Rather actual malice requires that the statement, when it is made, be made with *actual knowledge that it was false* or *with reckless disregard of whether it was false*. (See New York Times vs. Sullivan and Milovich vs. Lorain Journal Co.)

At a minimum actual malice requires that there ". . . be sufficient evidence to permit the conclusion that the defendant in fact entertained serious doubts as to the truth of his publication." See St. Amant vs. Thompson, a 1968 U.S. Supreme Court case. Also, according to said Court's ruling in the Milkovich case, "a public figure must prove actual malice by clear and convincing evidence . . ."[2]

To win a civil case generally the plaintiff must prove his or her case by a "preponderance of the evidence" which means the percentage of the evidence favoring their case must be over 50%. "By clear and convincing evidence" is actually a much higher standard. Thus, as

---

2 This requirement of proving actual malice was not in effect when President Jefferson sued The Hartford Courant for libel. He still lost.

The Truths of Justice

you can see, the United States Supreme Court, in interpreting freedom of the press under the First Amendment, has made it difficult for a public figure to successfully sue for libel.

As the late U.S. Supreme Court Justice William Brennan wrote in New York Times vs. Sullivan: "Thus, we must consider this case against the background of a profound national commitment to the principle that debate on public issues should be uninhibited, robust and wide-open and that it may well include vehement, caustic and sometimes unpleasantly sharp attacks on government and public officials."

It is against this background of the law that I tried the case of C. R. Jones vs. The Record, a libel case brought against a weekly newspaper. It was tried before me sitting as a court with no jury. The plaintiff, Mr. Jones, represented himself. *The Record* was represented by counsel.

Jones was intelligent, articulate, brilliant in his field of occupation, but highly emotional. He fervently believed he had been wronged by *The Record* and was determined to prove it. At the same time, in a colloquy with the court he stated that he realized the high burden of proof he had to overcome. Despite his lack of legal training he was a formidable party in court.

The first allegedly libelous statement was contained in what I found to be an editorial. It was on the editorial page in a column addressed "To our readers:" and signed by the publisher of the paper. It was dated September 14, 1995. The publisher's name was Smith. In paragraph 13 of his complaint, Jones alleged:

"In an editorial in the . . . *Record* dated September 14, 1995, Smith stated in reference to the suit against him "Now . . . Mr. Jones . . . has filed a nuisance lawsuit . . . . As many of you know, this is vintage Jones . . . file a frivolous lawsuit against anyone who disagrees with you."

The first issue the court had to consider was whether Jones, at the time of this publication and the other publication hereafter described, was a public figure. After some evidence had been introduced by Jones, I interrupted and asked Jones: "Sir, are you saying that on September 14, 1955, you were a candidate for election to the Town Council?" He replied: "yes." I was amazed.

I said then and in the written decision, "This court can think of no better example of a public figure than a candidate for public office. A candidate for public office puts his entire life up for review and analysis by the voters who are his/her potential constituents as well as the press which furnishes information and commentary about the candidates to the voters. This can include inquiries into and comments upon his/her educational background, business or employment history, military service, use of illegal drugs, fidelity to one's spouse, incidents of courage or cowardice, incidents of honesty or dishonesty, the reputation he or she enjoys in the community, his or her health; in other words, all facets of his/her life to permit the voters to make an informed decision on the candidate's qualifications for public office."

Jones claimed that he was a "limited" public figure and that the newspaper had no right to go into his dealings with his tenants (some of the lawsuits). I told him that I knew of no such category and that as a public figure, his entire life becomes subject to criticism and analysis *including his business relationships*. I cited as examples questions about Richard Nixon's finances (which produced the famous "Checkers speech"), John Kennedy's religion, Senator Thomas Eagleton's psychiatric history just before he was bumped off the ticket in 1972, Senator Gary Hart's alleged infidelity to his wife, and as to business relationships, he had to look no farther than the attacks on President Clinton for his involvement in the Whitewater matter which haunted him as a presidential candidate and through most of his presidency.

As for the article of October 20, 1994, Smith's comments were made in reaction to a law suit brought by Jones against Smith. Smith was quoted in *The Record* as saying that the charges in the lawsuit were "malicious, unfounded and completely in character." Although Jones was technically not a candidate on that date, he became a public figure by bringing the lawsuit which he knew would receive widespread publicity, he was writing a large number of letters to the editor which were published, he spoke at televised meetings of the Town Council on at least ten occasions at various times before October 20, 1994, he was chairman of the Conservative Party in town, and he admitted at trial that he was well known throughout town from the many mailings he had made to residents of the town.

From all of this, I concluded that he was a public figure on October 20, 1994, and stated in the decision that "From the totality of the evidence, this court concludes that the plaintiff has failed to sustain his burden of proof that either defendant acted with actual malice . . . no evidence was presented that either defendant entertained serious doubts as to the truth of the publications. On that basis alone, judgment is entered for the defendants."

I further found that the statements which were allegedly libelous were statements of ***opinion and not fact***. I cited the Connecticut Supreme Court decision in <u>Goodrich vs. Waterbury Republican-American, Inc.</u> which held that ". . . mere comment or opinion on public matters, even though defamatory, enjoys the ***unqualified*** protection of the First Amendment . . . . Under the First Amendment there is no such thing as a false idea. However pernicious an opinion may seem, we depend for its correction not on the conscience of judges and juries but on the competition of other ideas."

In closing, the decision stated: "This court recognizes the frustration a public figure encounters with coverage of him or her by the press. The press is not always accurate, it has a right to rely on its 'editorial judgment' which may easily differ from that of the public figure, and it can be highly critical, very annoying and sometimes unfair.

However, the First Amendment to the United States Constitution is both unique and at the heart of our guarantee of liberty. It is the price we pay to protect our liberty. Unlike other countries, freedom of the press and freedom of expression are vital to our liberty because they act as a watchdog on the conduct of our public officials so that any effort to deny us our freedom will be exposed."

The decision ended with these words: "The only comfort this court can offer to the plaintiff are the words of a former United States

The Truths of Justice

Senator from New York who said: 'Every time the **New York Times** criticized me in an editorial, I knew I must have done something right.'"

It is, of course, the press itself which is the strongest and loudest advocate for freedom of the press; and well it should be. However, there are times when the press goes too far.

It was during my first year on the bench, and only my third or fourth jury trial. The defendant, Frankie Jenkins, was charged with sale of cocaine by a non-drug dependent person, a felony that carried a five year mandatory minimum sentence. (See the chapter entitled *Illegal Drugs* for more on this case.) If he were drug dependent himself, he would be selling to get enough money to support his own habit. If he were not drug dependent, then he would be selling strictly to make money, and thus the five year mandatory minimum as a deterrent to those who sell without any reason than mere greed.

The "buy" or sale had "gone down" (taken place) after dark in the front of the apartment building in the housing project where Jenkins lived. Unfortunately for Jenkins he was selling to a police informant. Detective Corello who had witnessed the sale from an open window on the third floor of the apartment building next door was testifying as to how the sale took place. It turned out that a newspaper reporter, Nancy Brown, had been with him at the window. She was apparently doing research for a story on how the police were trying to deal with the sale of illegal drugs. The state's attorney had subpoenaed her as an additional witness to the sale.

The next morning, just after court opened, the attorney for the newspaper showed up, almost like clockwork, with a motion to quash the subpoena. The motion declared that requiring Ms. Brown to testify would be a violation of the First Amendment by invading the freedom of the press. She was not being asked to testify as to the identity of a confidential source which is usually the battleground for a freedom of the press argument. She was being asked to testify as a witness as to what happened. Counsel for the newspaper was one of the better attorneys in the state and was highly respected.

Nevertheless, I believed the motion to quash was a knee jerk reaction to something that was not really a First Amendment issue. Argument on the motion was deferred until the following Tuesday to give time to all parties, including the court, to research the issue. Suffice it to say that my research disclosed no court cases in which testimony in this kind of situation was considered a violation of the First Amendment. And there were no cases which held that it was *not* a violation of the First Amendment.

Counsel for the newspaper had cited several cases, including the famous Claus Von Bulow case, but I found the rulings in these cases to be irrelevant. The factual situations and the issues in these cases were different than the situation before me, and, therefore, the rulings in these cases were not applicable, probably, I believed, because no one had ever tried to apply the First Amendment to this type of situation, or if they had, it had not reached the appellate level where decisions were considered precedent. Nonetheless, I looked forward to debating the issue with such learned and articulate counsel.

After some preliminary sparring in which counsel had insisted the subpoena was a violation of the First Amendment even though there was no request to reveal the reporter's source or any other request except to testify as to what she saw, the colloquy between the court and counsel went something like this:

Court: "Tell me, counsel, supposing Ms. Brown had been sent to Waco, Texas to cover the stand off between the people in the Branch Davidian Compound and federal agents? She and other reporters were standing behind a rope to restrain them from getting too close to the Compound, when all of a sudden a man walked out of the Compound with his hands in the air proceeding toward the roped off area. When he was about one hundred feet away, he suddenly took out a gun and shot an F.B.I. agent who was walking toward him. Ms. Brown got a clear look at the shooter. Are you telling this court that she could not be required to testify as to what she witnessed?"

Counsel: "That's different, your honor."

Court: "In what way is it different?"

Counsel: "The agent was a federal officer."

Court: "Do you mean if the victim were a state trooper, she wouldn't have to testify?"

Counsel: "That's correct."

I was incredulous. I then described a scenario in which Ms. Brown was a customer in a bank when the bank was held up. This time counsel was forced to agree. "Certainly, she would have to testify in that case notwithstanding the First Amendment."

I ruled that Ms. Brown would have to honor the subpoena. The state then withdrew the subpoena, but shortly thereafter, Ms. Brown was served with a subpoena by the attorney for Mr. Jenkins. Counsel for the newspaper was still there as was Ms. Brown.

The following day was a holiday. I told counsel that Ms. Brown would have to testify in response to the defendant's subpoena for the same reasons I had already given concerning the state's subpoena. Counsel protested. I told him, loud enough so Ms. Brown could hear, that I was fully prepared to find her in contempt of court and send her to jail until she testifies. "She will have the keys to the jail. All she has to do is agree to testify, and she will be released."

The next day the defense attorney withdrew his subpoena. I assume he thought further about it and not knowing what she would say, he decided not to take a chance. What if she pointed at the defendant and said "That's the man I saw hand over the drugs?"

Change the First Amendment? **NEVER!** It has stood the test of time from the end of the eighteenth century to the beginning of the twenty first. It remains the foundation of our freedom.

Chapter Fifteen

SUING THE JUDGE

Judges are generally immune from being sued for what they do as judges, in court or out of court, as long as they are involved in their judicial duties. This is so because judges should not have to be looking over their shoulders wondering whether, or fearing, they will be sued for their decision-making. As noted throughout this book, judges are called upon to make some very difficult and sometimes controversial decisions that affect people's lives. They must be able to approach and conduct their duties with an open mind *free from outside pressure* that might affect their conduct and decision-making.

However, that does not stop individuals, usually those who are on the losing end of a lawsuit, from actually bringing suit against a judge for what they perceive as an injustice that affected them adversely. I have been subject to two such lawsuits while I have been on the bench.

The first involved an individual who I will identify here only as Mr. X lest he sue me again. X owned some vacant land fronting on a road in a rural area. Two teenage girls were riding their bicycles on the road in front of his land when a dog owned by Mr. X came off the land onto the road attempting to attack the two girls resulting in their being knocked to the pavement and suffering substantial injuries. Apparently Mr. X did not have liability insurance for such an event, he was subsequently sued for damages, and since he did not have insurance, another judge ordered that his land be attached to secure any judgment the girls might be awarded.

I had been assigned to conduct jury trials at the time this case came up for trial. We were about to begin jury selection. Mr. X was not represented by an attorney. Although he had a constitutional right not to be represented by an attorney, I urged him to obtain one.

"Sir, I recognize you have the option of proceeding in this case representing yourself, but jury trials are difficult to conduct by some attorneys. A layman, such as yourself, will be at a disadvantage against the plaintiff's attorney. There will be complicated issues of law that you do not have the training or experience to handle well in a courtroom."

He rejected my suggestion. I then told him that I would try to help him out with the procedural aspects of the trial but that I could not go so far that it would be unfair to his opponent. He then claimed that the lawsuit papers that had been served upon him by a sheriff had not been returned to the court clerk's office as required by law, and asked that I, therefore, dismiss the case. Plaintiff's attorney said that he had sent it to the clerk by certified mail but he did not have receipt of delivery with him. I continued the case for a week to give the attorney an opportunity to prove that delivery had been made and to give the clerk an opportunity to conduct a more thorough search for the missing papers.

A *copy* of the papers had been served upon Mr. X, but the law required that the original papers be filed with the clerk. The next day the original papers were found in a different file, namely the file that had been created when the attachment had been granted. The case was then ready for jury selection the following week. I was assigned to the criminal docket, and another judge actually conducted the trial. The jury eventually came in with a verdict in favor of the plaintiffs in the amount of approximately ninety thousand dollars. I don't recall whether the verdict was appealed, but the end result was that the verdict remained in place.

I promptly forgot about the case since I did not conduct the actual trial and was busy with other cases. I thought, at the time, I had been fair to the defendant. Imagine my surprise when a few months later I was served with a lawsuit brought by the defendant. There was small comfort in the fact that other judges had been named as defendants in the suit. These included the judge who tried the case, the judge who had ordered the attachment and any other judge who ever had anything to do with the case no matter how remotely.

The charges against the judges were essentially that we were all corrupt and conducted the affairs of a corrupt judicial system. I don't recall his getting more specific than that as to the judges. He also sued Connecticut's entire Congressional delegation including its two United States Senators as well as the media, including the television stations in the state and several newspapers. His claim against them was essentially that he had written to them advising them of the corruption that existed in the judicial system and that they had not acted upon his complaints.

I believe he also sued a few attorneys who had previously represented him. To top it off, *he was seeking damages in the amount of seven hundred and fifty million dollars* **($750,000,000)**. I didn't worry too much about the amount since I didn't have anywhere near the amount of assets he was seeking. The State Attorney General's office represented the judges. I don't know whether Mr. X prepared the lawsuit or he had help from an attorney. Although lacking in specifics against the judges, which he could have added later, the complaint in the lawsuit was done very professionally. About a year later a federal judge dismissed the lawsuit as to the state judges on the basis of judicial immunity. Mr. X, whose land is under foreclosure due to his failure to pay the judgments against him, currently patrols his property with a shotgun he is threatening to use against anyone attempting to evict him.

Sometime in 1994 I had tried a jury case in which the defendant was charged with relatively minor crimes, namely, reckless driving, driving while his license was under suspension, breach of peace and reckless endangerment. I dismissed the breach of peace charge on the basis of a recent state Supreme Court decision which essentially held that what might be offensive words to one may not be offensive words to another.

A town official had approached the defendant on a Saturday morning, the day of a special election, and informed him that he could not place a campaign sign in a certain snow bank which had occurred as the result of a snow storm the previous evening because it would impede the view of drivers leaving and entering the parking lot of the town hall where the voting was to take place. Defendant apparently responded with foul language, and when the town official went to look at his license plate, he gunned the motor in place causing the wheels to spin. This was the basis of the reckless endangerment charge.

Defendant then turned around and quickly left the parking lot - the basis for the reckless driving charge. He was represented by an attorney. The jury found him not guilty on the reckless driving charge but guilty on the charges of reckless endangerment and driving while his license was under suspension. I fined him a thousand dollars and thought that was the end of the matter. His appeal to the Appellate Court was turned down, and the Supreme Court refused to hear it further.

In late 1997, this defendant whom I will call Mr. Y, brought a lawsuit against me and other judges with whom he had dealt, various attorneys, members of his family, police officers, prosecutors, a public defender, a municipal official and a corporation. There were a total of thirty-two defendants. From the trial I was aware that he loathed the state police, but this suit went way beyond that trial and involved people not connected with it. In this civil lawsuit he claimed violation of his constitutional rights and that certain torts or civil wrongs had been committed against him. He was seeking one hundred and fifty million dollars (**$150,000,000**) in damages.

The suit was brought in the state superior court and was presented to a judge not named in the lawsuit. Motions to dismiss were filed. Mr. Y was not authorized to serve legal papers nor was Mr. V. who signed the documents as a *"Sovereign Man Of The Land"*. The judge either dismissed the suits or granted summary judgment for the other defendants for various reasons including improper service of the papers and an expiration of the statute of limitations. The suit was dismissed as to the various judges who had been sued for two reasons:

1. The State cannot be sued without its consent. The judges were and are officers or agents of the State, and although there are exceptions to this rule (i.e., defective highways), the State has never passed legislation permitting a suit for money damages against Superior Court Judges.

2. Absolute judicial immunity. This was addressed because it appeared that the judges might have been sued in their individual capacities. The court cited a Supreme Court case that stated: ***"The immunity rule is designed to promote principled and fearless decision making by removing a judge's fear that unsatisfied litigants may hound him with litigation charging malice or corruption."***

As I recall one of the claims against the judges, it goes something like this: "The American flag which is on a pole to the judge's right in the courtroom has a yellow fringe on the outer borders of it. This fringe is not part of the flag, and it is both illegal and unconstitutional to have it on the borders of the flag. Therefore, any proceedings conducted with such a flag are unconstitutional."

I'll let you be the judge of that claim.

I realize these kinds of experiences are all part of a judge's job, and "they go with the territory". But sometimes, I can't help but think: What a waste of time and money!

Chapter Sixteen

CIVIL LAW

"There are criminal cases. Everything else is civil."

Despite what you may have heard about reductions in the crime rate, criminal court dockets are overflowing. Criminal cases are the ones that get the headlines, and there is a certain fascination the public has with criminal law. This public interest in criminal law is supported by the emphasis given to it by the television networks. With a few exceptions, shows on television dealing with law focus on criminal cases. ***Law and Order, The Practice, Matlock, Perry Mason*** are shows that come to mind.

The same is true in news coverage of actual events. Murder and mayhem take center stage, particularly on local television news. Conflict, violence, disaster sell on television. Perhaps, it's because there is a mystery as to "who done it," perhaps it's because victims lose their lives in criminal matters, and the freedom, or even life of the defendant is at stake.

However, let me assure you that there is a tremendous amount of civil litigation in this country — probably much more than criminal. Family law is technically considered civil, housing law, usually disputes between landlord and tenant, is civil, parts of juvenile law are civil, and then there is the vast majority of cases that are called simply "civil" which involve conflicts between parties in a variety of ways, some of them very complex, in which serious injury or death is often involved. However, the dispute is primarily over money damages and not the loss of freedom by the defendant. It is this latter type of civil litigation upon which I will focus in this chapter.

Juries hear cases of wrongful termination of employment, sexual harassment and/or discrimination in the workplace, product liability cases and a plethora of other cases in which individuals and/or corporations are in conflict.

Some civil trials take two days, some two weeks, and some two months. The longest civil jury trial over which I presided (a civil arson case) took three months and ten days mainly because each side presented at least six expert witnesses.

AUTOMOBILE ACCIDENTS AND FALL DOWNS

These types of accidents constitute the majority of civil cases. The motor vehicle was invented to replace the horse as the main means of individual transportation. It was much faster and more comfortable, and with trucks commercial goods were transported further and faster than ever before. The motor vehicle industry also spawned the need for highways, gasoline, traffic laws, and although probably not envisioned by the inventors of motor vehicles, motor vehicle accidents became increasingly common.

These accidents not only produced automobile insurance, but the conflict as to who was at fault produced a surge in lawsuits that was, at the beginning, beyond anyone's belief. Today, with millions of people on the road every day, motor vehicle accidents furnish a major portion of civil litigation. State law requires that every motor vehicle be insured so the real battle is between the plaintiff and the defendant's insurance company. The plaintiff is usually represented by a private attorney. The defendant, if insured, is represented by an attorney who has a private practice but has the insurance company as one of his/her clients. If there is a counter-claim by the defendant that it was the plaintiff who caused the accident and that the defendant suffered damages, then the plaintiff may also be represented by an attorney who represents the plaintiff's insurance company to defend against the counter-claim. Unless the litigation is a suit directly against the plaintiff's own insurance company, for example a suit to recover under the uninsured motorist provision of the plaintiff's own policy, the fact that either party is insured is never mentioned in front of the jury. It is considered prejudicial to the defendant if the jury knows that the defendant is insured, the theory being that the jury is more likely to find the defendant liable for the accident and award higher damages if the jurors know that it isn't the defendant himself/herself who will have to pay the amount awarded. As a practical matter, however, it has been my experience, from talking to jurors after the trial, that most of them are aware that the parties carry insurance. They know that if the defendant didn't have insurance, the suit would be against the plaintiff's own insurance company claiming uninsured motorist benefits. Uninsured motorist benefits are due from your own company if the other driver is uninsured and you did not cause the accident yourself.

Speaking of civil juries, it has been my experience that the jurors who have been selected to serve are generally very intelligent, unbiased and have the ability to sort through the facts presented to them and reach a sound decision.[1] The plaintiff has to prove his/her case. There are two parts to the plaintiff's case. The plaintiff must prove that the defendant is liable (caused) the accident, and must prove the injuries/damages that were caused by the accident. In the several years I have conducted civil jury trials, there was only one time that I disagreed with the verdict.

Despite what you may have heard, huge verdicts are rare. Juries are generally skeptical and really put the plaintiff to his/her burden of proving his/her case. They do not "give away the store". Good plaintiffs' cases are usually settled before trial. If the liability issue favors the plaintiff, it is in the interest of the defendant's insurance carrier to settle — assuming it can settle for a reasonable sum. If the plaintiff is demanding much more than is reasonable, then there is no choice but to go to trial. The parties try to settle on their own, and if that doesn't work, a judge holds a pre-trial conference and usually recommends a figure. A recommendation from an experienced judge often produces a settlement.

However, when the issue of liability is seriously in question and both sides continue to maintain their positions, or when either side is unrealistic as to the value of the case, or both, the case proceeds to trial. This takes place after extensive discovery by each side. Parties and witnesses, including the doctors who will be called as expert witnesses, undergo depositions.

---

[1] The same is true of criminal juries. These qualities in the jurors who remain after jury selection is not surprising in view of the extensive individual questioning described in the chapter on Jury Selection, a process unique to Connecticut.

The Truths of Justice

These are usually held in the office of one of the attorneys where the subject testifies under oath in response to questions posed by the other side's attorney. Each side is generally represented by an attorney. In this way the other side will be able to get an idea as to how well the party or witness will testify during the trial. The person being deposed will have to give substantial information to the other side. If they are not candid, or if they are inconsistent with their testimony at trial, all of this can be used against them to impeach their credibility before the jury.

In discovery, each side has to disclose to the other side all relevant information regarding the case. It has often been said that trials are not to be conducted by ambush, that neither party should be unfairly surprised at the trial itself. With all of this information, whether gained by deposition, a review of the answers and documents furnished by disclosure and by the party's own investigation, each side should have a reasonably good idea as to how the trial will play out.

They should, therefore, be in a good position to settle before trial. When the judge directs the plaintiff's attorney to "call your first witness", if the case has not settled by then, it probably will not be. There are exceptions. When one side sees that his/her case is not going as well as expected, there could be a change in the offer of settlement. Of course, the other side is also able to detect the weakness of the opponent's case, and his/her position is likely to harden.

Since these cases are generally weaker, the better ones having been settled, the result is usually a defendant's verdict. ***The number of defendant's verdicts far outnumber plaintiffs' verdicts***. Further, even if the liability issue favors the plaintiff, juries generally award far ***less*** than is sought by the plaintiff. Recently, in a case involving an intersection accident where the defendant conceded she caused the accident, the plaintiff had demanded $12,000 to settle the case. The insurance company came up in stages with offers of $5,000 to $7,500 to $8,500. The plaintiff had dropped her demand to $10,000. They were $1,500 apart, and neither side would budge.

When they get that close, either figure is reasonable, but they still would not settle. The plaintiff was a young and attractive woman who had suffered some injuries but did not appear to be disabled. The orthopedic surgeon who had treated the plaintiff testified that she had a 4 percent permanent partial disability of her cervical spine (her neck). The defense attorney asked one question. "Isn't it true, doctor, that this was a subjective finding, that is that you based your evaluation solely on her complaints about her neck?" The answer was "Yes." Therefore, the jury, in order to believe the 4 percent had to believe the plaintiff had told the doctor the truth.

During a recess, I brought both attorneys into my chambers. Neither side saw any reason to settle at that point. Plaintiff's attorney asked permission to use the blackboard in his closing argument to describe how he had computed the damages. I granted his request. He then proceeded to tell me, and his opponent, how he was going to "go for broke" and compute the damages up to $240,000. I warned him that his client's permanency of her neck was at issue, and finished with the warning: "Dave, don't be greedy. Juries don't like greedy plaintiffs."

The defense attorney wisely said nothing no doubt thinking that plaintiff's attorney would hang himself. The jury, of course, did not know of the pre-trial settlement figures including plaintiff's willingness to take $10,000. Apparently, Dave thought he had nothing to lose. He did not take my advice.[2] During final argument he laid out on the blackboard how he had arrived at the $240,000, and then stated: "But if you're not convinced on these figures (pointing to a portion of the damages) then you should award $110,000" as he pointed to the figures making up the $110,000. The jury came in with a verdict of $1,377, the amount of Plaintiff's medical bills.

Of course, hard line positions taken by the insurance company can also backfire. Allstate Insurance Company had taken a position as to what they considered weak plaintiffs' cases — "Take them all to trial." It was a hard line position, but it was generally successful. Allstate won many more cases than they lost.[3] The case of John Doe v. Allstate was an exception. This was an uninsured motorist case in

---

[2] This is known as "Judge, you try your case your way, and I'll try my case my way."

[3] My experience with Allstate is that, for the most part, the cases that go to trial result in either a defendant's verdict or a judgment equal to or less than its last offer of settlement.

which Allstate was defending against its own insured.

Mr. Doe worked at the main Hartford Post Office. He was a letter sorter, machine operator, approximately fifty years old who was, on a Sunday afternoon, driving home from work. He was traveling north on I-91 between Hartford and the Massachusetts state line. He was in the far left lane proceeding at a speed of between 60 and 65 miles per hour when a Chevy Blazer suddenly pulled up behind him. The driver was apparently impatient with the plaintiff's speed and drove into the rear of the plaintiff's car before he broke to the right and pulled away.

The driver of the Chevy knew he had hit the plaintiff, couldn't stop on the highway at that point and couldn't safely get off the highway until two exits north. When he arrived home, he did report the accident to the police. He had no motor vehicle insurance, so the plaintiff made a claim against his own insurance company, Allstate, to pay for the damages he suffered in the accident. He had acquired approximately $6,000 in medical bills as a result of the accident, and the orthopedic surgeon who treated him evaluated the injury to his cervical spine as a 10% permanent partial disability.

During a pre-trial conference, another judge had recommended a settlement of $50,000. Allstate rejected that amount and offered $30,000. As I was leaving the courthouse the evening before the trial was to commence, I ran into plaintiff's attorney. I asked him if he was ready to start. He replied that Allstate had raised its offer to $35,000 and that he was going to recommend that figure to his client. Usually, the client accepts his attorney's recommendation, so I was surprised the next morning that the plaintiff (to his undying credit) had rejected the latest offer and was ready to proceed to trial.

Prior to trial, I heard contested motions. Plaintiff wanted Allstate's records as to how much it had paid the orthopedic surgeon, Doctor Roe, for conducting independent medical examinations of plaintiffs for Allstate including his charges for testifying. Defense counsel objected.

"I object, your honor. That's an invasion of privacy."

I overruled the objection on the basis that there was no such privacy in this situation and that what Allstate paid him was relevant to the issue of any bias he may have in favor of Allstate.

"But, your honor, we cannot distinguish between what we pay him for independent medical examinations, for legal defense matters and medical bills and what we pay for treatment of our insureds." Defense counsel stated.

I turned to the Allstate representative who was seated in the audience. "Have you ever heard of a 1099?" I asked. "When I was in private practice, a corporate client would send me an IRS form 1099 stating how much it had paid me in legal fees for the year, the original of which would be sent to the IRS. Don't you issue a 1099 to Dr. Roe just for the services he performs for Allstate separate from payment of medical bills incurred by your insureds?"

"Yes, your honor. I will provide it."

We then proceeded to trial. The plaintiff testified that his job entailed leaning his head down to type in the zip codes on the mail going through his machine, that this caused him to use his neck, and the pain was so severe that he could not function. As a result he claimed, and the records supported his claim, that he had to accept a reduction in grade and transfer to a branch post office as a counter man where he would not have to bend his neck. His doctor had given him 10% disability of his neck. Dr. Roe, who earned $99,000 a year from Allstate conducting independent medical examinations and testifying in court found no permanent injury to the plaintiff's neck. This was just not credible to the jury. Why would a man take a drop in grade and a lower salary if he had not been injured?

Next to testify was Dr. Ward Curran, professor of economics at Trinity College. Defense counsel objected stating he was not qualified to evaluate the plaintiff's lost income, past and future. I had read his curriculum vitae and listened to him describe his background and qualifications. I had no problem qualifying him as an expert witness. I overruled the objection.

Dr. Curran testified that as a result of the plaintiff's drop in pay, his lost income to date and his expected lost income until he reached the age of sixty-five was $99,000. The jury accepted that, added the

$6,000 in medical expenses and awarded $38,000 for pain and suffering and future pain and suffering as a result of his disability. The total verdict came to $143,000. The case was not appealed, and Allstate paid the verdict. My impression was that the plaintiff made a better witness than his attorney thought he would.

As for fall down or slip and fall cases, whether on snow and ice or because of defect in a sidewalk or stairs or a slippery condition on a supermarket floor, juries are even less likely to award damages to plaintiffs in cases that actually go to trial. Perhaps, jurors have the underlying belief in such cases that the plaintiff should have watched where he/she was going, but I can tell you that all of these types of cases that I have tried with a jury, and there have been many, have resulted in a defendant's verdict. Juries are obviously very skeptical about these types of cases.

There is only one case of a slip and fall that resulted in a plaintiff's verdict, and that was a case that was tried to me as a court without a jury. Somehow, the insurance company neglected to claim the case for a jury trial. The plaintiff, a middle-aged police officer, had slipped on a wet gangway leading to his boat at a marina. A gangway is movable at the bottom because the dock on which it rests rises and falls with the tide whereas a ramp is generally fixed at both ends.

After listening to the testimony of the expert witnesses, reviewing photographs and other exhibits, I concluded that the marina was negligent in not taking sufficient precautions to prevent someone from slipping on this particular gangway. In a civil case, the burden of proof is by a preponderance of the evidence (as opposed to the burden in a criminal case of proof beyond a reasonable doubt) which means that it is more likely than not that what the plaintiff claims is true. The plaintiff suffered a 10% permanent partial disability of his left knee, and underwent two significant operations on his knee during a period of a year. I found the marina 80% liable, and the plaintiff 20% liable and after a 20% reduction of the damages, I awarded the plaintiff $86,000. The award was not appealed.

MEDICAL MALPRACTICE

Here too, awards in the millions of dollars are rare. Cases holding the health provider liable are not common. The million dollar plus verdicts are the ones that get the headlines and the attention, but they are the exceptions rather than the rule. Keeping in mind that there are two elements to this type of suit, liability and damages, the plaintiff must first prove that the defendant was negligent and then prove the damages that were caused by the negligence.

With this background, here are some examples:

RES IPSA LOQUITUR

"The thing speaks for itself". The classic example given in law school is that of the surgeon leaving a scalpel in the patient's abdomen, then sewing him up and returning him to his room. This is a case in which the thing done (leaving the scalpel) speaks for itself. It is clearly negligence. It is obvious that such a mistake does not conform to the standard of practice of other surgeons in the area.

The damages can vary. If the patient complains when he/she comes out from under the anesthesia, x-rays are quickly taken and the scalpel is quickly removed without any damage to the body, such as infection or cutting of an important part of the body. Then, the only damages would appear to be the discomfort stemming from this foreign body remaining in the abdomen, and the discomfort of having to undergo another operation even if it's only to remove the scalpel. The damages would, therefore, be minimal.

Another example of res ipse loquitur is the case of the woman who was undergoing surgery when a fire broke out in the operating room. She was obviously not negligent. She was under anesthesia. Although it could have been the hospital equipment being defective, the issue of who was at fault was mainly a dispute between the surgeon and the anesthesiologist. The case settled for $250,000.

I can recall a potential client during my years as a practicing attorney walking into the office to complain about a mis-diagnosis at a

183

local hospital. His appendix was giving him pain so he went to the emergency room on a Saturday evening. An intern told him he had a light fever and a stomach upset and that he should take aspirin and get some rest. Sunday afternoon he came back with severe pain, and he was diagnosed with a ruptured appendix, which was quickly removed. He made a full recovery. I could see the dollar signs in his eyes. I told him that we could probably prove liability for the failure to initially diagnose the problem with the appendix. The defense would be that when he presented himself Saturday evening, his symptoms were mild and that the appendix had not swelled sufficiently to indicate any problem. More importantly, I said:

"What are your damages? How have you been hurt by this? Is your injury permanent?"

Instead of answering my questions, he proceeded to berate the hospital for the intern's alleged mistake.

"Sir," I replied, "Even if we can prove that the hospital made a mistake, the consequences are so minor, it isn't worth pursuing."

"What do you mean?" he asked. "I had to have my appendix out".

"True." I replied. "But if the intern had properly diagnosed the problem with the appendix, you probably would have been admitted to the hospital Saturday night, and depending upon how quickly your symptoms progressed, you might have had the ruptured appendix removed Sunday morning instead of Sunday afternoon. Your damages would have been the discomfort you were experiencing between Sunday morning and Sunday afternoon. The appendix would have had to be removed in any case. There was no permanent injury, you didn't lose any extra time from work. Your damages are minimal, you're fortunate it was caught in time and the problem resolved with no significant consequences. You should go home and forget about it."

He still looked unhappy so I said: "You can, of course, seek the advice of another attorney, although I think he/she will tell you the same thing; and certainly, if another attorney were persuaded to take your case, the attorney would be very unlikely to take the case on a contingency fee basis since the likelihood of winning is so small. Therefore, you should be prepared to pay the attorney a retainer of at least $5,000 in advance plus probably another $2,000 to cover the costs of depositions, filing fees, expert witnesses etc.," I bade him goodbye, and was not surprised to learn that he never did make a claim against the hospital. I believe it was the $7,000 up front retainer that had the most impact in dissuading him from proceeding further.

I found during my years as an attorney that when I had a difficult time trying to persuade a client that he did not have a good case and shouldn't bring suit, the demand for a substantial retainer was usually a good way to convince the client not to proceed. You see, the client is perfectly happy to have the attorney take the case on a contingent fee basis (the attorney utimately receives a percentage, usually one third or one quarter of what he/she collects) because there is no risk to the client. He is perfectly willing to take a chance on the attorney's blood, sweat and tears.

HOW TO DELIVER A BABY

This is a case brought against an obstetrician, Dr. D. who delivered a baby, Florence, vaginally instead of by C-Section (Cesarean section which is delivering a baby by surgical incision of the walls of the abdomen and uterus, so named because of the belief that Julius Caesar was born this way). It was alleged that as a result of Florence being delivered vaginally, she suffered serious injuries including shoulder dystocia[4] resulting in permanent damage to her left shoulder and arm. The case came before me on a Motion for Summary Judgment filed by the defendant's attorney. A motion for summary judgment claims that there are no issues of material fact and that the moving party, in this case the defendant, is entitled to judgment as a matter of law. In effect, the defendant is claiming that the evidence is so clear that there is nothing for the jury, which decides the facts, to do, and that under the law, which the judge decides, and based on these allegedly uncontroverted facts, there is no question that judgment should enter for the defendant.

[4] Dystocia results in the shoulder being crushed as the baby comes out. The most common causes are the pelvis being abnormally small, the womb muscles failing to contract or the neck of the womb failing to expand; or excessive size of the fetus.

The Truths of Justice

The plaintiff's expert witness was one, Dr. Julius, another qualified obstetrician, whose deposition had been taken by the defendant. Defendant claimed that by Dr. Julius' own statements in the deposition, he conceded that it was not a deviation from the standard of care if an obstetrician does not foresee a shoulder dystocia occurring. To decide this issue I, of course, had to read the transcript of the deposition which I proceeded to do. After considerable argument by both attorneys, I later issued a written decision. The important parts are quoted as follows:

"Proximate cause of the injuries sustained is a question of fact for the trier of fact, in this case the jury. Based upon defendant's motion, it is necessary to determine whether the **only** conclusion to be drawn from Dr. Julius' deposition is that the defendant's alleged negligence was not the proximate cause of Florence's injuries. Dr. Julius also testified that based upon the mother's advanced maternal age, her obesity, her excessive weight gain during her pregnancy as well as the failure of the defendant to timely apply an internal electrode to the baby's scalp to more accurately monitor her condition, the existing evidence of fetal distress, the high blood pressure reading of 202 over 118 creating a risk of a seizure, a reduction in the baby's heart rate all cried out for a C-Section to be done; that these factors could have caused a traumatic vaginal delivery which would have resulted in shoulder dystocia. Further, Dr. Julius, on page 79, included the risk of shoulder dystocia as one of the factors to be utilized in considering whether to do a C-Section instead of a vaginal delivery. The court finds that taking Dr. Julius' deposition as a whole the jury could conclude that he was saying that in view of all the existing conditions, including a risk of shoulder dystocia from a vaginal delivery, a C-Section should have been performed."

I further pointed out that the defendant will have an opportunity to impeach his credibility through cross examination after Dr. Julius' testimony at trial. It is up to the jury to evaluate the credibility of all witnesses. "The deposition is not sufficiently clear or consistent to support defendant's claim that there is no genuine issue of material fact. There is such an issue, and I cannot take that determination as to what the true facts are away from the jury . . . . Thus, the issues boil down to:

1. Was the defendant negligent in not doing a C-Section, and if so, was that negligence a substantial factor in causing the shoulder dystocia?

2. Was it foreseeable that harm of the same general nature would result even if the defendant did not foresee or could not have foreseen the extent of the harm or the manner in which it occurred?

3. Was there a chain of causation between the failure to do a C-Section and the resulting damages?"

I found that the jury could reasonably have answered yes to these questions and that the nexus between the negligence and the damages was neither too tenuous nor too remote. I also pointed out that the State Supreme Court had ruled that in regard to a summary judgment motion the facts must be viewed in the light more favorable to the nonmovant (the plaintiff in this case) who is to benefit from all favorable inferences to be drawn.

Defense counsel pleaded with me not to let this case go to the jury. He was undoubtedly concerned that the young girl with a shriveled arm would be more sympathetic to a jury than a doctor. Nevertheless, I denied the motion with the conclusion that there were genuine issues of material fact that the jury must decide. In a judge's instructions to a jury, we urge them to set aside any sympathy or bias they may have for or against either party and decide the case strictly on the facts presented in court. Apparently they followed these instructions as most jurors do. The jurors could not agree on a verdict in the first trial, and, therefore, a mistrial was declared. At the second trial, the jury rendered a verdict in favor of the defendant.

DENTAL MALPRACTICE I

During a visit to her dentist, the patient complained that two of her front teeth were protruding and a wisdom tooth was suspected as the cause. The dentist wasn't concerned, but he reluctantly referred her to an oral surgeon, Dr. O. When Dr. O examined her, he recommended that the wisdom tooth be removed, not because of the protrusion of the front teeth but because he discovered that a front molar was losing bone because of the wisdom tooth. He recommended that even though none of the wisdom teeth were causing the patient any discomfort, all of the wisdom teeth should be removed at the same appointment. The patient, a thirty-five year old woman, agreed, and she was scheduled for surgery in the oral surgeon's office.

As the surgeon was removing the wisdom tooth closest to the front molar in the lower part of the mouth, his instrument cut a nerve in her jaw that extended to her ears thus paralyzing her bottom lip and jaw. She was left with no feeling there, and when she consumed food or liquid, it dribbled from her lower lip. The injury was permanent. She eventually brought suit against the oral surgeon. She did not claim malpractice in the cutting of the nerve because that was considered a normal risk of surgery. She did claim malpractice on two grounds, one that the surgeon had not obtained her informed consent to perform the surgery and two that the surgery was unnecessary.

The case was vigorously contested. I presided over the trial with a jury of six. The plaintiff was represented by an experienced and capable trial attorney who had a dramatic if not flamboyant style. The surgeon was represented also by an experienced and capable trial attorney who was quieter and more methodical but, nevertheless, seemed to bore in with his questions until his point was clear. Of course, there were expert witnesses for both sides, both experienced oral surgeons from New York City who offered contrary opinions. The law requires that in a medical malpractice case, the plaintiff must offer testimony from an expert witness. That witness must testify as to the standard of care for, in this case, oral surgeons in the area and also that the surgeon deviated from the standard of care. (Often the experts are from out of state since generally local doctors do not wish to testify against their colleagues.)

Informed consent consists of the doctor advising the patient of the procedure to be used and pointing out the risks accompanying the operation. The patient then acknowledges her/his understanding of what has been told to her/him and agrees to go ahead with the operation notwithstanding what she/he has just been told about the risks. Today, most doctors obtain this consent in writing on a sheet of paper that contains the doctor's explanation and warning of risks.

However, in 1993 when this surgery took place many doctors did not obtain informed consent in writing. That was the situation here.[5] However, at the trial the surgeon produced blown up photographs of his office notes, and they purportedly showed that he had explained the risks to the patient and she had consented to proceeding. She denied this, so it was her word against his word, but he had a supporting document. The jury chose to believe the surgeon.

The second issue is whether the surgeon should have recommended the surgery even with her consent. Here was a thirty five year old woman who was not suffering any discomfort. The concern about the protruding teeth had somehow been discarded and replaced by the surgeon's concern for the loss of bone in the molar which he attributed to the presence of the wisdom tooth. However, the bone loss had occurred over the past fifteen years, and there was no indication that it was going to continue. The plaintiff's attorney argued that the surgery to remove the wisdom teeth was premature. There may not have been further bone loss and the surgeon could have monitored the molar frequently to see if it became necessary to remove the wisdom teeth. In view of the risk involved with the surgery, if the bone loss continued to occur, it might be better to lose the molar and replace it with a false tooth and, thereby avoid extracting the wisdom teeth.

That seemed to me to be the better argument.

However, the surgeon's attorney, through his lengthy and methodical questioning, focused primarily on the issue of informed consent, so it seemed that the issue of whether the surgeon should have recommended the surgery became insignificant.

---

[5] In 1996, I suffered a very mild heart attack. As I was being wheeled into the room for the angioplasty to be performed, the cardiologist asked me to sign an informed consent form. I looked at him. "What happens if I don't sign." I thought in that situation it was hardly a voluntary consent.

Of course, the jury may have considered this issue, believed that the removal of the molar, if it became necessary, was as much of a risk to the nerve as the removal of the wisdom tooth, or the jury may have believed that the patient wanted to go ahead anyway in order to eliminate the protruding of the front teeth, or the jurors may just have believed the surgeon and his experts that the surgery was necessary.

In any event, the jury's verdict was for the defendant. I'm not sure how I would have voted if I had been on the jury. I did not have the benefit of their discussion in the jury deliberation room, and, as is usually the case, I as the judge who had to rule on admissibility of evidence, probably knew some facts that the jury never heard because they were not legally admissible in the trial. The plaintiff was disappointed, but was satisfied that she received a fair hearing and at least had the opportunity to present her case to a jury. I'm not sure I would have been so forgiving.

DENTAL MALPRACTICE II

This was a case against a general dentist, Dr. G. The plaintiff was a man in his mid fifties, with white hair and a ruddy complexion. He was a bus driver, and had gone to Dr. G. to have one of his upper teeth extracted. During the extraction, the tooth broke off leaving bone in his upper gum which had to be removed. In the process of removing the bone, Dr. G. had accidentally cut through the roof of the plaintiff's mouth into the nasal cavity. Apparently, Dr. G. had tried to stretch the skin of the roof of the mouth sufficiently to cover the existing hole. This was unsuccessful although not known at the time. The patient waited a few days, but became increasingly concerned when whatever liquid he would drink would come out through his nose more and more frequently. The dentist claimed that he had scheduled the plaintiff for a follow up appointment, but the plaintiff never kept his appointment, and by the time the plaintiff did come in to see him, it was too late to cover up the hole completely.

There was a dispute at trial as to the facts surrounding the scheduling and keeping of the follow up appointment. The dentist then referred the plaintiff to an oral surgeon who also was not able to close the hole. Finally, the patient was fitted with an appliance that covered the hole. The plaintiff had obviously sustained permanent injury, his level of pain and discomfort following the surgery had been severe, and he was still suffering discomfort even with the appliance.

The plaintiff claimed that he had lost his job with the bus company as a result of having taken too many sick days and that the policy of the company was not to rehire any employee whose employment had been terminated. Driving a bus was the only thing he knew how to do claimed the plaintiff, and he could not get another job. He started drinking and ended up living in a shelter where he was presently residing. He blamed all of this on the alleged malpractice of the dentist. If he could prove the malpractice, then he would probably be entitled to substantial damages.

As I have indicated, a medical malpractice case can rise or fall depending upon the qualifications of the expert witnesses. The plaintiff himself did not make a strong witness, but this was nothing compared to what happened to his two expert witnesses. I had qualified both of them based upon their training and experience. The first expert to testify was a dentist who practiced in Stamford, Connecticut. The plaintiff's attorney then brought out more of the witness' background so it wouldn't appear that they were hiding anything which could later be obtained through cross-examination by the defense attorney. The problem was the witness' experience while he was practicing in New York City and then a New York suburb prior to his moving to Connecticut. While practicing in New York, he had been arrested and convicted of Medicaid fraud, and had served time in prison. He was then put on probation with the condition that he not practice dentistry while on probation. He maintained that during probation he consulted with another dentist but did not actually practice dentistry.

However, it was determined to the satisfaction of the New York court that he had actually filled some cavities. His probation was revoked, and he was not only imprisoned again but he was stripped of his license to practice in the State of New York. How he managed to obtain a license to practice in Connecticut was never revealed. For some reason he wanted me to look at the decision of the New York Court of Appeals which upheld his probation violation. I chuckled to myself when I read the decision. It was written by the Chief Judge of the Court of Appeals, the highest court in New York state. His name was Sol Wachner who had since been arrested, convicted and imprisoned in a federal prison for stalking and threatening his ex-girlfriend. His case received quite a bit of notoriety when this happened in the early nineties. What a coincidence!

From this record of the witness, Medicaid fraud and violating probation and lying about it, the jury rightfully drew the conclusion that he was not a witness who was likely to tell the truth. I asked the plaintiff's attorney after the verdict had come in why he had chosen to put this witness on the stand. He replied that he didn't learn of the prior convictions until it was too late to disclose another expert witness. I pointed out to him that the deadline for disclosing an expert witness is discretionary with the court, and under the circumstances, I probably would have given him an extension of the deadline, but, of course, I couldn't do it once the trial had begun.

The second expert witness was an experienced and highly competent general dentist from the local area. His credentials were impeccable, and he had a clean background. However, it turned out that the plaintiff's attorney was a patient of his, and the dentist was a client of the plaintiff's attorney. Although I believe the witness told the truth as he saw it, I can certainly understand why members of the jury might question his impartiality. Not surprisingly the jury returned with a verdict for the defendant.

OTHER CIVIL CASES

There is a large variety of civil cases in addition to motor vehicle accidents, fall down accidents and medical malpractice. Some are jury trials, and some are court trials. For example, foreclosures of mortgages are heard by a judge, whether or not to grant injunctions or restraining orders are heard by a judge. Appeals from decisions of zoning boards and other town and state agencies are heard by a judge.

The first selectman of a nearby town died. The second selectman took his place. He was of a different political party than the late first selectman. The vacancy on the three member board of selectmen was filled by a member of the late first selectman's party. Nonetheless, the chairman of that party sought a court order to have me declare the second selectman's assumption of the office illegal and void because of the minority representation statute. There was, of course, more to it than that. These were very complex issues of law. I found that the minority representation statute did not apply in this case and upheld the second selectman becoming the first selectman. The case was not appealed, and that individual was elected to a full term as first selectman at the next regular election.

A teacher in a local school system had been fired. The police in the community in which he lived, far from where he taught, had arrested him for possession of cocaine. He admitted committing this felony. He appealed his firing to the court claiming, among other things, that his firing was a violation of the Americans with Disabilities Act. I found that because the Board of Education, after public hearings, had determined that he no longer held the trust of at least half of the students and faculty, the Board was justified in terminating his employment. The decision was not appealed.

PRODUCT LIABILITY, NEGLIGENCE AND DEATH

One of the more interesting civil cases in which I was involved was **Janet May, Administratrix of the Estate of Robert May vs. ABC Laboratories and Urgent Medical Treatment.** The plaintiff's husband was a research doctor at a local company. He was an asthmatic. He and all other employees were required to be vaccinated on a particular day. They lined up in the cafeteria and received their shots. Early that evening Robert May suffered from a delayed anaphylactic (abnormal) reaction to the shot and experienced difficulty in breathing. At first he thought it was just another episode of an asthmatic attack that would soon pass. His breathing became even more difficult, and both he and his wife realized that he was in a serious condition. Instead of calling 911, his wife helped him into the family car and drove to an immediate medical treatment facility nearby on the mistaken assumption that it was an emergency room type of facility. The doctor and staff believed they were neither equipped properly nor in possession of sufficient medical skills to treat Dr. May. They called 911, the ambulance and paramedics arrived, but it was too late. Dr. May died on the way to the hospital.

He was in his forties, happily married with two children with a bright future. His employer was legally immune from suit, but subsequently, his wife as Administratrix of his estate, brought an action against both the Urgent Medical Treatment company (UMT) and ABC Laboratories (ABC). The claim against UMT was that it had falsely advertised itself as an emergency facility on the radio and that Janet May had heard the radio commercial and had relied upon it in deciding to take her husband there. There was no tape recording of the commercial still in existence. There was a copy of the radio script which had the word "emergency" in it but that word had a line through it indicating it had been eliminated from the commercial. The question that remained was when the word was crossed out, before the commercial was read on the air or afterwards.

The claim against ABC was more complex. It was primarily a claim that the warnings on the packages of the vaccine were inadequate. The employer claimed that Dr. May had signed a form in which the risks of the vaccine were explained and consent was given for it to be administered. One or two employees of the company were prepared to testify that they recalled Dr. May signing the informed consent form. The problem was that although forms signed by other employees had been kept in the company's files, the one Dr. May allegedly signed was missing. The plaintiff claimed that even if he had signed it, it was insufficient under what is called the "learned intermediary" rule. This rule developed through court decisions required that the person administering the vaccine have knowledge of Dr. May's medical condition.

The Truths of Justice

The informed consent form apparently did not warn of an adverse delayed reaction by people suffering from asthma, and even if it had, the question was whether it had been adequately explained to Dr. May prior to the shot being administered. If not, there had to be a warning on the package from ABC sufficient to alert Dr. May of this potential danger. If the shot had been administered by his own doctor who knew of his medical condition, then his doctor would be considered a "learned intermediary", and ABC would not be liable for the alleged inadequate warnings. Without the learned intermediary, ABC, it was claimed, had an obligation to inform the recipient of the vaccine directly of the risks described.

It did not put such a warning on its packages, and in all likelihood Dr. May had never seen the package that was sent to his employer. On the other hand, if the jury believed that the person who administered the vaccine had learned from Dr. May that he was an asthmatic and that person or his/her associate had warned of the potential for the delayed adverse reaction and Dr. May had understood and consented to the administering of the vaccine, then ABC would probably have been found not liable. Of course, there was no written form signed by Dr. May available, and it is questionable whether the person who administered the shot would have known of this risk if the label on the package from ABC had not contained this warning.

The case was hotly contested, and I heard pre-trial motions over a period of nearly a year. The attorneys for all three parties were very competent with excellent reputations that were well deserved. ABC was also represented by a highly competent attorney from out of state whose law firm served as general counsel to ABC. This resulted in hearings being held in my chambers so that we could bring the out of state attorney in by speaker phone. ABC fought hard to keep their documents secret because it did not want information disclosed to its competitors. This resulted in my issuing some protective orders and denying others.

I ordered disclosure of any information that was already on file with the Food and Drug Administration. ABC claimed that certain documents were privileged under the attorney-client privilege that prohibits disclosure of communications between the client and its attorneys. The documents were submitted to me "in camera" which meant that I would review them in my chambers and decide what was protected by this and other privileges. ABC did not want the plaintiff to see documents that were protected in an argument over whether they were privileged because then the plaintiff would learn this information even if I then ruled it was protected.

The documents amounted to three hundred and seventy pages so it took longer to review than I had planned; but there was no other choice. They had to be reviewed in secret by someone who was impartial. Depositions were taken of the expert witnesses, many of them out of state, as a result of which the pre-trial costs of the parties continued to mount. This was not a problem for the defendants who had substantial financial resources. It did appear to be a problem for the plaintiff, but I later learned that she was able to pay these costs from the proceeds of life insurance policies. Of course, the experts had to be paid as well, and their fees were high.

The plaintiff, whose attorneys did not have the same background in these issues as the attorneys for ABC, had a difficult time in obtaining qualified experts in the field. At one point it appeared from the deposition of one of the plaintiff's experts that his testimony would not be very helpful. However, I granted the plaintiff more time to retain another expert over the strenuous objections of the defendants who had both the resources and the knowledge to retain highly qualified experts in this field. I gave the plaintiff this latitude because I wanted this contest to be fought on a level playing field. After thousand of pages of documents had been produced and depositions of nearly twenty witnesses had been taken, the case was ready for trial.

As a last effort at settlement, the parties agreed to a mediation session with two former federal judges who, since retirement had gone into the business of mediation and arbitration. It appeared as if the mediation would not be successful. However, in a twelve hour marathon session ABC agreed to a settlement with the plaintiff for a substantial amount of money. The plaintiff had been rejecting offers of settlement from UMT in part, I believe, because the widow wanted a jury to hold UMT liable, thereby justifying her decision to go first to UMT rather than call 911.

The trial against UMT commenced in front of me and a jury, but after the first witness had testified, the parties settled also for a substantial sum although nowhere as large as that of the other settlement. I respected the plaintiff for hanging in there until she was able to reach a reasonable settlement. As I have said about divorce cases, the race does not always go to the swiftest, but rather to the one with the most stamina to keep fighting for what they think is right. I'm sure it was for the benefit of not only the widow but also the future of the children. It was the best they could do under the circumstances, for, in the end none of it could bring Dr. May back to life.

CASES OF FIRST IMPRESSION

In civil court, Mondays of each week are generally reserved for what is called "Short Calendar." Trials are not held on that day. Trials before a jury or a judge are part of the regular calendar (the list of cases that are expected to go to trial). Short calendar matters are not trials, and they are usually resolved on the same day although a written decision is obviously not forthcoming that day.

Short calendar generally consists of written motions on issues of law to be decided by a judge. They include motions to strike a complaint or answer or other written pleading on the basis that what is set forth is, even if proven, not sufficient to constitute a valid complaint or defense. Short calendar also includes motions to amend, motions for summary judgment and motions to dismiss. Summary judgment is granted, usually for the defendant, only if there is no disagreement as to the facts of the case, (which would otherwise be heard by the jury), and the only issue remaining is whether the claim or defense is a viable claim under the law even assuming that there is no question about the facts. Issues of law are decided only by a judge. The parties are required to submit memoranda as to what such party claims the law is with citations to statutes and other cases

197

that have been decided on the issue before the court. The judge then hears oral argument. If he or she has reviewed the memoranda (also called briefs, although they are hardly that) in advance of oral argument, he or she may rule from the bench after the conclusion of oral argument. If more research is necessary or the decision should be in writing, then the judge decides the issue later with a written memorandum of decision. This can result in the conclusion of the case or continuation of the case to trial depending upon the decision.

When the issues are clear, and the Appellate or Supreme Court has already ruled on the same issue in another case, and the facts are sufficiently similar to the facts of the case before the judge, the judge must decide the case, under the principle of *"stare decisis"*, which means that a decision on a point of law by a court (Appellate or Supreme) will be followed by a court of lower rank (Superior Court) in a subsequent case which presents the same legal problem although different parties are involved in the subsequent case.

What is not so clear are those issues on which a Connecticut appellate court has *never* ruled. The judge can look to decisions by appellate courts from other states or by federal courts for guidance but is not bound by those decisions. The judge is not bound by decisions of other Superior Court judges although he/she can look at them for guidance. Basically, the judge is left on his/her own to decide the case with no precedent to guide him/ her. That's why those cases are called cases of "first impression." Some of the more significant of these cases that I have had to decide follow. (See *The Catholic Church: Something To Hide* for another such case.)

NOT JUST A BYSTANDER

Madsen v. Setora is a case involving drunk driving. On the Friday before Christmas, certain employees of the same company decided to have a Christmas party. It started at the office of the employer and continued to the nearby home of one of the employees, David Black. Mary Smith who was eighteen, three years younger than the minimum drinking age in Connecticut of twenty one, drove her car to the party giving a ride to another employee, Nicholas Setora, who was nineteen years old. Setora left his car at the company parking lot. At the party, everyone consumed a substantial amount of alcohol including Mary Smith although she consumed less than Nick Setora. Setora then asked Smith for a ride back to his car.

She drove him to the company parking lot knowing full well that he was substantially intoxicated. She let him off next to his car, waited for him to start it, and then left. At about the same time Rebecca Madsen was driving east on I-84 toward Hartford until she ran out of gas near Exit 64. She parked in the right hand break down lane, and walked to the exit to obtain a can of gasoline warning her fifteen year old daughter, Leslie, to stay in the car with the doors locked. For some reason, Leslie got out of the car and was standing behind the trunk when, suddenly appeared an intoxicated Nicholas Setora, driving at a high rate of speed in the break down lane where he was not supposed to be. He saw the Madsen vehicle too late to avoid hitting Leslie straight on, cutting off both of her legs and killing her.

He stopped momentarily, then pulled out and drove toward the guard rail at the next highway light where he smashed into the guard rail and the light pole. He claimed he was not trying to escape, but rather, shocked by what he had done, he was trying to commit suicide. He failed at that, and ended up serving a few years in prison for what he had done.

Meanwhile, the attorney for Leslie's Estate brought suit against Setora, Black and Mary Smith. The claim against Smith was that she had knowingly assisted Setora in driving while intoxicated. Smith's attorney moved to strike the claims against her saying that she was just a bystander and bystanders were not liable for the negligence of others, such as driving drunk.

There was no Connecticut precedent on this issue, nor, under these facts, could we find any case law from other states. Thus, it was a case of first impression in Connecticut. I ruled in favor of the plaintiff and denied Mary Smith's motion to strike. I stated that if a third party knows that the defendant's conduct constitutes a breach of duty (to not drive while under the influence of alcohol, the duty being owed to other drivers or pedestrians whom he may hit and injure), *and that third party gives substantial assistance or encouragement to the defendant to so conduct himself, the third party is also liable to the plaintiff - victim.* Someone giving substantial assistance to a tortfeasor (a person committing a civil wrong) is also a tortfeasor.

Smith's attorney had argued that a bystander does not have to take preventive action to prevent the wrong from occurring. I pointed out the distinction between a bystander and someone who actively assists the tortfeasor by using an analogy. A man comes out of a bar and is so drunk he can hardly stand up. Someone standing outside the bar has no legal duty to stop the drunk from getting into the car and driving away, but if the drunk's car won't start and the bystander then drives his car up to the drunk's car and uses his battery to give a jump to the battery in the drunk's car thus enabling him to drive away and hurt someone, he is no longer a bystander but rather one who has actively assisted the drunk driver to drive.

Smith, knowing Setora was drunk, nevertheless, drove him to his car so he could drive away and hurt someone, thereby substantially assisting and encouraging him to operate his automobile on the highway while under the influence of alcohol. She, thereby, transformed herself from a bystander to a tortfeasor. As a result of my ruling Smith's insurance company and the other two insurance carriers reached a reasonable settlement.

TO CATCH A THIEF

<u>Andrea Peirolo v. American National Fire Insurance Company</u>. On June 22,1992 the plaintiff had parked her 1987 Chevrolet, a motor vehicle **owned** and operated by her, in front of the Mill Pond Store located on Rte. 19 in Stafford Springs, Connecticut. While she was leaving the store with her nineteen month old son in her arms, she saw a man, later identified as Robert Rivers, enter her car and sit in the driver's seat. As the plaintiff approached the car and opened the passenger door in an attempt to prevent Mr. Rivers from stealing it, he placed the car in reverse and began to back it up.

This knocked the plaintiff to the ground and she sustained injuries. Rivers was later apprehended and imprisoned. There is no dispute that the plaintiff did not know Rivers, that he did not have permission to use the car and that he had no insurance coverage of any kind. At the time of the incident, plaintiff's automobile was insured by the defendant, American National Fire, (ANF). Plaintiff was not covered under the liability portion of her policy because the driver of her automobile, which was in the process of being stolen, was clearly using it without permission. Plaintiff's claim under the uninsured provision of her policy was denied by the defendant, ANF.

ANF's major defense was that the motor vehicle that struck the plaintiff (her own) wasn't by definition an "uninsured" motor vehicle. The policy stated, in part: "However, uninsured motor vehicle does not include any vehicle . . . owned by . . . you." On the surface that would appear to deny plaintiff coverage under the uninsured motor vehicle provision of her policy. However, the policy also defined an uninsured motor vehicle as "a land motor vehicle . . . 1. to which no bodily injury bond or liability applies at the time of the accident." Under this definition, of course, plaintiff's vehicle qualified as insured. There was no liability coverage because the driver was using the vehicle without permission. These two provisions of the policy, which is a contract between the insured and the insurance company, are contradictory.

Therefore, the meaning of the contract is ambiguous. My decision stated in part that Connecticut law is very clear. "A limitation of liability on uninsured or underinsured motorist coverage must be construed most strongly against the insurer. Ambiguities in an insurance contract must be resolved in favor of the insured." That is so because under basic contract law ambiguities are resolved against the party responsible for drafting the contract. Certainly, the parties are not equal in their ability to understand the provisions of the contract. The insurance policy contains much technical language familiar to the insurance company drafting it.

Attorneys have a difficult time interpreting insurance policies. For the layman buying the policy understanding the terms is far more difficult. The decision goes on to say that "the plaintiff probably did not read or have explained to her the fine print in the subject policy setting forth the exclusion, and even if she did, it is unlikely that she expected to lose the uninsured motorist coverage for which she had paid under the circumstances of this case . . . . The legislative intent behind the uninsured motorist statutes has been defined repeatedly as to assure that every insured recovers damages he or she would have been able to recover if the uninsured motorist had maintained a policy of liability insurance . . . . When people are injured, they have an expectation that they are going to be covered by their uninsured motorist coverage . . . . The denial of liability coverage and then, because of the exclusion, denial of uninsured motorist coverage would result in this plaintiff not being able to recover at all for her injuries. This flies in the face of logic and the intent of the legislature to provide uninsured motorist coverage to someone who pays for that coverage but can't take advantage of it when her own car is stolen .

To deny her coverage under these circumstance simply because she owned the insured vehicle is fundamentally unfair and against public policy". I also noted that both the Texas and Colorado Supreme courts had reached the same conclusion under similar circumstances.

The duty of a judge is to see that justice is done. It would have been an injustice to deny the plaintiff recovery for the reason set forth by the defendant.

THE FIREFIGHTER'S RULE

Are police officers precluded from suing people for injuries that allegedly occur while the police officers are in the performance of their duties? This was the question before me in the case of Estes v. Holder in 1997. The Connecticut Supreme court, in 1959 in the case of Roberts v. Rosenblatt adopted the "firefighter's rule which generally applies to firefighters who respond to a fire and are injured by some defect on the property where the fire is taking place. They are precluded from recovering from the property owner for such injuries on the theory that the cause of such an injury is a risk inherent in the performance of the firefighter's duties, a risk he is employed to address on behalf of the public.

This rule was later extended to police officers, and although the rule initially applied only to liability of property owners, the defendant, in a motion for summary judgment, claimed that it extended to all injuries sustained by a police officer while engaged in the performance of his official duties. There were no Appellate or Supreme Court cases on this particular claim. Thus, it was a case of first impression.

The plaintiff, West Hartford police officer Stephen B. Estes, claimed that he injured his right knee at the International House of Pancakes (IHOP). An employee had called the police in June, 1994 to report a fight between the defendant, Michael Holder, and his estranged wife, a waitress at the restaurant. When Estes arrived at the scene, Holder resisted arrest and injured Estes' knee which injury eventually required surgery. Estes sued Holder, the tortfeasor, (not the IHOP) for assault and battery and negligence. The firefighter's rule was invoked by the defendant as a defense to the suit.

I denied the motion for summary judgment, stating that "The shield of the firefighter's rule should not be available to those who, in resisting arrest, commit either intentional or negligent acts that injure the police officer. Such police officer is acting in an effort to protect the general citizenry, and it is fundamentally unfair to protect from liability one who causes injuries to the police officer by interfering with such police officer's actions."

RECKLESS SUPERVISION

A bizarre accident was the basis for this decision. In August, 1995, the plaintiff was a patron of a hotel and needed help to jump start his automobile which was in the parking lot. An employee of the hotel, Edward Doe, used a golf cart's battery to start the plaintiff's car. After unhooking the jumper cables, Doe, not realizing the plaintiff was behind him, allegedly put the golf cart in reverse and backed the plaintiff up against the car, thus injuring his legs. Although the golf cart was not considered a motor vehicle subject to drunk driving laws, Mr. Doe asked the police to conduct a blood alcohol test to prove that he wasn't drunk. The test came back with a reading of .272, much higher than the drunk driving limit of .10.

Nevertheless, Doe insisted he was not intoxicated at the time of the accident. The plaintiff brought suit against the owners/operators of the hotel that employed Doe, identified here as "S", claiming negligent supervision of their employee, and in the second count, claiming reckless supervision of Doe. If the plaintiff succeeded on count two, he would be entitled to additional damages known as ***punitive damages*** which would include his attorney's fees as well as other damages. Plaintiff alleged that the injuries were caused by the reckless indifference of S to the rights of the plaintiff, more specifically that Doe was under the influence of alcohol at the time he was operating the golf cart, that S allowed him to perform his duties while under the influence and that ***they knew he was under the influence of alcohol and thus posed a danger to their patrons, including the plaintiff.***

The defendant moved to strike this count claiming that there was no legal cause of action for reckless supervision. No Connecticut cases decided this issue nor was I able to find any cases nationwide. Thus, a case of first impression in Connecticut and possibly in the United States was before me. For the purposes of the motion to strike I had to assume the facts alleged were true. An Appellate case in Connecticut had permitted a claim for negligent supervision of an employee. In a Supreme Court case in Connecticut not dealing with supervision of an employee, the court stated that "Punitive damages are awarded where the evidence shows a reckless indifference to the rights of others . . . ." I found that is exactly what the plaintiff alleged.

I further found that there was no decision or statute that excluded a claim for reckless supervision and that reckless supervision was a logical extension of the two cases cited. This was partly based upon the principle that the exclusion of none is the inclusion of all. I fully recognized that this ruling could put an employer in a difficult position. If an employer strictly enforces disciplinary rules and takes severe action against an employee who violates those rules, the employer may face a suit by the employee. If the employer does not enforce the rules, it may be liable for punitive damages. The answer is that the employer has to pay strict attention to the employee's background when he is hired and closely monitor his condition and activities. If the employer does this, this type of accident might not happen. Stricter rules benefit the innocent consumer, as they should.

DID THE SNOW STOP FALLING?

Not all of these issues are decided in favor of the plaintiff. In the case of <u>Sartorella v. XYZ Supermarkets</u>, the plaintiff had slipped and fallen on snow and ice in the parking lot of the supermarket on his way into the store. As a patron of the store, he was considered a business invitee, one to whom the supermarket owes the highest duty of care.

However, the Connecticut Supreme Court had established, in 1989, the rule of law that ". . . in the absence of *unusual circumstances*, a property owner, in fulfilling the duty owed to invitees upon his property to exercise reasonable diligence in removing dangerous conditions, the removal of an accumulation of snow and ice *may await until the end of a storm and a reasonable time thereafter before removing ice and snow from outside walks and steps . . . .*" In this case the evidence was uncontroverted that the snow continued to fall before and after the plaintiff fell although perhaps more lightly at the time of the fall and for an hour preceding the fall, but it still continued.

The issue then was what qualifies as "unusual circumstances". Plaintiff claimed the following as "unusual circumstances":

1. Other properties and land owners had plowed or sanded and local streets had been plowed or sanded.

2. The snow was extremely light for about one hour before the plaintiff's fall.

3. There was no alternative means of ingress and egress of the store.

4. The snow where he fell was packed down and slippery because of cars traveling over it.

I found all of this to be irrelevant because even though the snow was extremely light part of the time, there was no question that it was continuing. In point of fact, another 5.7 inches fell after the fall. Neither the Appellate nor Supreme Court had specifically ruled on what were "unusual circumstances". Thus, it was a case of first impression. I found nothing unusual about snow being packed down when cars drove over it, what the town did to the streets and whether homeowners plowed or sanded had nothing to do with the responsibility of a store owner where people were continually using the premises.

The Supreme Court case setting forth the rule described above indicated that a possible unusual circumstance would be evidence with respect to the changeover in precipitation *and* the availability of alternative means of egress from the store. This statement meant that a changeover in precipitation was still a necessary condition before the jury could consider whether there was an alternative means of egress to make it an unusual circumstance. The snow in this case had not stopped falling, and there was no precedent as to what constituted unusual circumstances while the snow was still falling. I found as a matter of law that the instances cited by the plaintiff did not constitute unusual circumstances and granted summary judgment for the defendants. The ruling was not appealed.

MISCELLANEOUS CASES

Rather than describe other cases in detail, I will summarize a few more that do not involve accidents. On June 1, 1994 Paul C., an employee of a major manufacturing company filed a complaint of sexual harassment and discrimination based upon sexual orientation with the Connecticut Commission on Human Rights and Opportunities. Paul C. was gay, and two employees had harassed him because of it, allegedly leading to his suicide on June 16,1994.

Shortly thereafter, Paul C.'s Estate brought suit against the manufacturer claiming that the manufacturer, through its employees, had discriminated against him in respect to conditions of his employment, and although he had complained to the company, the company failed to protect him against such discrimination in violation of certain state statutes. The defendant moved to strike the complaint claiming that certain statutes were not applicable because of the dates of their enactment, that Paul C. had not followed the proper procedure, and made other technical arguments.

Suffice it to say that there were several statutes which might be considered to be contradictory. I then embarked on comprehensive research on a variety of issues, including the intent of the legislature based upon statements of legislators during the debate on passage of the statutes. There were no Appellate or Supreme Court cases interpreting these statutes, in part probably due to the fact that some of the statutes were of fairly recent in origin. An analysis of all of the applicable statutes taken as a whole led me to conclude that the plaintiff did have a valid cause of action under these statutes. I denied the motion to strike and ordered the case to proceed on the factual issues involved. The decision was not appealed.

There are certain financial institutions in this country whose primary function is to buy mortgage debts at a discount generally from banks who are willing to give up what they consider a debt that is unlikely to be collected. If the buyers can then collect the debt in full, their profit is the discount for which they purchased the debt. Often, the seller is the Federal Deposit Insurance Company (FDIC) which has taken over a failed bank, is not in the banking business and is willing to sell the debt at a discount so it can obtain income more quickly to replace the money it had paid out to depositors.

In the case before me DEF, Inc. had purchased a mortgage from the FDIC at discount. The mortgage had already been foreclosed and the property taken or sold. However, the amount of the mortgage substantially exceeded the value of the property, and, therefore, the borrowers, real estate developers who had run afoul of the recession, were allegedly liable for the difference between the property value and the amount of the debt, commonly called a deficiency. DEF, Inc. was seeking that amount in what is called a deficiency judgment. As I recall, it was somewhere in the neighborhood of $1 million.

At the hearing before me, it turned out that DEF, Inc. no longer owned the mortgage, having sold it to XYZ Partners on September 21, 1994. The suit had been brought in the name of DEF, Inc. even though it no longer owned the mortgage. No one had ever moved to substitute XYZ partners as the plaintiff. When this was discovered, the defendants moved to dismiss the case claiming the court lacked jurisdiction to hear it. At that point everything stops, and the only matter to be taken up is the motion to dismiss. Any attempt to then substitute XYZ would be improper because if the court did not have jurisdiction over the case, it had no power to grant a motion to substitute plaintiffs.

There were several arguments put forth by XYZ which I found unavailing, and concluded that since DEF, Inc. did not own the mortgage which was the subject of the motion for deficiency judgment, the court had no jurisdiction over the case. Lacking a qualified plaintiff, and therefore, lacking jurisdiction, I dismissed the case.[6]

CONCLUSION

There is certainly variety in civil cases. I have overturned decisions of three different zoning panels for failure to follow their own regulations. These were relatively easy to handle since during my private practice of law one of my major clients was the town in which I lived, and as town attorney I had advised and defended in court various land use agencies of the town.

I have both granted and denied injunctions, and as a judge I have mediated hundreds of cases in a pre-trial attempt to settle them. Some I've settled, and some I haven't. The owner of apartment build-

---

[6] Most of these decisions were not appealed. If my decisions were upheld by the Appellate or Supreme Court, then it would be precedent and have to be followed by other Superior Court judges. If not appealed, the attorney for the losing party in my case could always argue in a similar case that my decision is not binding upon another Superior Court judge hoping, no doubt, that the judge will draw the inference that this is just a flawed decision by that crazy Judge Rittenband.

ings sought an injunction against a food supply company which had received approval to build a warehouse across the road, claiming that it would be unsightly for his tenants. I visited the site personally and found that the apartments were set back far from the road, most of them didn't face in the direction of the warehouse and that there were trees in between the apartments and the warehouse sufficient to prevent the warehouse from being noticed. I denied the injunction.

In a major case involving two supermarket chains, I had to decide the enforceability of a single sentence in a deed to one chain that restricted the seller from permitting the use of her remaining land for the retail sale of groceries and provisions. Only one witness testified in this court case (no jury), the attorneys were highly competent and submitted excellent memoranda of law. In a twenty-one page decision, I found that the restrictive covenant described was unlimited in duration, putting an unreasonable restraint on the use of the seller's remaining property, constituting an unreasonable restraint of trade, and was, therefore unlawful, void and unenforceable.

The case was appealed to the Supreme Court, but just prior to a ruling, the appeal was withdrawn, the parties no doubt having settled or the other chain having found a more suitable site for its supermarket.

Earlier in this chapter I indicated that civil cases are primarily about money as opposed to the liberty or life of the defendant in a criminal case. However, as you can see, people can still be seriously injured or die, and while there may be less publicity concerning the trial or result of a civil case, such civil matters nevertheless have a strong impact upon our society. Visit any courthouse in America today, and you will see the only forum in which some conflicts can finally be resolved. Civil cases remain a major part of our justice system.

The Truths of Justice

Chapter Seventeen

BAD LAWYERING

"Our profession is good if practiced in the spirit of it; it is damnable fraud and iniquity when its true spirit is supplied by a spirit of mischief-making and money-getting."
Daniel Webster

The most striking case of bad lawyering that was presented to me was the case of *Anthony Robinson v. Warden, State Prison.*[1] Robinson had been convicted after a jury trial in New Haven of Assault in the First Degree, three counts of Sexual Assault in the First Degree and one count of Kidnapping and had received a total effective sentence of fifty years in prison. Following the failure of his appeal to the state Supreme Court, he had filed a writ of habeas corpus. Such a writ is directed to the person detaining him (the Warden) commanding him to produce the body of the petitioner, Robinson, because as Robinson claimed, his confinement was illegal in that his right to effective assistance of counsel had been violated by the ineffective assistance of his attorney, Daniel Bennett, before, during and after the trial.

This right to assistance of counsel (the Supreme Court having interpreted it as meaning the *effective* assistance of counsel) is enshrined in the Sixth Amendment to the United States Constitution. The writ of habeas corpus is guaranteed by Article 1 Section 9 of the United States Constitution, and was called by Sir William Blackstone "the great writ of liberty." The matter came before me because the prisoner (petitioner) was confined in a prison located in the Judicial District in which I was sitting.

The essence of the petitioner's claims was that Attorney Bennett had a conflict of interest unknown to either the petitioner or the trial court at time of trial which conflict adversely affected Bennett's repre-

---

[1] The names of the parties and some of the attorneys have been changed to protect their privacy.

sentation of him. He further alleged that Bennett was ineffective by failing to conduct an adequate investigation of the complainant victim and in allowing the petitioner to be present at trial in prison garb.

FACTS OF THE CRIMES

During the evening of March 2-3, 1989, Robinson seriously assaulted Laura Schwartz on the second floor of her apartment in a New Haven housing project. Robinson claimed that he was Schwartz's lover and lived at the apartment with Laura and her eight year old daughter. Schwartz disputed that claiming that Robinson was a homeless man on whom she had taken pity and permitted him to sleep on a couch on the first floor. They had apparently been drinking during the night and had used cocaine. Schwartz claimed that Robinson wanted to have sex with her, that they had never had sex before, and when she rebuffed him, he lost control and in a wild rage had viciously beaten her, and then had proceeded to force her to have sex three different ways.

Robinson claimed that they had consensual sex, which they had been doing for several months, and when he told her he was going to marry one Dorothy Simmons, Schwartz lost control and started to attack him with her fists and anything else she could lay hands on. He defended himself, and in the process struck her several times forcefully. She was petite, and he was approximately six feet tall weighing in excess of two hundred pounds. When the police arrived, they were both completely naked and covered with blood. She was taken to the hospital, and he was taken to jail.

WHY HE RETAINED ATTORNEY BENNETT

Attorney Bennett visited Robinson in the Whalley Avenue Correctional Center, where he was being held pending trial. They were no strangers to each other, and possibly were distantly related. Robinson's father had been killed in an automobile accident the previous year, and Bennett had been appointed as administrator of the father's estate. The only asset was the wrongful death claim against the other driver, a claim which Bennett settled for $150,000.

After Bennett legitimately took a one third fee and funeral and medical expenses were paid, the balance left over was to be divided among Robinson and his three siblings. They were each entitled to $22,739.21. Robinson wanted to hire Attorney John Williams (his real name), an experienced criminal defense attorney with an excellent reputation who had represented Robinson in the past. Robinson had planned to use his inheritance to pay Williams a retainer. Bennett told him that the money had been attached by Laura Schwartz in a civil suit she had instituted against him. This was not true.

In fact, when the application for an attachment of the money had been made by Schwartz, Bennett had told the judge that he, Bennett, had already been paid a retainer by Robinson from those funds, which was also untrue. As was later revealed, Bennett had taken the money for his own use before the crime was even committed. Bennett told Robinson that he was willing to wait for the money (which, of course, he had already taken) when he won the civil case and the attachment would be released. Robinson reluctantly signed a retainer agreement. After Bennett left, Robinson had second thoughts and wrote to Bennett that he had changed his mind because he didn't want to risk his freedom on Bennett's admitted limited experience as a criminal defense attorney. Bennett returned to the jail, calmed Robinson's fears and persuaded him to continue Bennett's representation of him.

In September, 1995 the judge who had been hearing pre-trial motions in the habeas case was assigned to another judicial district. I was chosen to replace him in this matter. My first contact with Bennett was when he responded to a subpoena from the petitioner's attorney, Special Public Defender Denise Ansell (her real name) from New London. The state (warden) was represented by Assistant State's Attorney Alan Carter. Bennett had filed a motion to quash the subpoena.

I denied the motion telling Bennett he could say whatever he wished when under oath, he could even exercise his right not to testify under the Fifth Amendment right against self-incrimination, but he did have to take the witness stand. Note from this that he was very familiar with my feelings about the legitimacy of the subpoena.

Attorney Ansell was seeking copies of Bennett's checks to pin down what happened to the money due Robinson and his three siblings. Bennett told her that he customarily threw out checks that were more than three years old, and he didn't think he had retained any in his files. I ordered him to look again for them and to sign an authorization for Attorney Ansell to obtain the records of his accounts at Shawmut Bank in time for her to take his deposition on November 2, 1995. He did not comply and furnished the authorization only after being urged to do so by Attorney Carter.

By that time it was too late to take the November 2nd deposition. I then ordered Attorney Ansell to subpoena the bank records and directed both Ansell and Carter to issue subpoenas for Bennett's court appearance on December 5th. Although Attorney Ansell's sheriff was never able to find Bennett, Attorney Carter did have the subpoena served by hand to Bennett at his residence at the crack of dawn. Bennett then called Carter who confirmed to him that he had to appear in court on December 5th. Despite all of this Bennett did not appear.

As a result of this blatant ignoring of a court order, I directed that a *capias* be issued which means that a sheriff would take him into custody and bring him to court no later than the following day. To make sure he actually appeared in court, I set bond at $150,000.

Remember, this man was an officer of the court who was flagrantly violating court orders. The sheriff was never able to catch up to him and advised me that he thought Bennett was "ducking the capias". In February, 1996 Bennett's attorney called and said he would have him in court on February 21st. Again, Bennett failed to appear, later claiming an emergency.

Finally, on February 29th, he did appear, took the witness stand and promptly invoked his right against self incrimination under the Fifth Amendment to all questions. His excuse, through his attorney, for not honoring the subpoena was that he had taken the subpoena to his attorney's law firm and left it with another partner "to take care of this, get it quashed." I did not accept this excuse since Bennett already knew of my prior ruling denying an earlier motion to quash a subpoena of him. I found him in contempt and ordered him to pay part of Attorney Ansell's fees.

THE HABEAS TRIAL

The actual trial began on March 3, 1996. It took nineteen days over a period extending to November 15th. With substantial time needed for preparation of the transcripts, final memoranda of law were not submitted to the court until June, 1997. A thirty-two page Memorandum of Decision was issued on September 12, 1997.

Shawmut Bank, at the direction of the Court, did produce Bennett's bank records, and Attorney Ansell hired a forensic certified public accountant to audit the records. Based upon this audit as well as other testimony and records, I found that **Bennett had** "illegally and unethically *misappropriated Petitioner's inheritance . . . at least one to two months before" Robinson allegedly committed the crimes* for which he was arrested on the same day. Although the underlying case was a criminal case, *a habeas trial against the warden holding the prisoner in violation of his constitutional rights is considered a civil trial.* Therefore, the standard of proof is much lower than "beyond a reasonable doubt" which is the standard in a criminal prosecution. The standard in a civil case is "by a preponderance of the evidence", which means that the court (or jury in another type of civil case such as an automobile accident) has only to believe the petitioner's claims are more likely true than not true. In percentages, it must exceed fifty percent. It may be slightly more than fifty percent, but it still must be higher than an even fifty percent.

Further, in a civil case the court *may draw an adverse inference from the witness' invocation of his Fifth Amendment rights against self-incrimination.* In this case, I did just that. I also concluded that Bennett had engaged in an elaborate cover up of his activities. He had gone to the women's prison at Niantic and tricked Robinson's

214

sister into signing a statement that she had received all of her inheritance. Robinson's brother, an admitted alcoholic, was picked up by Bennett in downtown New Haven and taken to Bennett's residence where Bennett plied him with liquor but gave him little to eat. When the brother was drunk, he then signed a similar statement that he had received all of his inheritance. I concluded that Bennett's own pecuniary interest in the Estate funds that belonged to the petitioner was contrary to the petitioner's interest. Placing his own financial interests ahead of the interest of his client is the very heart of a conflict of interest by the attorney. This conflict adversely affected Bennett's performance in representing Robinson in the criminal case. It was plain that:

1. Robinson was denied the right to counsel of his choice, thereby depriving him of the services of Attorney Williams, a much more experienced and capable criminal defense attorney.

2. Bennett, because of his lack of experience, chose to use the defense of "not guilty by reason of insanity" whereas he should have used the consent defense at least as to the counts of Sexual Assault 1. Bennett was unable to make an informed decision because he did not conduct an adequate pre-trial investigation. He did hire a private investigator but told him there was "not much money in this case". Of course, there wasn't because all of Robinson's money had been misappropriated by Bennett.

He paid the investigator $1,000. He didn't use any more of the money he had taken from Robinson. As a result, the investigation was cursory. If the investigation had been done thoroughly, it would have revealed sufficient negative information about Laura Schwartz to undermine her credibility when she denied the sex had been consensual. Her credibility was already questionable. She had denied under oath using alcohol the evening of the crime which was inconsistent with the very high blood alcohol levels determined at the hospital that morning of .251 and .254. There was much more information that could have been produced through a comprehensive investigation, but having taken petitioner's money and spent it all on himself, Bennett didn't have the funds necessary for such an investigation.

3. Further, Bennett was ineffective in that he permitted Robinson to appear before the jury in prison garb. It is the law on both the federal and state levels that a defendant cannot be compelled to stand trial before a jury *dressed in identifiable prison clothes.* To do so was particularly prejudicial to this defendant because he was charged with crimes of violence. The jury is very likely to infer that a defendant in custody is dangerous and potentially violent, thereby giving credence to the charges against him.

It was disputed as to whether the labeling on the back of the petitioner's shirt identifying where he was being held and the shackles he was wearing were ever seen by the jury. However, there was no dispute that Robinson, throughout the trial, was dressed in a white tee shirt and khaki pants. State's Attorney John Corrigan, who prosecuted Robinson, stated in testimony before me that it would be very common to see a person similarly dressed walking across the New Haven Green especially in June when the trial took place. I pointed out to him that "the inside of a courtroom is *not* the New Haven Green, that Robinson was the only one wearing a white tee shirt and khaki pants, that every other male was dressed in a suit, a sports jacket or clearly identifiable summer clothes other than a white tee shirt and khaki pants . . . . In addition, Mr. Robinson was dressed in the white tee shirt and khaki pants *every day* of the trial which lasted from June 4, 1991 through June 28, 1991, a period of approximately three and one-half weeks including fifteen days of actual trial."

The petitioner's expert witness put it very well when he said: "When you have a trial that extends over a significant number of days, and you're wearing the same thing every single day, then it becomes "prison garb" because we assume that our jurors are not fools". Bennett, by failing to object to Robinson's appearance, did not preserve Robinson's right to appeal on this issue. Further compounding Bennett's misconduct, Robinson had requested that Bennett obtain civilian clothes for him, but Bennett refused telling Robinson that all of his money was tied up by Schwartz's civil suit.

I granted the petition for habeas corpus, vacated the convictions and sentences and ordered a new trial. I stayed the order until a final decision is rendered on any appeal taken from my decision. I ordered that the petitioner be released if the state did not retry him within one hundred and twenty days of my decision or if appealed within one hundred and twenty days of an unsuccessful appeal.

An appeal was taken by the State, but my decision was affirmed by the Appellate Court. The State did not choose to appeal it further to the Supreme Court, so the decision is final. Much of the credit should go to attorney Denise Ansell, who represented Robinson. She did a thorough and effective job. Her performance was outstanding. Robinson was released from custody pending a new trial. However, he has become seriously ill and the new trial has been postponed. While Robinson was in prison for fourteen years, the victim, Schwartz, died from a drug overdose. Her unavailability to testify may cause the state additional problems .

It is interesting to note that the appeal did not dispute the merits of my decision. Instead, it was on the basis that I had denied two motions to recuse myself from the trial. A motion to recuse is to request the judge to withdraw from the case because of a conflict of interest or established bias by the judge. The first motion brought by Attorney Carter claimed that I had said, once evidence was introduced concerning the alleged misappropriation of funds, that I had made up my mind that Bennett had taken the money. He cited a page of the transcript. What he failed to cite was the next page on which I said that "the evidence introduced so far doesn't look good for Attorney Bennett, but I haven't made up my mind. I would like to hear what Attorney Bennett's response is. I want to hear all the evidence in this case before I come to any final conclusion."

In the judicial district where I was conducting the trial, it was practice to submit the denial of a motion to recuse to another judge. That was done, and that judge upheld my decision.

The second motion to recuse came toward the end of the trial. In January, 1996 after evidence was produced regarding the missing money and Bennett had openly defied court orders to appear, I referred a summary of the evidence to the Chief State's Attorney to investigate for possible criminal action and to the Statewide Grievance Committee because of what appeared to be violations of the Code of Ethics. As a Superior Court Judge, I had a duty to do so, and neither party objected to the referrals.

The Grievance Committee did take action, and eventually Bennett was suspended from the practice of law by a judge in New Haven for the actions outlined in the habeas case. As for the Chief State's Attorneys office, I heard nothing for almost a year. Around October I received a letter from an assistant chief state's attorney advising me that her office did not believe there was sufficient evidence to apply for an arrest warrant, and she invited me to call her if I had any questions. Curious as to whether she had at least reviewed the audit of Bennett's check and the checks themselves, I called her.

Her response was that all of this information was confidential and could not be released even to the judge who had referred the matter. I told her I didn't agree with that position, and, perhaps, I sounded a little frustrated at being given no information when her letter had invited me to call her if I had any questions. Later, by voice mail I apologized if I had come on too strong, and dropped the matter. At the next court date, Attorney Carter moved to recuse me on the basis that I had told her I was upset because her office was not applying for a warrant. I informed him that what he was telling me was hearsay, and more importantly it was untrue. I told him that I did not protest the decision not to apply for a warrant. I did protest her refusal to give me any information. He, nonetheless, continued to claim that this showed my bias against Bennett. I denied the motion, and my decision was upheld by another judge and subsequently by the Appellate Court.

Also of note, at the beginning of the trial, Attorney Ansell had urged me to disqualify Assistant State's Attorney Carter. She claimed that there was a conflict of interest between the state's attorney's office defending Bennett's conduct on the one hand, and at the same time investigating him for possible criminal prosecution. I told Attorney Ansell that I did not feel I had the authority to disqualify Attorney Carter because that would leave the state with no representation. I also said that this was not Washington, D.C., and I had no authority to appoint a special prosecutor. I told Attorney Carter to take this issue up with his superiors, and I would leave it up to them to make a decision as to whether there was a conflict of interest.

In light of the close relationship with the assistant chief state's attorney who was investigating as to whether to prosecute Bennett and Attorney Carter's office which was defending Bennett's actions (evidenced by her prompt call to Attorney Carter to report the "contents" of our conversation), Attorney Ansell may have had a point, and, perhaps, I should have sought the intervention of the Attorney General whose office handles civil matters for the state and has no relationship to the state's attorney's office that prosecutes criminal defendants. As it turned out, the habeas decision has been upheld, and despite any possible impediments, justice was done.

This was the second case where I was presented with the issue of recusal. It was presented to me during a civil trial in which the plaintiffs were seeking to recover attorney's fees from a contractor they had represented against a major construction company that had refused to pay fees for work done on the construction of the Yale Molecular Medicine building. The plaintiffs' client, (the contractor I mentioned who was actually a subcontractor to the major construction company), had eventually settled its claim on its own. In reading the settlement agreement, I learned that certain moneys due the client were to be held in escrow to make sure that other subcontractors hired by the plaintiffs' client were paid. Included was a subcontractor which I had represented as an attorney.

I brought this to the attention of the defendant in the case before me. I informed him that I used to represent this company, but I had no knowledge of its dispute with the defendant. I also told him that the owner of the company was a friend of mine, and that I customarily had breakfast with him every Saturday or every other Saturday. However, I had not discussed this case with him and had no intention of doing so. I didn't feel it was necessary for me to recuse myself because the involvement of my former client was a peripheral matter that had nothing to do with the issues in this case. I then asked him if he wanted me to recuse myself.

The defendant's attorney, after conferring with his client said no, that they believed I would be fair. Following thirty days of actual trial, I issued an eighty two page decision finding for the plaintiff on all counts. With attorneys fees and interest as well as punitive damages, the judgment came to well over $300,000. Immediately, the defendant moved to set aside the verdict on the basis of the "bias of the trial judge". When defense counsel appeared in court, I said to him: "Counsel, you declined to make a motion to recuse me during the trial. What has changed?" His reply was priceless: "Well, your honor, the only explanation for your draconian decision has to be your bias toward my client." That case was appealed, but my decision was upheld by the Appellate Court.

Following the subsequent motions to recuse in the habeas case, I commented to another judge:

"Remember, Johnny Cochran's famous phrase? 'If it doesn't fit , you must acquit.' Well, I have a new one for you. If you think you're going to lose, move to recuse!"

There are, of course, other instances of bad lawyering although not as dramatic as the habeas case of Robinson v. Warden. There is the case of a tax attorney who knew little about criminal law and who initially represented the defendant in the murder case described in the chapter entitled *"Murder in the Connecticut Woods."* The defendant's conviction was overturned because the attorney had pleaded his client guilty without considering the defense of "extreme emotional disturbance".

There is the case of the wife's attorney in the chapter entitled *"Family"* who neglected to determine the value of the husband's pension which, without intervention by the court, would have resulted in the wife receiving less than that to which she was entitled. There is the attorney described in *"Civil"* who was willing to take $10,000 in settlement of a minor accident claim. The insurance company had offered $8,500 which was rejected. At trial, the attorney was greedy and asked the jury for a verdict of over $200,000. It responded by coming in with a verdict of approximately $1,300; the amount of the plaintiff's medical bills.

There are other instances as well. However, these attorneys are in a very small minority. Then there are attorneys who steal client's money. They are not ineffective, rather, they are dishonest. It is still bad lawyering. These are the ones that produce the headlines. Nonetheless, the overwhelming majority of attorneys take their oaths very seriously. They stay abreast of the law, they work hard, and they give effective representation to their clients. They are vigilant in protecting their clients' rights. Notwithstanding a few bad lawyers, it is an ethical and honest profession that remains crucial to our justice system. The honest and effective attorneys should be admired for their professionalism, their integrity, their knowledge, their creativity, their skills and for their dedicated work on behalf of their clients.

Chapter Eighteen

SENTENCING

"The mass of men lead lives of quiet desperation."
Henry David Thoreau

Nearly 25 percent of respondents to a 1996 Gallup poll of adults in the workplace indicated that they were "generally at least somewhat angry at work." Not surprisingly, the actions of supervisors or managers was cited as the most common cause of workplace anger.

There are those who have been the victims of corporate downsizing in recent years and become unemployed. When they finally are rehired, it may be at a different, less satisfying job for less pay. Corporate downsizing has destroyed the myth that working hard and being loyal to the company means that you will continue to have a safe job until retirement age. Workers who believe that myth overlook the creed of company presidents: a more profitable bottom line.

Working at an unsatisfactory job to get through the day and earn the necessary paycheck is the frustration that Thoreau had in mind when he wrote of lives of quiet desperation. Apparently that desperation is no longer so quiet as evidenced by the number of recent killings in the workplace by disgruntled employees. The killings in Honolulu at Xerox, the killings at a shipyard in Seattle, the day trader in Atlanta who lost a lot of money in the stock market and returned to shoot up the office where he traded come to mind. Closer to home, a few years ago, a terminated employee came back to the headquarters of the Connecticut Lottery and killed the director and several other employees. These are just a few recent examples of what has caused violent attacks to become the second most common cause of serious injury and death in the workplace.

Of course, violence extends far beyond the workplace. The killings in high schools in this country by other students, notably Columbine High School in Colorado, have become rampant in the last few years. This extremely violent society is unique to the United States. In a journal called "*The Responsive Community*", its authors, Franklin Zimring and Gordon Hawkins, point out that ". . . the rate of violent death from assault in the United States is from 4 to 18 times as high as in other G7 nations . . . ." They don't blame it all on guns. "Americans are also more likely to kill people with knives than citizens of comparable countries . . . . There is something in our culture that makes us much more likely to consider it legitimate as part of getting into a fight to use means that threaten deadly results."

The *Minneapolis Star Tribune*, in an editorial, tried to explain some causes of violence. "Surely American culture has become more vulgar: the language, the messages on T-shirts, the loutish talk shows, the crude movies and music, the rowdy audiences at sporting events, the road rage, the gun worship, the gruesome video games, the sex-obsessed television sitcoms, the general meanness that seems to escalate to domestic abuse and to verbal and physical assault."

By some measurements, the crime rate has gone down, but that should not lead to complacency. According to Jack Maple, a former Deputy Commissioner of the New York Police Department, violent crime in America is still 3.5 times higher than it was in 1961. He points out that "Twenty or thirty years ago, criminals used Saturday night specials or revolvers. Now, with automatic and semiautomatics, not only is the bullet more powerful but the round capacity is much greater. The shooter can change magazines much more quickly than he can reload a revolver. So, he lets more rounds go and more people are killed."

I do not pretend to be an expert on the causes of violent crime although the reasons I have given, mostly from experts, do seem to make sense. However, as a judge who is about to impose a sentence on someone who has committed a violent crime, I naturally take into account the cause of the crime. It is certainly not the overriding factor, but it is relevant and must be considered on a case by case basis.

Abraham Lincoln said that the function of government is to do for the people those things that the people cannot do for themselves. The major political parties seem to agree on this. The disagreement appears to be different interpretations as to what the people can and cannot do for themselves. However, there is no dispute that it is up to the government to protect its citizens from crime and violence. In today's modern society the people are no more equipped to protect themselves from crime and violence than they are, individually, to protect themselves from foreign aggression against their country.

The portion of government that is designed to protect our citizens from crime and violence is the criminal justice system. Although as a judge, I try to be a zealous protector of a defendant's constitutional rights, once the defendant is convicted, ***my primary purpose as a sentencing judge is to protect the public from crime and violence, with emphasis on the word "violence".*** Another purpose of imposing severe penalties for crimes of violence is to send a message to those of the public who tend toward violence that such conduct will not be tolerated. Hopefully stiff sentences will act as a deterrent.[1] Compassion is also appropriate in certain cases as it was in the Kathy Gerardi case mentioned in the chapter entitled "***Stalking and the Strange Case of Kathy Gerardi.***"

BOND: Of first concern are the decisions that must be made in setting bond for those people who have been arrested for a violent crime. The two main factors a judge should take into consideration in determining what bond (bail) should be set are the danger to society if the defendant is released and the likelihood he/she will flee the jurisdiction (state) if released.

I am forever mindful of an instance several years ago in which a man had threatened to kill his wife and children. A high bond was set, and the man was incarcerated pending trial. Through his attorney, he moved to have the amount of his bond reduced. For some reason, the judge agreed to reduce the bond to an amount that he could post. Shortly after he posted, he made good on his threat, killing his wife and children that same night. I never want to be responsible for that result.

As noted in the chapter on domestic violence, when a man who had stalked and tried to kill his ex-girlfriend was presented before me, I set bond at $2 million. I set a very high bond on a man who had broken into his estranged wife's apartment and beaten her male companion

---

[1] In my own experience, sending violators of domestic violence protective orders to jail seemed to lessen further incidents of domestic violence and/or violation of protective orders.

within an inch of his life and later threatened a police officer.

In another case, a man used a shotgun to shoot a woman in her buttocks and her back. Fortunately, the wounds were not fatal. The bail commissioner recommended a bond of $50,000. The prosecutor agreed. I tripled it to $150,000. When the man protested, saying that he could never raise the ten percent required by a bondsman, I told him: "Sir, that's exactly why I raised it to $150,000. I don't want you to get out. You're too much of a danger to society."

A woman allegedly killed her newborn baby and stuffed the fetus in the trashcan. I didn't necessarily think she would do it again (she wasn't pregnant and she was unlikely to kill anyone else), but she initially faced the death penalty for what she allegedly did and was, to my way of thinking, a flight risk. I set bond at $1 million.

A couple accused of killing an individual in their apartment for the thrill of it ("This was a better high than I get from cocaine") appeared before me. I set bond at $1 million.

A local attorney, now deceased, whom I respected very much and who was highly competent and enjoyed an excellent reputation, used to say that the bonds I set were too high. Part of his reasoning was practical. If the defendant somehow raised sufficient money to be released, he did not have money to hire a private attorney. The attorney was not talking about himself. He had plenty of business and didn't need more clients. His point was well taken, but I still had to consider the defendant's danger to society.

SENTENCING: In federal court there are sentencing guidelines which judges are supposed to follow, although if they see good cause, they can impose less time or more time in a particular case. The purpose of these guidelines is to make sentencing more equal. The idea is to prevent one judge from imposing a very harsh sentence and another judge from imposing a much lighter sentence for the same type of crime, although each judge has a certain amount of leeway.

Some states permit the judges to impose a *range of years* as a sentence, such as twenty-five to life or fifteen to twenty-five and then leave it up to the parole board to release the prisoner at what it considers the appropriate time depending upon the circumstances of the crime and the inmate's record while in prison. Connecticut does not follow these procedures. Judges have more discretion.

Most crimes are designated by categories, i.e., Felonies are class A, B, C or D. A D felony carries a maximum of five years, such as Burglary 3rd degree. Burglary 2nd degree is a C felony carrying a maximum of ten years. Burglary 1st Degree is a class B felony carrying a maximum sentence of twenty years. There are certain mandatory minimums, such as nine months may not be suspended if the crime is Sexual Assault in the 2nd degree. Sale of cocaine *by a non drug dependent person is a mandatory minimum of five years*, presumably on the theory that a non drug dependent person is doing it just for the money whereas someone who is a drug addict is doing it to obtain more drugs to feed his addiction. Sentences can be imposed either concurrently or consecutively.

With this background, recognizing that taking away someone's liberty is an awesome responsibility, but keeping in mind that the main goal is to protect society, here are some sentences I have imposed:

1. David Copas, as described in the chapter, *"Murder in the Connecticut Woods"*, had, at age twenty-five, brutally murdered a sixteen year old girl by stabbing her at least twenty-two times and then, to finish the job bashing her in the head with a huge rock. After reviewing the pre-sentence investigation report, I saw no hope of rehabilitation and believed that he would continue to be a danger to society if released. I sentenced him to life in prison (which is sixty years in Connecticut), and under present statutes he is not eligible for parole. In the event the statute is changed, I put on the record my feelings that he should never be released because parole boards generally take into account the comments of the sentencing judge.

2. Kerwin Sands, convicted of two separate counts of sexual assault in the first degree, as described in the chapter entitled *"Sexual Assault and Pedophiles"*, was sentenced to forty years, execution suspended after twenty-four years. The sentence would have been much higher except that the victims did not want to testify.

3. A sixteen year old boy had been dating the daughter of a police officer. Incredibly, he had written to the father requesting permission to

use condoms. This resulted, as you might imagine, in the father forbidding the boy to have any contact with his daughter. The boy responded with flyers distributed at the school urging violent harm to the father. He then obtained a rifle from a friend in Hartford and stored it in a friend's house in the town in which he, the father and the daughter lived. I was troubled by this because of the boy's age and his apparent psychological problems. However, I could not overlook the danger to the girl's father. I sentenced the boy to the maximum of three years and ordered psychological counseling while he was in jail and after his release.

4. A man in his early twenties had a fetish for women's underwear, underwear that was being used. He did not want to buy underwear at the store because it would be new, and he did not want underwear from the female members of his family. This resulted in his breaking into the house across the street and stealing a young woman's underwear. His parents had tried everything. They had sent him to several inpatient facilities, one as far away as New Mexico, all to no avail. There was no medication that would control this addiction, although supposedly research was being done to find the proper medication.

What disturbed me was his statement to the probation officer who was conducting the pre-sentence investigation that if anyone tried to stop him while he was stealing the underwear, he would use physical force if necessary against that person. I admired his candor, but in view of this attitude, he was an assault waiting to happen. I could not release him because he was by his own admission too dangerous.

I sentenced him to five years suspended after serving three years and five years of probation. Judges in Connecticut cannot change a sentence they impose that is in excess of three years. I wanted to keep control of this case. I informed his attorney that if he could produce satisfactory evidence that a cure or a controlling drug had become available, I would consider modifying his sentence. This did not occur. I felt sorry for the defendant and his parents because the young man was afflicted with a disease not of his own making for which there was neither control nor cure. However, in keeping with my duty to protect society, I felt had no choice but to send him to prison.

5. A married couple had robbed four different convenience stores. They used a gun even though they claimed it was not loaded. They said that they were doing it to get the money to buy drugs. The husband was the principal perpetrator. Although I sympathized with their alleged addiction, these crimes of violence were too serious for any leniency. The husband was sentenced to ten years and the wife to eight years.

6. A student at the University of Connecticut ("A") had become involved in an argument with another student ("B") at a Subway Sandwich Shop. The two had been physically separated by bystanders but not before B had pushed A. Now A sought revenge. He and his brother and another student burst into B's dormitory room and hit him with a hammer, a bottle containing a soft drink as well as their fists. Two other students had accompanied them, but had stayed outside the room. Fortunately, B did not suffer any permanent injury. Although none of the students had a prior record, I considered this premeditated act of violence to be very serious. I sentenced the three who had entered the room each to three years in prison.

7. A mid-level employee of an insurance company had become addicted to heroin. Upon returning home from work one night he approached a local gang from whom he had been buying drugs, seeking more heroin. They refused because they claimed that he still owed them money. They roughed him up a little and warned him not to return without the money. Later, however, his addiction got the better of him, and he returned for more heroin but without any money. This infuriated members of the gang, and they started to assault him.

One of them hit him over the head with a tire iron causing him serious and permanent injury. The members of the gang that were present were all arrested. Because the state had some problems with proof such as the victim having a difficult time positively identifying which assailant had hit him with the tire iron, the assistant state's attorney had worked out a plea bargain arrangement with all of the defendants calling for a sentence of ten years suspended after five years. By some means, through subsequent admissions or through pre-sentence investigations, it became clear that Defendant J was the one who had used the tire iron.

The Truths of Justice

Therefore I rejected the plea agreement as to Mr. J. I told the defendant's attorney and the prosecutor that in view of the circumstances, the sentence was too light. I suggested the attorney convey to his client that he could withdraw his agreement to plead guilty and go to trial or he could agree to a sentence of ten years suspended after eight years. I informed the attorney that if Mr. J. was convicted at trial of assault in the first degree, he would be facing a sentence of at least twenty years. Mr. J. then accepted a sentence of ten years suspended after eight years.

Even though he knew that I was the one who had demanded the sentence of eight years to serve, Mr. J., shortly after arriving at prison, wrote to me asking me to modify his sentence and give him less time. I denied the motion advising him that I was prohibited from modifying a sentence in excess of three years. I wouldn't have modified it even if I did have the power to do so. I did not decide on eight years lightly. I suggested that he might wish to apply to the Sentence Review Panel of three judges. If he did, he was unsuccessful.

8. A nineteen-year-old young man had been convicted of a motor vehicle violation. He was angry about his conviction, and surprisingly he called the police station seeking to talk with the officer who had arrested him. When he was informed that officer was not on duty, the young man proceeded to leaving a threatening message that "no one pushes me around. He better watch out. I'll get him for this." Incredibly, he left his name with the officer to whom he spoke.

He was later stopped by the police and a sawed off shotgun was found in the back seat of his car. His attorney plea bargained for a sentence of three years. When he appeared before me, he begged: "Please don't send me to jail. I won't do it again. I promise I'll be good". He sounded like a little boy who was about to be punished for dipping into the cookie jar. I informed him that threats of violence against police officers could not go unpunished, and that I could not give him a suspended sentence because despite what he said, I could not take a chance with the police officer's life. I sentenced him to three years.

9. Five young men from Massachusetts, aged between eighteen and twenty-two years old, were on the University of Connecticut campus on a Saturday night looking for some fun. They were not U-Conn students, but they were apparently trying to find a party they could attend. Whether there was an admission fee or they needed money for something else, they were short of funds.

They noticed a man seated near the soda machine at the University Co-op store, which, at that hour was closed. They approached him and demanded money. When he replied that he didn't have any, they beat him, and two of them kicked him while he was on the cement floor of the small plaza that extended from the building. The victim was handicapped although apparently the defendants were unaware of this. He sustained serious but not life threatening or permanent injury. The perpetrators (defendants) were caught and arrested by the campus police.

They eventually all pleaded guilty to the robbery. Some, such as the ones who did the kicking, were more involved than the others. This was a classic case of unprovoked and cowardly violence. Even though they had no prior record or the records were minor, I sentenced the two who had done the kicking to five years in prison and the other three to sentences ranging from two years to four years.

10. Perhaps the most striking example of a violent crime other than murder is the case of Ronald Chandler. Chandler had had an on again, off again relationship with his wife. They had been separated for approximately six weeks when Chandler decided to confirm his suspicion that his estranged wife was having sexual relations with another man, although apparently he saw no problem with his own extra-marital relationships.

He suspected a close friend of his of being his wife's paramour. On a Friday night about midnight or shortly thereafter, he drove to the apartment complex where his friend lived and found his wife's car parked in the parking lot. He said later that all he wanted to do was confirm his suspicions, and the car parked there late at night would normally have confirmed what he suspected. However, not satisfied with this knowledge, he proceeded to the front door of his "friend's" apartment. Hearing no sound from inside he probably realized that his wife was not attending a party with other people present. Nonetheless, determined to gain further knowledge (they could just be reading the comics over a cup of coffee) he banged on the door.

There was no response, so he kicked the door in and rushed into the bedroom where he found his wife and "friend" in bed together. Here, the stories differed. Chandler claimed that he caught them in the nude in the middle of sexual intercourse. Mrs. Chandler claimed that they were each dressed in sleep wear and were in fact sleeping. Of course, if Chandler's objective had been only to confirm his suspicion that they were having an affair, at that point he had accomplished his goal.

Instead of leaving, he became enraged, pulled his wife from the bed and threw her against the wall, jumped on his friend, picked up a trophy that was on the night table and began to hit him on the head with it. The trophy struck the victim's eyes. The chief medical examiner described the injuries as bilateral orbital fractures as well as orbital rim fractures which could only be produced by a blunt instrument used with a great deal of energy. "They represent a potential significant loss of function of the eyes. Similar degrees of energy applied to other parts of the head have the potential to produce loss of brain function, either temporary or permanent. In some cases, energy of this magnitude applied to the head could produce death." The victim stated to the probation officer who conducted the pre-sentence investigation that he now has "a permanent steel plate, wires and screws which are holding his left eye in place." He said that his "night vision is still affected, and his eye does not look the same as before the assault".

The victim, lying on the floor, begged Chandler to stop. The victim managed to get up and run out the opening created by opening the sliding doors, but fell on the ground. With the neighbors watching, Chandler continued to kick him and yelled that if had a gun he would kill both of them. Someone had called 911, so Chandler, apparently realizing the police were on the way, fled the scene in his pick up truck. It was later revealed that when he arrived earlier, he disabled his wife's car.

Chandler was interviewed by two psychiatrists from the Institute for Living. The one for the state found no evidence of a major mental illness, that his rage was not the product of a mental disease or defect, and Chandler was not in a state of mental dissociation. The psychiatrist

for the defendant found that Chandler was in a state of "mental dissociation" at the time of the attack. "The mental dissociation constituted
a partial fugue state with a lack of awareness or understanding for his
situation and a substantial impairment of his controls, resulting in
explosive acting out that would be tantamount to a trance state. The
mental dissociation occurred in the psychological context of a man
with underlying emotional problems of a depressive nature. These
problems are long term and stem from a dysfunctional family setting
and emotional trauma from a mentally ill mother which left him psy-
chologically vulnerable." (These are the same two psychiatrists who
testified three months later in the murder trial of State v. Copas
described elsewhere in this book. The state's psychiatrist again testified
for the state, and the defendant's psychiatrist testified for the defendant
in the murder case.)

An insanity defense was not offered in this assault case. The defendant had a minor record. After considerable negotiations, a plea bargain was struck. The defendant would plead guilty. The agreed sentence would be fifteen years suspended after twelve years. This was the
cap or maximum sentence under the agreement, and at the time of
sentencing, the defendant had a right to argue for a lesser sentence.

I reviewed the pre-sentence investigation report, letters from the
victims and letters in support of the character of the defendant. I was
not impressed with the claim of mental and emotional problems of
the defendant. It appeared to me that this was another circumstance
of the defendant being portrayed as a "victim" whereas the real victims were the two people who had been brutally attacked. However,
I maintained an open mind and looked forward to the arguments
put forth by the parties.

I was dismayed by the remarks of the defendant's attorney and an
attorney who spoke on the defendant's behalf. An attorney whom I
knew and respected said that he had known the defendant for a long
time, that this was out of character for him, and he concluded with the
comment that we all have a genie in our bottle, and sometimes the
genie erupts and blasts out of the bottle, and that's what happened with
the defendant. The defendant's attorney concentrated on what led to

the outburst, the defendant finding his wife in bed with another man, his "best friend", that what the defendant did was natural in response. The defense attorney concluded with: "I challenge any man in this courtroom not to have done what the defendant did under the same circumstances."

I didn't buy any of it. I pointed out to the attorney that this couple was separated and about to get a divorce, and it's not as if the defendant, shocked to learn that he had been betrayed for the first time by a wife to whom he thought he was happily married, came home from work and found the couple together in his marital bed.

I sentenced the defendant to the agreed upon maximum of fifteen years suspended after twelve years. I told the defendant he had committed a vicious, premeditated crime, and that he was lucky that his attorney had worked out an agreement for a cap of fifteen years suspended after twelve years. Otherwise, I would have sentenced him to a minimum of eighteen years suspended after fifteen years and possibly even more.

11. Finally, the case of State v. Sam Keyes. Mr. Keyes had pleaded guilty to three counts of burglary in the third degree and had admitted to a violation of probation under which his three year sentence was suspended. He was thus facing a maximum sentence of eighteen years. There was no agreement on sentencing. The state and the defendant were free to argue for whatever sentence they believed appropriate.

Both the state's attorney and the public defender were highly competent and very eloquent. The state recommended ten years to serve with no portion of the sentence being suspended. The prosecutor's comment was that probation will never benefit this young man.

The defendant's attorney conceded that the pre-sentence investigation was one of the most discouraging that he had ever read. He also conceded that Keyes had a bad prior record starting with three counts of burglary and one of possession of hallucinogenic when he was sixteen years of age. He was now twenty-two years old. Defense counsel then went into the defendant's personal background. He'd been in twelve different schools and been beaten and abused by three alcoholic stepfathers. His parents were divorced when he was ten years old, his mother was an alcoholic and his own father, also an alcoholic, had abused him. The mother then married three additional times prior to the defendant's fourteenth birthday, moved to three or four different states and put him in twelve different schools. He noted that the report said that "counseling had little effect", and then stated sarcastically that it was "shocking to find out that, after 14 years of being beaten by five or six alcoholic parents and stepfathers that a slight bit of counseling would have little effect." The counseling was with the local Youth Service Bureau for approximately one year.

According to defense counsel, he had never had any psychiatric treatment or substance abuse counseling and had been incarcerated from age sixteen to the present. The attorney proposed a ten year sentence totally suspended and that his probation be subject to the rules of the Alternative Incarceration Center. I told him that I could not give him a totally suspended sentence. "I sympathize with what happened here, but, I as a judge, have a responsibility to the community . . . . I'm concerned about burglary. Fortunately, in these instances no one else was present, but what I fear is a future situation where some home-owner is there and that person ends up getting killed." I ended up sentencing the defendant to a total of ten years suspended after seven years with five years of probation. The conditions of probation were restitution within the first two and a half years of probation and that he submit to such psychiatric, substance abuse, alcohol abuse evaluation, assessment, treatment and counseling, in-patient or out-patient as may be directed by the Office of Adult Probation.

I stated to the prosecutor that "I don't agree that probation is totally lost on this defendant. I want to make one more attempt to see, even though it's only three years we're holding over him, to see if something can be done." I wish I could say that this case had a happy ending. The next time I saw Mr. Keyes was when he testified eight or nine months later in a jury trial I was conducting. A defendant was charged with escape from a half-way house. He claimed that he accidentally violated one of the rules and that he feared going back to prison because he was afraid of Mr. Keyes. He claimed that Keyes was the head of a gang in prison, and he had once been beaten by other inmates upon Mr.

The Truths of Justice

Keyes' orders. I warned Keyes of his Fifth Amendment right not to testify, but he testified anyway.

He denied that he was either a member or the head of a gang. However, he said that he was in a position in which he demanded and received respect. If someone disrespected him, he would inform other prisoners of that and what they did or didn't do was up to them. He never ordered anyone to do anything. I would not have been surprised if the theme from the Godfather suddenly started to play throughout the courtroom as he testified.

I later learned from another judge that Keyes had appealed the sentence I gave him to the Sentence Review Panel and was turned down. Apparently, another judge had given him an additional sentence for another crime subsequent to the sentence I had given him. Hopefully, he won't get into more trouble and will eventually get the treatment and counseling he needs. He's still a young man, and hope does spring eternal, but whether treatment will be effective after so many years in prison for multiple offenses is questionable. By the way, the defendant on trial for escape was convicted.

I'm generally confident that the sentences I've imposed have been fair and reasonable, and as Harry Truman said, "make your decision and never look back." There are, however, three decisions that I have made in sentencing which continue to give me pause. The first of the three was a case of Robbery in the Second Degree.

A young man had waited in the parking lot of a Kentucky Fried Chicken until closing time. When the manager got into his car with the day's proceeds, the defendant approached him, demanded the money and punched him when he initially refused. The defendant did not have a weapon. He then ran to his accomplice who was waiting in a car, and they drove away. This was certainly a serious crime of violence and normally would have meant jail time. The prosecutor urged incarceration. The victim had, surprisingly, sent a letter which did not ask for the defendant to be imprisoned.

What made me pause on this one was the pre-sentence investigation report. The young man had totally turned his life around during the eighteen months between arrest and sentencing. Why there was such a long delay I don't recall, but whatever the reason, it served the defendant well. He had a very minor record prior to this incident and had hardly been an outstanding citizen. However, he had gone to counseling and received treatment for substance abuse. He was now clean of illegal drugs and alcohol. He had gone back to school and was doing well. He had been employed part time from shortly after his arrest to the present. He was very active in his church. He volunteered substantial amounts of time there and worked hard in other charitable endeavors.

It was a glowing report. He had completely rehabilitated himself and had become a contributing member of society. My concern was that if I sent him to prison where he would be in with hardened criminals, there was a good chance that the rehabilitation he had achieved would be lost and that he would commit crimes again upon his release. I gave him a suspended sentence with five years probation and set conditions on the probation that would result in his being closely monitored to prevent him from straying from his path of rehabilitation. It has been several years since this occurred, and I believe he has stayed out of trouble.

The second case involved assault with a motor vehicle. The defendant was driving while intoxicated and hit another car at an intersection causing relatively minor injuries to the other driver. As indicated in the chapter *"You Ruined My Life"*, I usually imposed a three year sentence for assault with a motor vehicle. What changed my mind in this particular case was that the driver, a mother of three young children, was the primary caregiver for three children. The husband worked during the day, there was neither sufficient money for babysitters with experience nor relatives nearby. To put the defendant in jail would devastate these children I reasoned.

The victim, through her attorney, appeared to have made only a perfunctory objection to a suspended sentence. The defendant was in a wheelchair apparently having suffered some temporary injuries of her own. I wondered at the time whether her visible emotional distress was real. Her husband stood behind the wheelchair massaging her neck and shoulders. I almost told him to stop because I had the feeling that the massaging was being done just for show. I said nothing because I didn't want to incite an emotional outburst if the massaging was necessary. I knew she would lose her license so I wasn't too worried about her driving again.

I gave her a suspended sentence, put her on probation with some very strict conditions and warned her that any violation could land her in jail, and next time she would not receive any kind of break. Later, I wondered if I had been had. I was especially annoyed when she called the clerk's office requesting that a condition of probation be eliminated. I told the clerk to tell her "absolutely not", and if she still wanted a modification, she should contact her attorney and file a formal written motion and we would then schedule a hearing on it. In retrospect, I wish, at the very least I had sentenced her to five days to serve to commence on a Friday morning so that the husband would have to take off from work only three days. That way she would have at least gotten a taste of jail which would have made her think twice before drinking and driving. This decision still bothers me.

The third situation occurred within two weeks of my first day on the bench. The defendant, Steven Cannon, was seventeen years old. He had been charged with sexual assault in the form of sexual touching of three young girls. This had occurred earlier that summer in a field where three girls between five and nine years old had been playing. Steven wandered over there and apparently touched them on their private parts. He denied it, but was being held on $15,000 bond.

His newly appointed special public defender (a *special* public defender takes the place of a regular public defender who either has a conflict or is overburdened with other cases. The special P.D. is paid on a per diem basis) had moved to have him released without bond. I was informed that because he was an alleged pedophile, other prisoners would beat him up despite the efforts of the guards and the sheriffs to prevent it. I ordered the sheriffs to lock him up downstairs away from the other prisoners at least while he was awaiting his court appearance.

The problem was that the defendant was mentally retarded. I did not feel that I could let him out because of the danger he posed to the community. At the same time, I didn't want him to be housed with the other prisoners because of fear for his safety. I asked the attorneys, the

Alternative Incarceration Center representative, probation and the bail commissioner for suggestions. No one had a satisfactory solution. I ordered a representative of the State Department of Mental Retardation to be present at the next hearing, which I scheduled for the following Monday. This was on a Friday. The representative showed up and informed me that the DMR did not handle sex offenders. I suggested several state hospitals, but none of them were suitable for one reason or another. The mother and stepfather were of no help. They could barely subsist themselves. I had ordered these various officials to do some research in the interim and come up with suggestions. No one had an answer. Frustrated, I said: "Do you mean to tell me that this is the first time this situation has come up anywhere in the state?"

Apparently it was. Later the statewide directors of the Alternative Incarceration Program had a special meeting to discuss this case. I was present. Nobody had ever encountered this specific situation before, and they really had no meaningful suggestions as to how to deal with it. But, back to Monday morning where he was presented before me following the weekend. I had thought about it, and had fashioned my own solution.

I ordered that he be released on the following conditions: that he is under a curfew from 9:00 p.m. to 8:00 a.m., and that he was never to go anywhere unless accompanied by an adult, preferably his mother or stepfather. His mother was to present him to the Alternative Incarceration Center by 9:00 a.m. He was to remain there subject to their rules, regulations and activities until closing time at 9:00 p.m. On the weekends when the AIC was not open he and his mother were to call into the AIC every hour to make sure he was not on his own. It was not a perfect solution, but it was the best I could do. I was transferred to another court before his case came up again, but it's my understanding that he did not cause any trouble under the conditions I had ordered.

I do not pretend to be a Solomon. You may disagree with some of my decisions, and you may be right, but you really have to be there to understand all the factors that go into making a decision on sentencing. And make a decision you must. Making decisions promptly and fairly is one of the primary duties of any judge.

Chapter Nineteen

IS REHABILITATION POSSIBLE?

What do we do about the huge prison population who got there because of their addiction to drugs or alcohol, because they are sexual offenders, because they are angry people who just "lost it" or because they have mental problems? The current system is to give them some sort of treatment while in prison and, then, follow up with either out-patient or in-patient treatment while they are on probation. How effective has this been? Has it reduced the rate of recidivism? Has society been made safer?

The Department of Corrections oversees prisoners while they are incarcerated and while they are on parole, and the Judicial Branch oversees those on probation after they are paroled. It should be noted that the Judicial Branch is responsible also for those offenders who do not go to jail but rather receive a suspended sentence and go directly to probation. My experience as a judge on the firing line every day is that these programs are often effective, but are not as effective as they could be.

Alcoholics who have been through programs still drink and drive, drug addicts have not kicked their habits and still commit crimes to obtain more drugs, and sexual offenders, despite treatment, strike again. Some progress has certainly been made, but more needs to be done if we are to stop people from offending again. In some cases, it is probably hopeless. I refer you to the case described in the chapter *"Lying Under Oath"* in which a defendant while on probation had been sent to three different in-patient drug treatment centers and had failed at all of them all. These centers are usually non profit and **are not lock down facilities**. Thus, the patient can walk out at any time and can commit additional crimes before he is caught and arrested for those and for violation of probation.

There has to be a better way. I recommend the following:

The Truths of Justice

1.   Put more emphasis on treatment while the offender is in prison. You have, if you'll pardon the expression, a captive patient who is subject to the strict rules of the prison. From July 1, 1998, to June 30, 1999, the budget for the Department of Corrections was approximately four and a half million dollars ($4.5 million) for addiction services. I am certainly not one who says throw money at the problem. However, because these problems are so dangerous to our society, the addiction services budget for the Department of Corrections should be increased.

2.   The prison system should be revamped. In each prison there should be a separate unit for the following:[1]

a.   Alcoholics.

b.   Drug addicts including those addicted to cocaine, heroin, marijuana, LSD and any other drug for which there is a high rate of addiction.

c.   Those needing anger management, treatment and counseling.

d.   Sexual offenders — although I believe it is very hard to cure them, and if the offender does not respond noticeably to treatment, such offender should, at the end of his prison term, be transferred to a mental health facility until he/she is cured. As suggested in the chapter "**Sexual Offenders and Pedophiles**", if the offender is never cured, he/she remains locked up, for life if necessary. It is too dangerous to have sex offenders, particularly pedophiles, on the streets again if they have not been cured. This is further explained in that chapter.

e.   Gang members. They should be segregated from the other prisoners to reduce their influence on prison life. It should be done so that they cannot threaten other prisoners nor carry out those threats. If they decide to continue their violent ways, at least they can hurt only each other.

There must be strict rules for compliance. For example, visitors should still be subject to search and should be prosecuted for trying to sneak alcohol or illegal drugs into prison. Incentives should be made available to prisoners to persuade them to successfully complete the courses of treatment, such as influencing the parole board. Although good time credit is no longer available and there

---

[1] An alternative could be to use different prisons solely for a specific type of prisoner, i.e., alcoholics, drug abusers, sexual offenders, etc. The state has made a positive step in this direction. Four community justice centers were to be in operation in 2002. Probation and parole violators who are drug addicts will be sent to these lockdown facilities for treatment rather than be returned to prison. This will also prevent further prison overcrowding.

is a certain minimum time that violent offenders have to serve, the Department of Corrections should be able to come up with some type of effective incentive that will help to make these programs successful.

There should also be a mandatory program of education for those who do not have high school degrees so that they can qualify for their G.E.D. In addition there should be job training and job placement programs so that when prisoners are released, they can more quickly become productive members of society, thereby removing another temptation to commit crimes.

As for the Judicial Branch, funding should also be increased to provide for more lock-down facilities so that in-patient treatment of those on probation can really be mandatory. Until there is a significant drop in drug, alcohol and sex related crimes, increased funding is neccesary to deal with those who go directly to probation.

Of course, I realize this will cost substantial sums, particularly at the commencement of the prison segregation system I've described, just to cover the cost of expansion of present prison facilities and/or to build and staff separate units to cover the entire prison population. However, the return on our investment will be well worth it. It will mean a dramatic decrease in the number of repeat offenders, a corresponding reduction in the crime rate (which means reduced pressure on law enforcement,) fewer people to be supported by the state and an ultimate reduction in our prison population.

If drug addiction is substantially reduced, the demand for drugs could slacken which would lead to a drop in the drug trade. There will be savings in law enforcement and in the cost of the criminal justice system as well as the need for more prisons. Most importantly it will mean more safety for the citizens of our state, freedom from fear and violence, and that alone is worth the cost of this investment.

I don't pretend to have all the answers nor the right answers. However, I have seen offenders presented to me in court who scoff at the effectiveness of treatment of their addiction while in prison. I have seen thousands of repeat offenders who have spent time in prison who can't seem to shake their addictions. I have seen too many people convicted of manslaughter with a motor vehicle, robbery, burglary, sexual assault and other crimes that might have been avoided if the offenders had received successful treatment for their addictions. I would hope that my recommendations merit consideration.

The Truths of Justice

CONCLUSION

You have now had a view of how the justice system really works. If you have found the realism interesting, I urge you, if at all possible, not to turn down an opportunity to serve as a juror. All jurors with whom I have talked have found trials a fascinating experience, whether it be a motor vehicle accident or a murder case. It is an experience you will never forget.

The Truths of Justice

APPENDIX A

(Author's note: The names of the parties involved, and certain places and dates, have been changed to protect their privacy. But in all other respects, this is an actual decision of mine.)

Connecticut Trial Ct. Unpublished Decisions
DOE v. DOE
JOHN DOE vs. JANE DOE
Superior Court
Judicial District of Tolland, at Rockville

MEMORANDUM OF DECISION

RITTENBAND, J.

This is an action for dissolution of marriage (of approximately 10 1/2 years) brought by the plaintiff Husband, hereafter "Husband" against the defendant Wife, hereafter "Wife" in August, 1993. It is a matter that consumed many days of pre-trial motions, depositions, negotiations, etc., and fourteen (14) days of trial before this court over a period of four (4) months in a limited contested action that was hard fought, very contentious and at times even bitter. Both parties are highly intelligent and well educated. Wife is a nurse. Husband is a medical doctor and is an expert in his field with a nationwide reputation.

The court finds the allegations of the complaint and cross-complaint (paragraphs 1 through 7 of each) have been proven and since paragraph two of each have been proven, the court has jurisdiction in this matter. Accordingly, judgment of dissolution of marriage is hereby entered on the basis of paragraph 3, irretrievable breakdown of the marriage with no reasonable prospect of reconciliation.

As to child support, alimony, award of assets and attorney's fees, the court has considered the criteria set forth in §§ 46b-84, 46b-81, 46b-82 and 46b-62 which has incorporated by reference the criteria set forth in § 46b-82, all of said sections being those of the Connecticut General Statutes.

In applying these criteria, the court has considered the totality of the evidence including the exhibits and the testimony of the witnesses, including the Husband and Wife. Much of the Court's decision is based upon the credibility of the witnesses, in particular the credibility of each of the parties to this action. The court's evaluation of their credibility is based upon their demeanor and attitude on the witness stand, the manner in which they responded to questions and the instances where their testimony conflicted with other evidence, including exhibits; their recollection or lack of recollection of certain events and the interests of the witnesses or lack thereof.

Although the court is not convinced the Wife's outbursts in court were totally credible, and although there appeared to be a conflict between her deposition and court testimony concerning her expectation of and goal of billable hours, the court finds that on the whole the Wife was candid, forthright and consistent in her testimony. She was an honest, reliable and credible witness. This is in sharp contrast to the clear lack of credibility of the Husband who was less than truthful and who often told or committed what Winston Churchill has called "terminological inexactitudes". A few examples thereof are as follows:

1. The Husband, on Memorial Day weekend, 1993, spent time with one Deborah Smith, hereafter "Smith", while they were both at a convention in Chicago. Husband denied any sexual relations or sexual contact with her during that weekend.

However, when confronted with his love letter to her of June 20, 1993 (Defendant's Exhibit 38 A), which date was approximately three weeks after returning from that weekend in Chicago, the Husband's reply was "I was desperate".[1] In an apparently subsequent undated letter from Husband to Smith (Defendant's Exhibit 38 C) Husband refers to his not having wanted to experience her sexually, "although

---

[1] It is hard for the court to believe Husband's original claim that he did not have sexual relations with Jones in Minneapolis, with only telephone and mail contact thereafter, when he, in approximately three weeks, (June 20, 1993), pledged his love to her.

you changed all that in Chicago". The court concludes from the contents of these and other very expressive love letters and the Husband's attitude and responses on the witness stand, that the Husband did have an intimate relationship with Smith, including sexual relations, in Chicago, Memorial Day weekend, 1993 despite his earlier protestations to the contrary.

2. In a letter from Husband to Smith of August 11, 1993 (Defendant's Exhibit 38 D), Husband indicates that he wants to have sexual relations with her again; and he subsequently admitted in court that he had sexual relations with Smith in July, 1993, at a convention in Toronto. He claims that that was after the marriage had broken down irretrievably. However, he was planning their sexual encounter in his letter to her of June 30, 1993 (Defendant's Exhibit 38 B), prior to the time in July when the parties hereto agreed that the marriage had broken down. In this letter, he talks about Smith and himself being booked on the same flight to Toronto. Despite evidence that sexual relations had occurred between Husband and Smith in Toronto in the middle of July and that there were subsequent love letters from him to her referring to their sexual relations (Defendant's Exhibits 38 D, 38 F and 38 G) and his admission in court that he did have sexual relations with her in Toronto in July, Husband in effect denied this affair in a November, 1993 deposition under oath, comparing his relationship to her with that of a professional colleague and friend, Dr. Gary Brown and with a platonic relationship he had with his friend, Sylvia Hart. He also stated that she was merely an acquaintance when in fact he had had and continued to have sexual relations with her and continually made protestations of love to her in various letters. The court can understand Husband's desire to keep his affair with Smith secret, but the court cannot condone his lying under oath at the deposition.

3. The court finds his claim that the marriage broke down because the Wife did not want Husband's brother, David, who had AIDS, to move in with them in their new home in Bolton to be without foundation. Wife cared for her brother-in-law and went out of her way to help him to obtain medical care for him, prepare meals for him while

they were living together in Vernon, having a birthday party for him and, generally, being very attentive to his needs. She had a very close and good relationship with him until he died in March 1991. In September 1991, Husband told Wife he didn't love her anymore. He subsequently claimed it was because she didn't want David to live with them in Bolton. However, as early as Mother's Day, 1992, he was writing notes to Wife expressing his deep love for her. In early 1992, he looked forward to the coming year "I only want to share this love with you". November 21, 1992, in his card on their anniversary, he again expressed his love, specifying inter-alia "the constancy, depth and strength of my love". This card was accompanied by a diamond anniversary band, and in the card he stated that his love for her would last longer than the diamonds. In a Valentine card, February, 1993, a little over three months prior to the beginning of his affair with Smith, he again wrote expressions of love to his wife, even using the phrase "with more love than you'll ever know", which is similar to the ending of his love letter to Smith of June 20, 1993, "I miss you more than you will ever know". See Defendant's Exhibits 35 A, B, C, and D. Either he was not telling the truth about Wife's alleged treatment of David as being the cause of the breakdown which he seems to claim started in September 1991, or he got over it very quickly as evidenced by his cards and gifts to Wife starting in early 1992 and going to at least February 14, 1993 in which he expressed his devotion and permanent love for her.

4. Husband's testimony concerning the policy at Newington Children's Hospital as to filling out time cards is another example of his untruthfulness under oath. He claimed, in court, that there was a policy that allowed him, if he worked ten hours in a day, to put down only eight hours and add two hours to the following date, which would be, of course, a falsifying of records. His testimony was clearly refuted by Dr. Malloy, the head of his department at that time.

5. There were instances of non-compliance by Husband with some, but not all, discovery requests, contradictions in his testimony as to what he had furnished as well as failing to furnish items ordered by this court during trial.

The Truths of Justice

The court does not find Husband to be untruthful in the refusal of contract work with the Middletown Board of Education. The court finds the testimony of Ms. Orlowski to be not sufficiently credible to contradict Husband's testimony. He may have come across as arrogant to her, but that is not unusual when a leading expert in his field or any other field has his or her opinion challenged by someone who is essentially a lay person in that field.

There were other instances of lack of credibility by the Husband, but suffice it to say that frequently he showed his disdain for the truth as well as a pattern of being not willing to accept responsibility for his actions.

With the above in mind and considering the criteria set forth in §§ 46-62, 46b-81, 46b-82 and 46b-84 of the Connecticut General Statutes, and based upon the totality of the evidence, including the credibility of witnesses as described above, the court makes the following additional findings of fact:

1. Fault

Having found that the Husband had an intimate relationship, including sexual relations, with Smith at least as early as Memorial Day weekend in May of 1993, the court also finds that such adultery by the Husband was the primary cause of the irretrievable breakdown of the marriage. Between September, 1991 and May, 1993 the parties were trying to keep the marriage together; and it was working as evidenced by Husband's cards and gifts to his Wife, the latest the court has seen being on February 14, 1993 in which Husband expressed his everlasting love for his Wife. According to the Wife's testimony, which the court believes, things were getting better and it appeared that the marital relationship was improving with every prospect that the marriage would stay together. This was right up to and including the end of May, 1993. Then, commencing the first week in June, 1993, right after Husband's affair with Smith began at the end of May, 1993, "everything started to go down hill". While Wife was doing everything she could to keep the parties together, Husband became much more difficult and withdrawn no doubt caused by his desire to continue his relationship with Smith. He had found someone else with whom he had fallen deeply in love and who seemed to meet his perceived needs more than his Wife. Because of this affair with Smith all progress toward and hope of reconciliation with his Wife were shattered. This affair as described above was what primarily caused the marriage to break down irretrievably. Accordingly, this fault or cause by the Husband will be a factor in the court's consideration of alimony, assignment of property and award of attorney's fees.

2. Earning capacity:

Based upon the totality of the evidence, including the credibility of witnesses, and after consideration of the exhibits and lengthy testimony concerning earning capacity, the court finds that the Husband has an earning capacity of $201,400 gross annual income.[2] Husband's age is still young at 42, his health is good, his skills and employability are excellent. He is a brilliant doctor with a rare expertise in his field. He is one of two or three experts in this field in Connecticut. In 1989, his book was published, it sold well, and he became a nationally renowned expert in his field. This resulted in his speaking at seminars and conferences throughout the country and bodes well for an increase in his private practice. Husband has admitted to presently being able to work 32 billable hours per week. The court finds that he could realistically be expected to work 35 billable hours per week, and based upon testimony and review of his bills in evidence, he could realistically be expected to bill an average of at least at $110 per hour. This would result in $3850 per week. For fifty weeks (allowing him two weeks vacation),[3] that would result in a gross annual income from his private practice of $192,500. In addition, Husband has been receiving royalties from his book for four years. He has been receiving approximately $8900 per year.[4] Royalties that have been steady and have provided a continuous source of income

[2] "Earning capacity is an amount which a person can realistically be expected to earn considering such things as his vocational skills, employability, age and health". Lucy v. Lucy, 183 Conn. 230 (1981).

[3] The court has considered but has not accepted Husband's argument that he is entitled to more than two weeks vacation and most holidays, nor does the court accept his argument as to the amount of non-billable time he must work to support the billable time.

[4] The court has not included royalties from his new book not yet published because it would be too speculative.

over an extended period of time may be included in determining gross income for the purpose of establishing alimony and child support just as bonuses and contractual rights (which include royalties) are includable. Accordingly, the court finds the Husband's annual earning capacity to be $201,400. A reasonable amount for business expenses (on the $192,500) is $40,000 per year, giving him a net earning capacity before taxes of $161,400 annually.[5]

As for the Wife's earning capacity, her age of 40 is still young, her health is good, but her skills and employability are far less than that of the Husband. She is a registered nurse of which there are many in the State of Connecticut, and does not have the expertise and reputation enjoyed by the Husband. The court finds that the Wife has made every reasonable effort to increase her income. Based upon Wife's increases of approximately $3,000 per year in income over the past few years, the court finds her earning capacity to be $40,000 per year gross income. Taking nineteen billable hours a week at an hourly rate of $45 less 6% under new contracts would reach essentially the same result of $40,000 per year earning capacity, less business expenses of $2,000 a year, for a net annual income before taxes of $38,000.

Based upon the above, the court finds that the Husband should pay the Wife $543.00 per week in child support. This is based upon the child support guidelines.

3. Real Estate of the Parties:

Based upon the appraisals submitted, the court finds the value of the Briggs Road property to be $233,000. There is a mortgage balance of $221,726, leaving an equity of $11,274. This property is jointly owned. The 200 Spring Drive property in Manchester in the name of the Husband, has, based upon the appraisals, a value of $180,000. There are mortgages totaling $165,344 leaving an equity of $14,656.

4. Ability to Acquire Assets and Income and Needs of the Parties:

Based upon the substantial disparity in the parties' incomes and

---

[5] Husband may have to work harder than he would like, but it was his actions as aforesaid that were the primary cause of the irretrievable breakdown, and it was he who put himself in more debt following the separation by buying a house for $185,000 and by purchasing other expensive items all of which may not have been necessary. It is an eight room house on 2.8 acres with three bedrooms.

earning capacities now, and in the future, the Husband is in a much better position to acquire assets and additional income, and the Wife, for the same reasons, is in much more need of income and assets.

Accordingly, based upon the totality of the evidence and the aforementioned findings, the court hereby enters the following orders:

1. Judgment of dissolution of the marriage is granted on the grounds of irretrievable breakdown.

2. The parties shall have joint legal custody of the minor children with their primary residence with the Wife who shall be the custodial parent. Visitation shall be in accordance with orders hereinafter set forth on Schedule "A" hereof.

3. Husband shall pay child support of $543 per week for the support and maintenance of said children commencing on the Friday following the date of this judgment. The court has taken into account the Husband's obligation for alimony hereinafter set forth.

4. Husband shall pay to the Wife Twenty Thousand Dollars ($20,000) as lump sum alimony, one half ($10,000) by April 10, 1996 and the other half ($10,000) by July 1, 1996, for her support and maintenance. [6]

5. Husband shall pay periodic alimony to the Wife in the amount of $500 per week for her support and maintenance, commencing on the Friday following the date of this judgment. This alimony shall terminate upon the death of either party or the remarriage of the Wife.

6. Husband's pension/retirement fund with Vanguard shall be transferred to Wife pursuant to a Qualified Domestic Relations Order. Wife shall own said Vanguard pension/retirement fund free and clear from any claim by Husband. Husband shall retain, free and clear from any claim by Wife, his pension/retirement fund with TIAA CREF.

7. Husband shall quit claim all of his right, title and interest in the marital home at 65 Briggs Road, Bolton, Connecticut to the Wife who

---

[6] Husband was able to raise approximately $20,000 of his own money for his down payment on the purchase of his house in Tolland between September 1993 and May 1994.

shall be responsible for paying all expenses associated with said residence, including the mortgage, taxes, insurance, repairs and maintenance thereof.

Husband shall retain all of his right, title and interest in and to his residence at 200 Spring Drive, Manchester, Connecticut. In light of the larger equity in the Manchester property and in consideration of the criteria set forth in the Connecticut General Statutes as described above, if a sale of the marital home in Bolton, Connecticut takes place within two (2) years of the date hereof Husband and Wife will share equally in all costs associated with the sale of said home including any deficiency and any major repairs necessitated by the sale and in any capital gains taxes resulting from said sale. The Husband shall be entitled to deduct for tax purposes the interest portion of any mortgage payments made by him on the Briggs Road property under the pendente lite orders to the date hereof.

8. The Husband and Wife shall share equally in the cost of enrichment activities for the minor children (i.e. musical instructions, summer camp, educational enrichment programs).

9. Husband shall provide medical and dental insurance for the benefit of the minor children in at least as good coverage as on his present policy. The parties shall share equally the cost of all unreimbursed medical, dental, orthodontia, optical, psychiatric and psychological services and expenses including medicine by prescription. The provisions of General Statutes § 46b-84 shall apply.

10. Husband shall maintain a minimum of Three Hundred Thousand ($300,000) in life insurance naming as beneficiary the Wife as the Trustee for the benefit of the minor children of $200,000 and naming Wife as the beneficiary of $100,000. Wife shall maintain a minimum of Fifty Thousand ($50,000) Dollars in life insurance for the benefit of the minor children. The children and the Wife as Trustee for the children shall remain irrevocable beneficiaries until they attain the age of 23. The Wife shall remain an irrevocable beneficiary until her death. These policies are not to be encumbered further.

11. As to both health and life insurance policies, at the request of

either party at any time, the other party shall provide proof of such policies to and an authorization for the requesting party to communicate directly with the issuer (i.e. insurance company) of the policies within twenty days of such requests.

12. The parties, through their attorneys, have stipulated in open court that the attorneys' fees of each other's attorneys for this case are fair, just and equitable. The court from its own knowledge of attorney's fees in the applicable areas finds the hourly rate of Wife's attorney ($175) to be fair, just and equitable. Additionally, the court has itself been present for fourteen (14) days of trial. Based upon that and a review of the court file which has made the court aware of motions filed, hearings held, pre-trial conferences held, negotiations held and from the file and the testimony aware of depositions conducted, the court finds the number of hours spent by Wife's attorney to be fair, just and reasonable. Further, in light of the criteria for attorney's fees set forth in General Statutes § 46b-62 which has incorporated by reference the criteria of § 46b-82, and in light of the court's now finding from the totality of the evidence that the Husband unnecessarily prolonged this action in terms of the time spent by the attorneys (i.e. causing the Wife's attorney to prepare and argue issues which should never have been raised by Husband and to find and bring in witnesses necessary to contradict untruths of the Husband), the court hereby awards the sum of Twenty-Five Thousand ($25,000) Dollars which Husband shall pay toward Wife's attorney's fees in monthly installments of $600 commencing August 1, 1996 until paid in full. The court finds that in light of the Husband's large earning capacity as well as his assets (i.e. cash value of life insurance, personal property, etc.,), he has the resources to pay these attorney's fees.

13. Husband shall complete the paperwork necessary to obtain a Jewish "Ghet" within 30 days of the date hereof. Additional proceedings required by conservative Jewish law shall be completed within three (3) months of the date hereof. Husband will cooperate in these proceedings. Wife shall bear all costs associated therewith.

14. Husband shall assign the title of the 1988 Volvo to the Wife who shall indemnify and hold the Husband harmless therefrom. Wife shall be responsible for all costs associated with the maintenance of said automobile. The Husband shall retain the 1994 Jetta and assume the loan thereon and hold the Wife harmless therefrom and from any costs or liabilities concerning said automobile.

15. The parties shall exchange their entire federal tax returns on a yearly basis within ten (10) days of their filing with the IRS. Any modification granted relative to child support shall be retroactive to the April 15th filing deadline so that any modification based upon said tax returns will not be delayed because of delay in filing same or furnishing same to the other party.

16. Wife and Husband shall each be responsible for $500 of the First Card (formerly Chevy Chase Visa) balance, and $500 of the outstanding loan with Savings Bank of Manchester, and will hold the other harmless for failure to pay the 50% which they are obligated to pay. Each party shall be solely responsible for any other debts appearing on their respective latest financial affidavits as well as individual debts incurred subsequent to the separation of the parties, and will hold each other harmless from the said debts on their own financial affidavits and any individual debts incurred subsequent to the separation.

17. Husband shall be entitled to the tax exemption for Seth and the Wife shall be entitled to the tax exemption for Evan. The parties shall execute any and all documents required to effectuate this provision.

18. Any bonds, stocks and/or savings accounts for the children shall continue to be so held for the children's private school and college education costs only, and the party holding them shall share any and all information relating thereto with the other party.

19. Except as specified herein and on Schedule B (Division of Personal Property), each party shall retain all other assets listed on their respective financial affidavits.

20. All transfers shall be made, documents signed and delivered and necessary steps taken to comply with these orders within two (2) weeks of the date hereof.

Judgment is entered in accordance with this Memorandum of Decision.

Rittenband, J.